April 2013

For Cecilia —
Thank you for ...
enthusiasm. You are a ...
Thank you for being you.
On the journey together —
With all good wishes,

Challenging Conflict
Mediation Through Understanding

GARY FRIEDMAN
JACK HIMMELSTEIN

To Cecilia —
your being so enthusiasm
much infectious
and depth to this
Best
Gary

ABA
Defending Liberty
Pursuing Justice

ABA Section of
Dispute Resolution

Program on
Negotiation
at Harvard Law School

Cover by Nicholas Coley.

The materials contained herein represent the opinions and views of the authors and/or the editors, and should not be construed to be the views or opinions of the law firms or companies with whom such persons are in partnership with, associated with, or employed by, nor of the American Bar Association or the Section of Dispute Resolution, unless adopted pursuant to the bylaws of the Association.

Nothing contained in this book is to be considered as the rendering of legal advice, either generally or in connection with any specific issue or case; nor do these materials purport to explain or interpret any specific bond or policy, or any provisions thereof, issued by any particular franchise company, or to render franchise or other professional advice. Readers are responsible for obtaining advice from their own lawyers or other professionals. This book and any forms and agreements herein are intended for educational and informational purposes only.

Printed in the United States of America

16   15   14   13   12   10   9   8   7   6

Library of Congress Cataloging-in-Publication Data

Himmelstein, Jack, 1941–
  Challenging conflict : mediation through understanding / by Jack Himmelstein and Gary Friedman.—1st ed.
      p. cm.
  ISBN 978-1-60442-052-4
  1. Dispute resolution (Law)—United States. 2. Mediation—United States. I. Friedman, Gary J. II. Title.

  KF9084.H56 2008
  347.73'9—dc22

                                                                              2008022247

Discounts are available for books ordered in bulk. Special consideration is given to state bars, CLE programs, and other bar-related organizations. Inquire at Book Publishing, ABA Publishing, American Bar Association, 321 North Clark Street, Chicago, Illinois 60654-7598.

www.ShopABA.org

Contents

PART 1
THE CHOICE TO MEDIATE   **1**

Chapter 1
Standoff at the Ranch: Who Decides?   **3**

Chapter 2
Radix and Argyle: The Choice to Work
Through Conflict Together   **17**

Chapter 3
A Holocaust Memoir: What It Takes to Mediate   **41**

About the Section of Dispute Resolution

The ABA Section of Dispute Resolution, established in 1993, is the largest dispute resolution membership organization in the world, with over 18,000 members. The Section's objectives include maintaining the ABA's national leadership role in the dispute resolution field; providing information and technical assistance to members, legislators, government departments, and the general public on all aspects of dispute resolution; studying existing methods for the prompt and effective resolution of disputes; adapting current legal procedures to accommodate court-annexed and court-directed dispute resolution processes; activating state and local bar involvement in dispute resolution; and conducting public and professional education programs.

The Section provides members with accessible, relevant, and cutting-edge information, practice tips, and skill-building opportunities. It is a vibrant forum for networking and professional development that bridges together unique and diverse perspectives. The Section of Dispute Resolution is relied upon as a leader in shaping policy that impacts dispute resolution practice in a variety of arenas.

About the Program on Negotiation at Harvard Law School

Founded in 1983, the Program on Negotiation (PON) at Harvard Law School is a world-renowned interdisciplinary research center dedicated to improving the theory and practice of negotiation and conflict resolution. PON is a consortium of faculty and students from Harvard University, Massachusetts Institute of Technology, Tufts University, and other Boston-area schools. Drawing from numerous fields of study, including law, business, government, psychology, economics, anthropology, the arts, and education, PON encourages collaboration and provides a forum for the discussion of cross-cutting ideas.

Preface

This path-breaking book, *Challenging Conflict: Mediation through Understanding*, articulates in an easily understandable way a radically innovative vision of how professionals concerned with dispute resolution should operate. Gary Friedman and Jack Himmelstein are master teachers and great mediators, and this book encapsulates their hard earned wisdom. I can personally attest to the model's usefulness, not simply pedagogically, but in practice.

Full disclosure requires that I acknowledge my personal debt to both Gary and Jack, for I have had the great good fortune to have collaborated with them both. At Harvard Law School the three of us have taught together a mediation workshop for practicing lawyers. Each year for more than two decades Gary and I have shared a classroom. During the years I've been a law professor at Stanford and now at Harvard I have mediated scores of complex disputes, including two cases with Gary described in this book. Many elements of the understanding-based approach are now very much a part of my professional repertoire both as a mediator and a teacher.

Gary and Jack gave birth to some of the ideas underlying this work nearly a generation ago, and as the model's parents they have overseen its development and refinement in the intervening years. With the publication of this important book, the understanding-based model of mediation has come of age. Like a proud uncle, I take avuncular pride in the publication of this important book.

But be forewarned: the word "challenging" in the book's title might be aptly applied to the approach itself. This approach is premised on four core ideas, each of which challenges conventional wisdom. It emphasizes

- The power of understanding rather than the power of coercion
- That the parties themselves must take primary responsibility for whether and how the dispute will be resolved
- That the parties are best served by working together and making decisions together
- That conflicts are best resolved by uncovering what lies under the level at which the parties experience the problem

For disputing parties, for the lawyers representing them, and, most of all, for mediators, the implementation of this understanding-based approach requires change. Let me briefly elaborate.

A party in the middle of a difficult dispute usually yearns to be better understood but typically has little interest in trying to understand the other side. Many disputants resist even being in the same room with their opponent, much less really working together with them in a problem-solving way. A party in conflict will often try to avoid primary responsibility for resolving the dispute, preferring to shift that responsibility to his or her lawyer or a neutral—whether mediator, arbitrator, or judge—who is expected to announce what should be done. Many disputants (and some lawyers and mediators as well) see mediation as a form of non-binding arbitration in which a wise and well-informed neutral will take responsibility for deciding the proper outcome on the merits.

The understanding-based approach of mediation will also prove challenging for many lawyers called upon to represent a client in this process. A lawyer may view the dispute solely in terms of the legal arguments; he or she may measure opportunities and risks only in terms of possible resolutions a court might impose, and he or she may value an outcome only in dollars and cents terms. The understanding-based approach does not deny the importance of money, and it acknowledges the relevance of thinking hard about the legal opportunities and risks involved in adjudicating a dispute. But the model also asks lawyers to support a process in which the parties (not the lawyers) are center stage for much of the time; a process that explores the parties' underlying interests; a process that searches for opportunities to create value and expand the pie and thus do more than resolve how much money one disputant should pay the other. The understanding-based model will support parties who may choose to repair their relationship and who may wish to fashion a resolution that reflects values that are important to them but are not necessarily reflected in the formal legal norms that a court might use.

Last, and perhaps most importantly, this model is challenging—and radical—because of the role it defines for the mediator. It urges the mediator to explore with the parties the psychological, emotional, and value-laden issues that may lie *beneath* the stated conflict. It asks the mediator personally to forgo and resist the use of coercion and manipulation. And what is most challenging to today's conventional wisdom is the idea that the mediator should work with the parties *together, in each other's presence*, to create a resolution based on a deeper understanding of the other side.

Managing conflict is much more difficult when you must work with the parties in the same room. Disputants are often very angry with each other. They may know, consciously or unconsciously, how to push each other's "hot buttons." Their ability to communicate effectively with each other is typically badly impaired. Facilitating a process where the parties work together is extremely challenging, and it will require even experienced mediators to develop new skills. This approach also diminishes the mediator's power to manipulate the parties. Using caucuses gives the mediator an opportunity to communicate different messages to each party, because of the acoustic separation. One party never learns what has been told to the other. With an understanding-based approach, the mediator must forego the temptation of purposely creating in the opposing parties radically different perceptions of the mediator's view of the opportunities and risks of continued litigation.

Because the understanding-based approach to mediation is challenging, and because it asks for disputants, lawyers, and mediators to approach conflict in a new way, I expect both professional resistance and even conflict. But like Jack and Gary, I deeply believe that conflict in and of itself is not bad. Indeed, it is my hope that the publication of this new book will foster productive dialogue about the comparative advantages and disadvantages of alternative means of dispute resolution.

Robert Mnookin
Williston Professor of Law
Chair, Program on Negotiation
Harvard Law School
Cambridge, MA
March 2008

About the Authors

Gary Friedman and Jack Himmelstein are co-founders and co-directors of the Center for Mediation in Law. For the last quarter century, they have been training thousands of lawyers, law teachers, judges, and other professionals in their unique approach to conflict resolution throughout the United States, Europe, and Israel—working through the Center and also in cooperation with other educational institutions in the United States and abroad including Harvard's Program of Instruction for Lawyers and the American Bar Association.

Prior to their practicing and teaching conflict resolution, Gary was a trial lawyer in Bridgeport, Connecticut. Jack, after practicing law with the NAACP Legal Defense and Education Fund, taught clinical law at Columbia Law School for ten years and was then one of the founding faculty of the CUNY School of Law. Gary taught mediation as an adjunct at Stanford Law School and currently teaches each year at the World Intellectual Property Organization in Geneva.

They have written several articles on mediation and conflict resolution, and Gary authored A Guide to Divorce Mediation (Workman Publishing, 1993) in collaboration with Jack.

Prologue

We met in 1976, living on opposite coasts and both searching for ways that lawyers might better serve the deeper aspirations of the profession as well as those of the people they serve.

Gary had recently moved to California from a practice as a trial lawyer for five years with his family's firm back East, after having become increasingly disheartened with the human cost of adversarial litigation. He was in his second year of exploring different possibilities for how he might practice law in a way truer to himself and had tentatively started providing services to parties in conflict in what he was soon to term mediation. Jack had been teaching at Columbia Law School for three years after having practiced civil rights law with the NAACP Legal Defense Fund for six. At Columbia, he was directing a clinical program that included a focus on exploring what it meant personally to the students to become a lawyer. In those days, we like many others in law were asking whether the law was really a "helping profession" and what might make it more so. While the traditional legal approach was clearly essential and had long played a critical role in our society, in far too many cases the way lawyers worked on behalf of their clients had become excessively adversarial. Coercion, manipulation, even dirty tricks were all too acceptable means for "winning." There were tradeoffs and compromises, winners and losers. And "resolution" often came with deep wounding—psychological, emotional, financial—and not only for "the loser."

We believed that ways could be found to restore or engender a kind of humanity that so often seemed absent in the hashing out of solutions. And though it may seem paradoxical, we were also interested in the possibility of something good coming out of conflict, in reaching beyond win-lose or compromise toward ways of working through legal conflicts that had a greater sense of integrity in both the process and outcome.

We weren't the only ones thinking this way. We knew from our colleagues, students, and friends that the impulse toward service and justice, toward care and helping others, ran deep in the profession. We were searching for a better way.

As part of our professional and personal quests, each of us had been exploring educational approaches to understanding the psychological and spiritual dimensions of human identity and human relationships. It was in one such course of study that our paths crossed, and our colleagueship and friendship have continued since.

At that time, Jack had just started work on Columbia's newly created Project on Humanistic Education in Law to help develop approaches to law teaching focused on the human dimensions of the teaching and practice of law. With funding from the National Institute of Mental Health, the Columbia Project over a five-year period undertook research and conducted a series of intensive two-week summer training programs for teachers from law schools across the country. There we inquired together into the possibilities for humanistic, experiential, and participatory methods of legal education as well as for a deeper understanding of the underlying purposes, principles, and practices of lawyering. Gary joined Jack as resident lawyer member of the teaching staff for those summer programs, and the circle of learning and innovation expanded.

Colleagues we came to know in those first trainings became indispensable allies in the inquiry, and our friendships and associations with them continue to this day. Howard Lesnick, Jefferson B. Fordham Professor of Law at the University of Pennsylvania School of Law, worked closely with us in understanding the assumptions underlying the legal system and the traditional role of the lawyer as well as those that might underlie alternatives to both, including the possibilities for tapping the spiritual dimensions inherent in lawyers' work.[1] Jack was later to join Howard as part of the founding faculty of the City University of New York School of Law where Howard led the effort to bring a new pedagogy to CUNY's vision of "Law in the Service of Human Needs."[2]

Other participating legal educators from those first days who became central to the evolution and development of these ideas and trainings included Carrie Menkel-Meadow,[3] A.B. Chettle Jr. Professor of Law at the Georgetown University School of Law, Beatrice Moulton,[4] Professor of Law at Hastings College of the Law, and Len Riskin,[5] Chesterfield Smith Professor of Law at the University of Florida College of Law. All were to become leaders in articulating the vision and evolving practices of experiential learning in legal education and in what was then the emerging field of alternative dispute resolution.

Each of these four colleagues joined us in planning and conducting either, or both, those early summer intensive trainings or other programs soon to follow for both law teachers and lawyers. These included some of the first national trainings for law teachers in mediation and the application of models of human understanding to alternative dispute resolution as well as our earliest trainings and workshops for lawyers on mediative consciousness as applied to dispute resolution and other aspects of lawyering.

---

1. *See e.g.* DVORKIN, HIMMELSTEIN AND LESNICK, BECOMING A LAWYER (West Publishing, 1981); HOWARD LESNICK, LISTENING FOR GOD: RELIGION AND MORAL DISCERNMENT (Fordham Press, 1998).

2. Howard Lesnick, *The Integration of Responsibility and Values: Legal Education in an Alternative Consciousness of Law and Lawyering*, 10 NOVA L.J. 633 (1986); *Infinity in a Grain of Sand: The World of Law and Lawyering as Portrayed in the Clinical Teaching Implicit in the Law School Curriculum*, 38 U.C.L.A. L. REV. 1157 (1990).

3. Carrie Menkel-Meadow, *Toward Another View of Legal Negotiation: The Structure of Problem-Solving*, 31 UCLA L. REV. 754 (1984); DISPUTE PROCESSING AND CONFLICT RESOLUTION: THEORY, POLICY AND PRACTICE (2003); CARRIE MENKEL-MEADOW ET AL., DISPUTE RESOLUTION: BEYOND THE ADVERSARIAL MODEL (New York: Aspen Publishers 2005).

4. GARY BELLOW AND BEATRICE MOULTON, THE LAWYERING PROCESS (Foundation Press 1978).

5. Leonard L. Riskin, *Mediation and Lawyers*, 43 OHIO STATE LAW JOURNAL 29 (1982); *Mediator Orientations, Strategies, and Techniques: A Grid for the Perplexed*, 1 HARVARD NEGOTIATION LAW REVIEW 7 (1996); *Decision-Making in Mediation: The New Old Grid and the New New Grid System*, 79 NOTRE DAME LAW REVIEW 1 (2003).

As Gary's practice developed to what he felt was properly termed mediation and Jack's teaching evolved, the two of us continued to explore together the premises, principles, and methods by which lawyers might approach legal conflicts differently. We were joined in this ongoing inquiry by Harry Sloan, a personal and relationship counselor who we had met in our psycho-spiritual studies. Harry's gentle and piercing insight into the deeper aspirations that are within us and link us all were only matched by his vital humor. He always sought to evoke the possibilities for how things might be, and the impact of his belief in and support for evoking the possibilities inherent in our work with people in conflict continue despite his untimely death at an early age two decades ago.

Along the way, we founded a non-profit educational institute— the Center for Mediation in Law—with the core goal of developing this different understanding of working with conflict and conducting training programs in the principles and practice of mediation for lawyers, law teachers, and other professionals in dispute resolution. And we started to conduct these trainings that, in turn, challenged us to further articulate our ideas.

In 1985, Gary was asked by Bob Mnookin,[6] currently Samuel Williston Professor of Law at the Harvard Law School and Chair of the Harvard Program on Negotiation, and then a Professor at Stanford Law, to teach a mediation seminar for his law students. Bob had a longstanding expertise in negotiation, was and continues to be open to new ideas, and was intrigued by mediation. Bob had the courage both to challenge us as we developed our model and to support a "radically different" approach to conflict. Our association with Bob continued to develop after his move to Harvard Law School, and his contributions both to our understanding of conflict and to the evolution of the Understanding-based model have been invaluable. He has also supported its dissemination through trainings and the creation together of an educational video.[7]

---

6. *See, e.g.,* Robert Mnookin, *Why Negotiations Fail: An Exploration of Barriers to the Resolution of Conflict,* 8 OHIO STATE JOURNAL ON DISPUTE RESOLUTION 235 (1993); ROBERT MNOOKIN ET AL., BEYOND WINNING: NEGOTIATING TO CREATE VALUE IN DEALS AND DISPUTES (Belknap Press of Harvard University Press, New Ed Edition 2004).

7. *Saving the Last Dance: Resolving Conflict Through Understanding* (Harvard Law School Program on Negotiation and the Center for Mediation in Law, 2001). The three of us have taught mediation together at Harvard's Program of Instruction for Lawyers, and Bob and Gary have also taught regularly at the World Intellectual Property Organization (WIPO) in Geneva.

At the same time we were trying to understand conflict and how to work with it more effectively, we were also trying to understand how to do so more compassionately. This meant continuing our effort to understand what was going on within us and within the parties when we seek to support them in working through their conflict—what we call understanding the inner world of conflict. Buddhist inquiry has been one of several paths of human understanding that has been particularly helpful in our work, and we have benefitted greatly in this part of our journey by the active support and friendship of Norman Fischer. A Zen Buddhist priest and former abbot of the San Francisco Zen Center, writer and poet, Norman has dedicated his work to the application of Buddhist meditation practice and principles to everyday life through an organization he founded called Everyday Zen.[8] Our collaboration with him has deepened our appreciation of the importance of self-reflection and awareness of the subjective level of experience in our approach to mediating conflicts and in our educational programs, with Norman joining us as part of the teaching staff at different Center advanced trainings.

Many of the ideas, principles, and practices described in this book were developed through years of engagement with this group of dedicated friends, colleagues, fellow educators, and lawyers along with other pioneers in this field.

Today is very different from thirty years ago. Over these last three decades, different experiments and approaches to mediation have spread across the country born out of a common desire within both the professional community and the general public to find a less coercive and grueling, and more equitable and efficient, process to settle conflict. Today, countless disputes are resolved through mediation, and most people have at least a passing understanding of mediation as an alternative to going to court. But few know how many different types of mediation there are or what

---

8. See, e.g., NORMAN FISCHER, TAKING OUR PLACES: THE BUDDHIST PATH TO TRULY GROWING UP (San Francisco, Harper Collins, 2003). The Everyday Zen Foundation applies the insights of Buddhist practice and thinking in a variety of settings. For a comprehensive look at the possible applications of meditation to the work of lawyers and others in dispute resolution, *see* Leonard Riskin, *The Contemplative Lawyer: On the Potential Contributions of Mindfulness Meditation to Law Students, Lawyers, and Their Clients,* 7 HARVARD NEGOTIATION LAW REVIEW 1 (2002).

their options are for mediating. Nor are they aware of how much coercion that was the source of the initial dissatisfaction with the traditional ways conflicts have been resolved has crept back into the process.

This is particularly the case as increasing numbers of former judges have become mediators, mimicking the courtroom experience where the parties' lawyers put their cases up for judgment. It is also true when mediators, whatever their original professions, are hired simply to broker a deal, putting them in a position of power above the parties. In these cases, the ultimate authority to accept or reject a resolution may lie with the parties, but the mediator is all too likely to engage in coercion and manipulation in trying to reach an agreement or compromise. Pressuring the parties may be more subtle than what takes place in court, but the need to apply pressure is often viewed as no less essential. In this context, the understanding-based approach presents a real alternative.

We did not start out trying to develop a model of mediation. What we were searching for was a way of working with parties in conflict that had integrity for us and for them. As we develop throughout this book, that has meant supporting the parties in their making voluntary decisions together based what is important to both (all) of them. It has also meant ensuring that the parties are fully informed about whatever they might find relevant to the decisions they will be making. And as we shall develop in detail, that information includes the law but without the process becoming dominated by the law (or the lawyers).[9]

As we searched for what made sense for us in working with parties in conflict, we found that many, not all, of those who participated in our trainings were drawn to this approach or at least to parts of it. We continue to say to participants in our trainings that they should use as little or as much of what they learn with us as they believe has meaning for them and the parties they seek

---

9. Len Riskin, in trying to place us on the facilitative/evaluative continuum of his grid, has remarked that while our approach is generally facilitative, the inclusion of the law has the potential to introduce an evaluative element. He concludes, however, that in this approach the mediator "evaluates in order to free the parties from the potentially narrowing affects of the law." Riskin, *Mediator Orientations, Strategies, and Techniques: A Grid for the Perplexed, supra* note 3, at p. 37.

to support. If it does not, we do not seek a forced fit. Indeed, the whole point of the search for alternatives over these decades, as we view it, is that professionals and parties should be searching together for ways of working through conflict that seek to honor the best in the human spirit and provide professionals with a way to be authentic and true to themselves in that search.

In the attempt to capture both the spirit and practice of the approach that we have been working with over these years, we have "recreated" ten commercial conflicts that Gary mediated. In each case, except for The Symphony and The Neighbors for which we were granted permission to publish, all names, identifying characteristics, and circumstances have been changed to thoroughly protect the parties' privacy and the confidentiality of the mediations in which they participated.

After an Introduction to the Understanding-Based Model in which we set out the central aspects of the approach and its underlying principles, we develop the model in action through these ten conflicts. The scenes and dialogue that comprise these mediations are interspersed with our comments on the dynamics of conflict and the mediator's choices as the different aspects of the model unfold from start to the finish. Most chapters are followed by a section of "Commentary" in which we discuss in greater depth one or more of the central concepts for working with conflict in this way.

As our model of conflict resolution has evolved, so has the Center for Mediation in Law. We now conduct training programs not only in mediation, but also in the newly developing area of collaborative practice, and have also been actively working with non-profit and spiritual organizations wanting to learn the skills of dealing effectively with interpersonal conflict.

We feel a particular debt of gratitude to the many colleagues who have supported us, sometimes by challenging us, and contributed to the development of the model, the training programs, and this book. These include Peg Anderson, Nancy Barash, Barry Berkman, Jill Cohen, Catherine Conner, Dana Curtis, Liz Dvorkin, Laura Farrow, Marc Fleisher, Lauren Friedman, Marcia Goffin, Trina Grillo, Susan Keel, Joan Lieberman, Trish McCall, Chris Anderson McDonald, Katherine Miller, Steve Neustader, Maude

Pervere, Martina Reaves, Elizabeth Reingold, Peter Renkow, Amy Rodney, Kathy Stoner, Peter Swords, Mathew Wilkes, and many others in this country, and still others in our work abroad.

Through the telling of these stories and the development of the model, we also wish to express our appreciation for these and other parties and lawyers who seek to work through their conflicts together and for the many conflict professionals who seek to support them.

For further information about the Center and its training programs, we have a website, www.mediationinlaw.org. We welcome your contact.

Introduction to the Understanding-Based Model

For more than three decades, we have worked with people in conflict and taught professionals how to deal with conflict. Understanding conflict and how it works has been our preoccupation. Studying conflict has clarified how profoundly it impacts all of us in our lives for better and for worse. We were drawn to this work from our background as lawyers, and as people often caught in the grip of conflict, struggling to free ourselves, our families and friends, our clients, our colleagues, and our students from the restrictive and stifling hold conflict can have over all of us.

Throughout our work together, we have found a stance toward conflict that has been of enormous value to us and, we would like to think, to the people with whom we have been working: parties in conflict and the professionals seeking to help them. That stance is one of dealing with conflict itself in an effort to understand how we can relate to it, not just to survive, but to use it to improve our lives and those of the people we work with as well.

Allowing conflict to victimize us and others leaves us trapped in its grasp and diminished by it. *Challenging conflict* itself has provided us with tools for understanding it and for opening doors for ourselves, our clients, colleagues, and students that likely would not have occurred were it not for the power of that stance.

What we have come to understand is that, if unexamined, conflict has a way of readily enveloping us and taking over our lives. When conflict takes over, it creates its own reality. It dictates the terms on which we experience a conflict as well as those on which we try to deal with it. And it often does so in insidious, unseen ways that make us and others hardly recognizable to ourselves, never mind to each other.

Its terms include the need to think, feel, and speak based on right and wrong, winning and losing. Certain emotions, such as anger, rage, and righteous indignation are evoked and readily escalate. Fear is often felt, but hidden. Hurt as well is often denied and unseen. Compassion, understanding, and caring disappear, as if they don't exist. They are simply not felt or are quickly repressed if they try to sneak in. "Clothe yourselves in anger," conflict demands. "You can feel fear if it helps to maintain the anger, but make sure it remains hidden."

Within conflict's grasp, it seems the only way out is to win through pressure, persuasion, or manipulation. Or dig in your heels and wait the other side out until they come around. And if you become enmeshed in a prolonged stalemate, you can at least feel the satisfaction of righteous victimization. If that doesn't work, well surely, a third party decider will vindicate you, because indeed there is one right and one wrong, and you are the one who is right.

These are the terms that conflict presents. We don't accept those terms, not because they don't capture so much of the reality that we experience, but because they lead to a dead-end or lack of resolution and because they are woefully incomplete. If we accept them as *the* reality, we are trapped in conflict. We challenge those terms. It doesn't have to be that way.

You might conclude from this that we mean to eliminate conflict because of the harm that it does. Not at all. That is neither possible nor advised. We believe that the problem is not conflict itself, but the willingness of people to accept conflict's terms and succumb to its downward spiral.

Challenging conflict's terms allows us to see it as an opportunity for people to enhance their lives and deepen their understanding of themselves, each other, and the reality that they experience. As you will see, that is an essential part of our definition of mediation—for the parties to gain understanding of their conflict and use it to enhance their lives. Not that we recommend choosing conflict. It simply means when conflict enters our lives that we face it and try to find a way to move through it with understanding.

We seek to do that by making the participants to a dispute aware of how they, both parties and professionals, can become ensnared in what we refer to as a *conflict trap*. With that awareness, we can use the conflict to bring out the best in ourselves, rather than spiral down to our worst. Seen in this way, conflict can become an invitation to accept the reality of our automatic response to it and move beyond the confines of that response, to rise to the challenge of finding within us the understanding and compassion that liberates us from conflict's hold.

The Understanding-Based Approach to Mediation

One of the keys to the power of the Understanding-based model of mediation is that it is a real alternative. Parties have a variety of choices to resolve their dispute, in particular, proceeding through the adversary system either by having their lawyers negotiate for them or, ultimately, having a judge decide the matter. The Understanding-based approach poses a very different possibility and opportunity, one that we believe deeply respects and honors parties and leads to better solutions.

Understanding-based mediation offers people in conflict a way to *work together* to make decisions that resolve their dispute. This non-traditional approach to conflict is based on a simple premise: *The people ultimately in the best position to determine the wisest solution to a dispute are those who created and are living the problem*. They may well need support, and we seek to provide them support in helping them find a productive and constructive way to work together, to understand their conflict and the possibilities for resolving it, and to reach resolution.

So it was in the Radix and Argyle case, which is one of those we will explore in this book. The executives at these two large companies had been suing each other for years over $300 million, producing an endless stream of allegations and proceedings. Throughout the long history of their conflict, they and their lawyers were focused on the objective reality of the $300 million and the moves and counter-moves in legal battles. Each had again and again vilified the other, each resting assured that the actions and positions taken by the other were at the root of the conflict. That was the tone when the mediation began. Each saw the other as the enemy; nothing would change until the other changed; and that was unlikely to happen. They were trapped inside their conflict, stuck, as they had been for years.

But once the mediation started, a difference emerged. They were there in the room together, and when the question was posed whether they might want to explore a way out—together— a slight but noticeable shift took place. They sensed the possibility that they could come to understand how they and their companies had become caught within a web of assumptions, beliefs, attitudes, and feelings that had them ensnared in their conflict *and* that there might be a way out that could work for both. Those are our words. Theirs would likely be that "perhaps things could change." That glimmer gave us all the ability to make a choice about how we could proceed. Without the understanding that they were caught, the reactive stance would likely have continued to enmesh them in conflict.

In Radix and Argyle, initial changing perceptions led quickly to different possibilities. How the dialogue unfolded and how that shift began to take place will soon be explored. When the business executives and their respective counsel worked together and participated actively in the dialogue, they quickly came to a common initial realization—that it was in large measure their possible over-reliance on their attorneys, and their attorneys' espoused desire to protect their clients, that had fueled and prolonged the conflict for years at enormous cost to both companies, blinding them to the possibility they could find a common resolution. They were beginning to see the assumptions about their conflict that had them trapped and to join in the challenge to conflict's terms. That was only a start, but it was an important start. Much hard work would need to be done that would deepen and expand that understanding and translate their motivation into a practical solution.

This book is about evoking that start, deepening and expanding that understanding, and working together to create enduring solutions to conflict.

To pursue this path, we work from a base of four interrelated core principles.

- First, we rely heavily on the power of **understanding** rather than the power of coercion or persuasion to drive the process.
- Second, the primary **responsibility** for whether and how the dispute is resolved needs to be with the parties.
- Third, the parties are best served by **working together** and making decisions together.
- Fourth, conflicts are best resolved by **uncovering what lies under** the level at which the parties experience the problem.

These core ideas are radically different from the traditional way in which most people think about dealing with conflict. They call and build upon the motivations of both mediator and parties to work in an alternative way, and we have found that for many that motivation is there once they see the possibility. These ideas in action challenge conflict.

The Power of Understanding

In the traditional approach to resolving conflict, the coin of the realm is the power of coercion. When parties disagree, the exertion of control through the use of threat, persuasion, manipulation, or the imposition of an external authority is considered inevitable, necessary, and proper. That is true not only in the traditional adversarial model of resolving disputes but also in many of the seemingly differing models of alternative dispute resolution that have evolved. While we do not pretend to be able to totally eliminate coercion in our approach, we try to bring the power of understanding to bear wherever possible as the gateway to resolution.

Understanding proves central along several dimensions of helping parties to deal with their conflict. One, of course, is the substance of the conflict. We support each party in gaining as full an understanding as possible of what is important to him or her in the dispute, as well as what is important to the other party. Understanding is also critical in creating a working relationship between the parties and the mediator that makes sense to all. And understanding can prove crucial in helping the parties to recognize the nature of the conflict in which they are enmeshed and how they might free themselves from its grasp.

We want *everything* to be understood that may be important to the parties in resolving their differences, from how we will work together, to the true nature of the conflict in which the parties are enmeshed, where it came from, how it grew, and how they might free themselves from it. We believe the parties should understand the legal implications of their case, but that the law should not usurp or direct our mediation. We put as much weight on the personal-, practical-, or business-related aspects of any conflict as on the legal aspect. In finding a resolution, we want all parties to recognize what is important to them in the dispute and to understand what is important to the others. We strive for a resolution to satisfy each.

Party Responsibility—Let the Parties Own Their Conflict

"Let the parties own their conflict" means it is important to remember and honor that it is the parties' conflict. *They* hold the key to reaching a resolution that best serves them both. And *they* have the power and responsibility, if they are willing, to work together toward that resolution. For us, that does not mean simply that the parties must ultimately agree to any final settlement of their dispute. *Party responsibility* means the parties understand what is substantively at stake for both and craft a resolution best for all. It also means the parties actively participate in shaping the mediation process by making ongoing choices, along with the mediator, as to the course it will take.

Thus, the *parties exercise responsibility* not only in determining the substantive result—the *what* of the problem, but they also participate actively in deciding the *how*—the way the mediation proceeds. For us, the *what* and the *how* are inextricably related; and the parties' active involvement in shaping the *how* is more likely to lead to their creating a better result on the *what.*

This does not mean that the mediator plays a passive role, yielding to the parties in determining the course of the mediation. Rather, as you will see throughout this book, we view the mediator's role as both active *and* interactive with the parties. This stands in contrast to the assumption within the traditional approach to conflict that it is the professional who needs to assume active responsibility for the resolution of the controversy. Within this traditional framework, clients (or parties) are seen to properly yield a great deal of control and responsibility to the authority whether in the person of their lawyers, a judge, or even a mediator. In our approach, the parties are responsible and active, as will be evident in the cases that unfold in this book.

The mediator, too, is responsible. The mediator's responsibility is directed to supporting the parties in *their ability to make choices together based on their growing understanding. Understanding* ensures that those choices will be informed.

Working Together

We believe that the best way for mediators to support parties in resolving their dispute is for the parties to *work together* and make decisions together. We appreciate that for many professionals, this is one of the most striking and questionable aspects of our approach. Most mediators regularly meet separately with the different parties ("caucusing"). Our goal is to *work together* with the parties directly and simultaneously. We will address at length in this book *why* we work in this way and *how* we do so. Here we highlight a few of the bases on which this core principle rests.

We work in this way because it creates better solutions for the parties. We do it also because we believe it best honors the parties while also contributing to what we view as a critical need in society for developing better ways for people to go through conflict.

We do not believe that our approach to mediation with its emphasis on the parties *working together,* or any particular approach to mediation, is the answer to all conflicts. We do think that for those people who are motivated and capable of working together, there are many benefits. We have seen that succeed for thousands of individuals and organizations, some of whose stories, like Radix and Argyle, make up this book.

It is clear that the mediator *working together* with all the parties is quite different from someone from the outside making decisions for them, whether that someone is a judge, lawyer, or mediator. But we don't believe that a laissez-faire approach that might countenance one party yielding their decision-making authority to go along with the other makes sense either. As will be clear in the cases we explore in detail in this book, we work hard to make sure that when the parties *work together* and make decisions together, they are each able to act responsibly and are sufficiently informed to exercise independent judgment. While we seek to honor the parties' relationship by *working with them together*, we do not wish them to yield their autonomy.

Indeed, underlying our entire approach to mediation is a view about individual autonomy and relationships. In the mediation world, we find ourselves in a position between those who see the goal of mediation as only supporting the parties as separate beings who need to stand their own ground and those who believe mediation is really only about the relationship between the parties. We believe that a positive tension exists in recognizing the importance of both the individuality of the parties and their relationship. Both are essential and we need not be forced to choose between the two.

Ultimately, we are both separate *and* interconnected. Autonomy finds its fullest expression in the context of connection and connection finds more power and richness to the extent it embraces autonomy. The stories in this book illuminate how this approach can make a difference in people's lives.

Going Under the Conflict

Einstein is credited with saying that "you cannot resolve a conflict at its own level." The point for us in Einstein's words is that when it comes to dealing with conflict, we need not only breadth of understanding but depth as well. That means recognizing that conflict has an inner life and being open to that dimension. Repeatedly, we find that the basis for resolving conflict comes from examining with the parties, as best as we are all willing and able what *underlies* their dispute.

With this fourth principle, our focus returns to *understanding* but at a *deeper level*. This deeper level of understanding can make all the difference and therefore merits a special place in our core principles. The inquiry into what lies beneath takes place in each aspect of the conflict.

First, we work with the parties to understand what *underlies the substance of the conflict*. As we noted earlier, we help both sides identify what is truly important to each in the dispute—not only *what* they want but *why* they want it. In more traditional approaches, understanding is directed more to the surface of the problem—most frequently, how much money one side wants and how much the other is willing to give—as the professionals apply pressure on the parties to move to a compromise solution.

As we seek to deepen the parties' *understanding of what lies under the surface of their conflict* in terms of the substance of their conflict, the goal is for the parties to ultimately be able to take each other's views into account along with their own as the foundation for a solution that is individually suited to all parties. When the pressure is lifted and understanding is expanded and deepened, many mediations result in creative ideas that neither party had considered before the mediation began and that are ultimately more satisfying to each of the participants.

Second, we work with the parties to understand *what underlies their conflict* in terms of how it may have them trapped in their dynamic. Since almost all our work takes place with the parties together, and because the parties participate actively in that work, the mediation process readily becomes an education in going through conflict, and valuably so. In our experience, we have found again and again that *understanding the conflict* can provide the key to resolving it.

That is so because while conflict can be multi-layered and complex, certain restrictive patterns of behavior and ways in which people experience conflict play out frequently, but their source is usually hidden from view. Just as the roots of a tree hidden below the earth are the powerful life force to what we see above, what lies *under the conflict* is what gives it shape and force.

Conflict is rarely just about money, or who did what to whom. It also has a subjective dimension—the emotions, beliefs, and assumptions of the individuals caught within the conflict. This subjective dimension includes feelings, such as anger and fear, the need to assign blame, and the desire for self-justification. It is also grounded in certain assumptions about the nature of conflict that support the conflict and keep it going, such as the reliance on right and wrong. These are conflict's terms, and we join together with the parties in challenging those terms.

Beliefs about how conflict should be resolved need to be addressed if people are to move beyond the places where they have become stuck. Typically, these include the belief that the other person, or the other's position, must change, the need to protect oneself against risk, or the belief that an authority must make the final decision.

What often leaves both sides stuck in the conflict is that the subjective assumptions, attitudes, and feelings on one side are usually matched by similar ones on the other. Anger engenders anger, blame is answered by blame; efforts at self-protection on one side compel a similar reaction by the other in what often becomes ricocheting and escalating reactivity. The subjective dimension *underlying conflict* is not only at work for the parties, but is also very much present for the mediator and other professionals involved. Appreciating what is going on within us as conflict professionals—our judgments about one or both parties, identification with one or the other, anger or fear, or compassion and empathy—can hold the key to our work with the parties.

Our view is that an inescapable and critical relationship between the objective and subjective dimensions of conflict needs to be understood to effectively deal with most conflicts. Many approaches to conflict focus on one to the exclusion of the other, leaving out this essential inter-relationship. We believe the challenge is to understand both and their relationship. Put simply, to resolve conflict, it helps to *understand* it.

We are not suggesting that the answer to every conflict is that a little understanding magically changes the dynamics between the parties and resolves the problem. What we are suggesting is that understanding can begin to help the parties appreciate how they have become caught in this ricocheting trap and lead to a way out. It will take *breadth and depth of understanding* to hope to break out of such a complex and multi-layered situation. Repeatedly, we find that *the basis for resolution comes from discovering together with the parties what lies at the very heart of their dispute,* which is often a surprise, and which often has a profound effect on our work together.

The Goal of This Book

In the understanding-based approach to mediation, the four principles work in dynamic interaction with each other.

- understanding

- party responsibility   *- working together*

- going under the conflict

In the 10 cases we present in this book, these principles and that dynamic interaction come alive. Our goal is try to explicate not only why we view them as so central but how they work in practice.

Before starting that journey, we want initially to highlight two significant aspects of the understanding-based model that follow from these principles and distinguish it from other approaches and also begin to respond to some common concerns that have been expressed about working in this way. These points will be developed in greater depth in a number of the mediations that unfold in the book.

The Non-caucus Approach

Many other approaches to mediation recommend that the mediator shuttle back and forth between the parties (caucusing), gaining information that he or she holds confidential. Our central problem with caucusing is that the mediator ends up with the fullest picture of the problem and is therefore in the best position to solve it. The mediator, armed with that fuller view, can readily urge or manipulate the parties to the end he or she shapes.

The emphasis in our approach, in contrast, is on *understanding* and *voluntariness* as the basis for resolving the conflict rather than persuasion or coercion. We stress that it is the parties, not the professionals, who have the best *understanding of what underlies* the dispute and thus are in the best position to find the solution. *Meeting together* with the parties (and counsel) follows from these assumptions about people in conflict. These and other points underlying this approach are developed in greater detail in the chapters that follow.

To work in this way is challenging for both the mediator and the parties. The parties' motivation and willingness to *work together* is critical to the success of this approach. Mediators often assume that the parties (and their counsel) simply do not want to work together, and therefore keep the parties apart. In our experience, many parties (and counsel) simply accept that they will not work together and that the mediator will be responsible for crafting the solution. But once educated about how staying in the same room might be valuable, many are motivated to try it. If the parties (and the mediator) are willing, *working together* throughout can be as rewarding as it is demanding, as the mediations recounted in this book illustrate.

Role of Law and Lawyers

Mediators tend to be divided in how they approach the role of law in mediation. Some rely heavily on what a court would decide if the case were to go to trial, authoritatively suggesting or implying that law should be the controlling standard used to end the conflict. Other mediators, concerned that the parties might simply defer too readily to the law and miss the opportunity to find more creative decisions, try to keep the law out of mediation altogether or only bring it in at the parties' request.

As developed throughout this book, we welcome lawyers' participation *and* we view it important to include the law. We do not, however, assume that the parties will or should rely solely or primarily on the law. Rather, the importance the parties give to the law is up to them. Our goals are (1) to educate the parties about the law and possible legal outcomes and (2) to support their freedom to fashion their own creative solutions that may differ from what a court might decide. In this way, the parties learn that they can together reach agreements that respond to both their individual interests and their common goals while also being well informed about their legal rights and the judicial alternatives to a mediated settlement.

We also want to respond to a common perception and challenge that working in this way is simply not realistic for most conflicts and most people. When we hear that critique, we are reminded of similar statements three decades ago when it was the legal profession directing the challenge at the very idea of mediation where parties would decide for themselves. Now, too, the challenge is from many lawyers (not all), and they are joined, ironically, by a good number of mediators. Our response now—as it was then—is that many parties in conflict, if given the opportunity, can and want to do it. That response is now backed by thirty years of our experience and that of many other professionals who have integrated this approach into their practice. And it is backed by the parties who we and many others have worked with together in mediation.

In developing this approach, we have not felt so much that we are inventing something new, but rather that we are evoking and supporting a natural impulse of people in conflict to want to be able to *work together*, even in the face of having significant differences in their perspectives. The impulse may more often than not be obscured by the feelings of dissonance that are inevitably a part of conflict. But even if not in the foreground, that impulse is waiting to be tapped and given room for expression, even if only in the form of a wish of what might be if things were different. The same is true for the parties' capacity to *work through their conflict together*. If given the opportunity and necessary support, many are both willing and able. Our work with parties in mediation seeks to tap that impulse and give expression to that capacity.

This point is crucial because, as we said, the understanding-based approach builds upon the motivations of both mediator and parties to work in this different way. That motivation is often there *once the parties see the possibility*. But they will only be open to seeing it if the mediator believes it might be there and creates a context where the possibility of working in this different way can be evoked, as in the mediations recounted in this book.

The Choice to Mediate

Part

1

Standoff at the Ranch: Who Decides?

Settling into the nine-hour flight to "a little piece of paradise" in the hills of a South American country, as it had been described to me, I started to think about what I would likely encounter upon my arrival. I was making the trip at the urging of a good friend who travels two weeks every year to retreat and write at a remote inn called *La Finca* (the Ranch), perched high above the sea. My friend had suggested, somewhat wistfully, that I might be the last hope for the brother and sister owners who had become inextricably locked in conflict.

Graziella and Ricardo had inherited the land from their parents and divided it into two parcels. Over the years, La Finca's organic vegetable and flower gardens, the main inn building, and its cottages and outbuildings sprawled across both tracts. Ricardo took care of the land, gardens, groves, and buildings, while Graziella handled the management of the inn and all finances. Initially, they worked well together, building their combined efforts into what promised to be a long-term, successful business. But increasing disagreements and ill feelings between sister and brother over the management of and conception for the inn and gardens had grown into friction and enmity.

At this point, the viability of their joint endeavors was threatened and the atmosphere so poisoned by their mutual recriminations that my friend and other "regulars" were talking about not coming back.

Even while urging me to make the trip, my friend was not optimistic. "Too many words have been said that cannot be taken back. They can't even talk with each other any more. They're both good people, but they're so steeped in their battle. I hope I'm wrong." With the way he uttered those last words, I understood just how much he wanted this brother and sister to find a way out of their predicament. The fact that they had both separately confessed to him their desperation and interest in any help I might provide gave me hope that they both might have at least some motivation to work things through.

As I drove along the bumpy road leading up to the Ranch, I recalled what an Israeli colleague had once told us about a talk she had had with the then chief Rabbi of Israel. After listening to our colleague describe her work in mediation, the Rabbi threw out a challenge: "What did Cain say to Abel or Abel to Cain that led up to the slaying?" As she struggled to recall, he reminded her that the Bible, and commentaries on it, were exquisitely detailed on such matters as who said what to whom. But try as she might, she could not recall a word. "No surprise," the Rabbi exclaimed. "Nothing was said! Cain became jealous of Abel, and he slew him. Not a word! No dialogue. So maybe you're onto something."

Upon arriving, I saw at once why this idyllic spot was so dear to my friend, and why he wanted so much for the brother and sister to find a way out of their predicament. After Graziella and Ricardo gave me a gracious welcome, it quickly became evident that they were prepared to talk to anyone but each other. Each tried more than once to get me alone to plead their case in private, while I repeatedly said it would be best to wait until we could find a time to talk together. It wasn't until the afternoon of my second day there that they both agreed, somewhat reluctantly, to sit down together with me the next morning.

■ ■ ■

Their stance of mutual hostility was hardly surprising, nor was their desire to plead their case in private. When two or more people are in conflict, their instinct is usually to attack–defend–counterattack. Many of us will try to avoid the direct confrontation, preferring instead to argue our case to anyone who might lend a supportive ear. "I'm right; he's wrong," we protest to friends, family members, or anyone who will listen, laying out our grievances and hoping that our cause will be recognized as true and just. This conflict was no exception.

It was fairly easy for me to notice in this way just *how* Graziella and Ricardo were dealing or failing to deal with their dispute and to ask myself *how* that could change. That's a natural focus for me. But for the two of them, their attention was elsewhere. They were totally caught inside the conflict, preoccupied with the substance or *what* the other did wrong or was threatening to do. In our work in the understanding-based approach, this distinction between the *what* and the *how* can prove critical as we try to help people understand how they can deal with conflict differently. Having the ability to focus on both the *what* and the *how* is what we call *bifocal vision.*

In trying to avoid dealing with each other while seeking to win me over to one side, Graziella and Ricardo were, in effect, approaching me as they would a judge. That was hardly surprising. I have always been struck by just how much parties seeking resolution of a dispute outside of court continue to act as if they are still in the traditional system, appealing to me and expecting that I will pass judgment, as I gently try to return the responsibility to them.

For years I had made this point to parties in mediation reluctant to take responsibility for resolving their differences as well as to professionals in conferences or training programs who might be all too willing to assume that responsibility. But I had never been presented with such an immediate and dramatic illustration of just how powerful a backdrop the courthouse can present as when I came face to face with Graziella's and Ricardo's conflict the morning of my third day at *La Finca.*

■ ■ ■

I was having breakfast before our scheduled 11 o'clock meeting when Graziella arrived at my table, breathless and in obvious distress.

"Please come with me right now! We're in the middle of a fight!" Graziella addressed me in English, which both she and her brother spoke quite well. Outside, a dozen or so people, most seemingly Ranch employees, were watching a voluble argument in Spanish between Ricardo and a bus driver who had come to pick up some guests and had parked off the driveway among some small trees. There was a third man to whom Ricardo and Graziella seemed to be addressing their mutual recriminations. On the ground behind the bus was a bird's nest that must have fallen from one of the trees. Ricardo kept pointing emphatically at the bird's nest while shouting in Spanish. He looked surprised to see me there. I was a bit surprised myself.

"Look at what her people have done." Ricardo yelled toward me in English, red-faced. "We agreed no one would park there."

Graziella snapped back, "The bus had to be parked off the road. It was nothing intentional. It's just an old nest. Nothing was even in it. This is so crazy."

"You know nothing about birds and their nesting," he retorted. "There are laws to protect the environment—"

"—and about having ample parking at public establishments," Graziella interjected, "if you want to go on with your silliness."

Ricardo turned back toward the man, seemingly making his same point in Spanish.

I suspected that the focus of their upset at the moment might be emblematic of many of their differences, which was later confirmed, but at the moment I was more focused on *how* they were dealing with those differences.

"Who is this gentleman?" I asked.

"He's the judge from town," Ricardo said.

"The judge? And, if I may ask, why is the judge here?"

"I called him. There has been a serious breach of the law."

Graziella and Ricardo then started speaking angrily to each other in Spanish. The judge appeared impassive and quizzical.

I intervened again, in English, which the judge understood as little as I could understand his Spanish. "Would you ask the judge if he is here to make a decision?" It was hard for me to imagine that he was, but this was clearly a different culture.

Graziella and Ricardo had a rapid exchange with the judge in Spanish, to which he responded (translated for me) "likely not at this time."

I decided to take a different tack. "So let me ask both of you," I said. "Do you want the judge to do something here? To make a decision?"

> *Ricardo:* Not really.
>
> *Graziella:* The judge doesn't really have the power to make a decision here, and I don't even know why he is here. But I'm not about to let Ricardo get away with his attacks on me.
>
> *Mediator:* So, if neither of you wants the judge to make a decision at least at this point, perhaps you no longer need him here.

They seemed startled for a moment but then quickly began to redirect their arguments toward me.

> *Mediator:* My suggestion is that the three of us meet in an hour as we scheduled, without the crowd or taking up the judge's valuable time. I think this can wait until then.

Ricardo and Graziella looked surprised at the idea that they could stop their verbal warfare, or at least pause. They hesitated momentarily and then agreed. As I turned, they went back to talking to the judge.

I was not sure what they were saying, but I hoped they were both thanking the judge for his time.

■ ■ ■

While the possibility of the parties going to court is often somewhere in the backdrop of many conflicts that appear in mediation, the choice confronting Graziella and Ricardo that morning presented itself with particular starkness. They could turn to the judge to decide for them or deal with their conflict themselves and do so together. An hour later, I intended to waste no time helping them understand their choice of *how* they might proceed.

■ ■ ■

Entering the room, they were still steaming.

> *Graziella:* I'm glad you had a chance to see Ricardo in action. That's what I have been dealing with.

Ricardo: My sister keeps doing things to provoke me.

Mediator: So you are each starting to direct your arguments to me. Before the three of us can begin to understand the problem between the two of you and begin to deal with it, the two of you need to decide whether you want to continue talking to the judge or together with me. As you know, the judge's job and power is to decide who's right. Mine is different.

Graziella: You come highly recommended by someone we both trust, and we're paying you a lot of money, so maybe it would be better if you figured it out for us.

Mediator: I can help you figure it out for yourselves. I am not a judge. I don't have a judge's power, and I wouldn't want to decide which of you is right.

Ricardo: I'd rather talk to you. That's why we hired you to come so far to help us.

Mediator: I appreciate that, but do you have the impression that I would make some kind of decision?

Graziella: You might have to, because as you can see, we don't know how to talk to each other without getting very upset.

Mediator: I noticed that, but I also notice that you aren't eager to give up the power to decide to the judge.

Graziella: Right. I don't think he can make a very good decision for us.

Ricardo: We'd just keep fighting with each other, even after he made his decision.

Mediator: Would you like a process where the two of you can talk together without simply fighting back and forth and actually make decisions together, even though you may be upset with one another?

Ricardo: Of course. That sounds good. But I'm not going to be a pushover.

Mediator: I noticed that; nor will your sister. I think that's great. So it seems as if you both would like to make decisions together if you could. My job would be to help you do that.

Graziella: But we can't even talk together.

Mediator: Would you like to be able to?

Graziella: I have to tell you something. When my brother gets angry and yells at me, I get really scared. I hate it, and I won't stand for it.

Mediator: So if you were going to be able to work together, you'd need some way of communicating where you're not scared. And the question would be whether that is something you would want.

Graziella: Sure, and I'd prefer the weather was always perfect.

Mediator: You can't control the weather. The two of you can control how you deal with this conflict, but you would both need to be willing to try to do that.

Graziella: He is who he is.

Mediator: So you might need to know that Ricardo could act differently and would want to. And Ricardo would likely want to know the same about you.

Ricardo: And I would need to know that she's not going to leave as soon as it gets hard.

Mediator: Good. You're each telling me what you need from each other to be able to have a chance of working together. What would you need from me?

Graziella: If you're not going to decide who's right and who's wrong, what are you going to do?

Mediator: My job will be help you talk together, to provide a sense of safety where you each feel free to speak openly, help you create as full an understanding as you can, and put you in a position to make decisions together.

Ricardo: How do you do that?

Mediator: By continuing to do what I'm already doing, trying to understand both of you, giving you each the room to say what you want, and ultimately helping you reach an understanding of your conflict and how it looks from both sides, which may be something you haven't ever been aware of. All this would provide the basis for you to make the decisions you need to make together.

Ricardo: I hope you can get Graziella to see how badly she's been behaving by refusing to deal with me and going behind my back.

Graziella: And I hope you can get Ricardo to stop bullying me.

Mediator: Finding a different way that you can both deal with one another while in conflict is a good goal, and I think I can be helpful. So far, however, I have the sense that what you would each like is for me to be on your side. But for me to help both of you, I can't be on one side against the other. I'm going to stay here in the middle and give you each a sense of confidence that I can understand and support you, but without taking sides. If I actually move to one side or the other, I'll become part of the problem. A judge can do that and decide for you. If either of you felt that I was on the other's side, this process would fall apart. In fact, if you ever felt I was not in the middle, I would hope that you would tell me so we can keep that from happening.

■ ■ ■

It was clear to all of us that their sharing the power to decide would be preferable to giving it away to somebody else. By helping Graziella and Ricardo to look at the *how,* I was giving them a palpable sense of the difference between the traditional judicial system and the alternative posed by our working together.

These siblings were both powerful presences. But like most people caught up in conflict, their power was pitted against each other, leaving them stalemated. The real or imagined resort to the judge or other outside decision maker did not seem a viable way out. I had a clear sense that if their power could be redirected toward cooperating with one another, they would be able to turn their conflict around. To do that, we would have to discover how they had trapped themselves inside the conflict and see if they were both motivated to work through it together. When we return to the Standoff at the Ranch later in this book, we'll see how they took on that challenge.

Commentary: Who Decides?

In our approach to dealing with conflict, we have found one concept particularly helpful: the *conflict trap.*

Put simply, the ways in which people typically deal with conflict often keep them trapped within it. The more they struggle with one another, the more the trap tightens its hold. As we view it, parties often need to understand that it may be *how* they are dealing with their conflict that traps them, and the way out of their trap can lead them to *what* the solution to their dispute might be. That was exactly the focus the mediator tried to bring to the initial dialogue with Graziella and Ricardo.

A *conflict trap* is a set of mutually reinforcing responses to conflict that keeps the parties locked in battle even when the moves and countermoves are seemingly designed, as they often are, to end the struggle. These interlocking actions and reactions are in turn supported by any number of underlying, mutually reinforcing premises and assumptions the parties have about one another and about conflict. In order to understand how people become caught in *conflict traps* and how through *understanding* they can be released, we find it helpful to contrast the traditional ways of dealing with conflict with the alternative posed by the understanding-based approach.

The Traditional Approaches to Conflict

Two approaches to conflict dominate. In the first, the two sides are locked in a standoff, each attacking or trying to convince the other and neither backing down. In the second, the two sides try to appeal to a third party to resolve the conflict. Each can present its own *conflict trap*.

The Standoff

Graziella's and Ricardo's standoff in the Ranch's driveway that morning is typical of the way people deal with conflict in most cultures.

The disputants are pitted against one another. Attack–defend–counter-attack. The goal may well be to end the conflict by compelling the other to acknowledge being wrong or to just give in or give up. But the other responds in kind. In an escalating pattern, both parties assert their own view, defend against the other, vilify, refuse to listen to the other, and feel justified in doing so by the words and actions of the other and by the refusal of the other to listen or respond to them. Neither seeks to understand or be receptive to the view of the other. Standoff! They become trapped inside their conflict, as illustrated in Figure 1.1. Barring some change, they are likely to remain so.

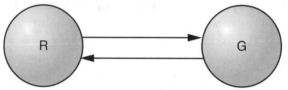

FIGURE 1.1 The Standoff

Given human nature, this dynamic seems as natural as it is inevitable, and it has played out in conflicts big and small through-out history. Each party to the conflict is simply trying to protect self, family, possessions, or country. Given the harm suffered or threatened, "the other side" and its actions must be condemned.

Both sides may well want to be understood by the other. "Don't you see: I'm right! You're wrong!" But they themselves are not interested in understanding. Reactively they seek to convince, attack, defend. Their defensive behavior is mirrored by the other. While neither grasps this, their actions inevitably reinforce it. Neither is understood; neither feels understood. Standoff!

The Appeal to an Outside Decision Maker

In the second mode, the parties seek to convince a third party of the essential rightness of their view. If the dispute is serious enough and the disputants cannot work it out on their own, they, or their lawyers, can decide to turn the dispute over to a third party who has the power to decide.

Here, the decision maker sits, as shown in Figure 1.2, figura-tively and often literally, above the disputants, with the power

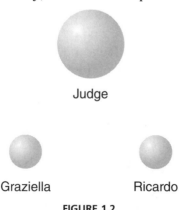

FIGURE 1.2

to make decisions regarding their conflict. The presence of the third-party decision maker invites, at the same time it justifies, the exclusively right–wrong view of the conflict.

This model of dispute resolution is so familiar that it reflexively becomes the basis by which many disputants approach their conflicts. For some conflicts, this model does in fact make great sense and should not automatically be dismissed in favor of some sort of mediative alternative. The point is rather that disputants should not automatically and axiomatically accept this traditional approach. Unfortunately, many do accept it, and once they've embarked on the path to the courthouse, frequently they find themselves trapped within the restrictive confines of that approach as the battle lingers on and on. Even when the matter is decided by a judge, often the conflict is left fundamentally unresolved.

The Understanding-Based Alternative

The understanding-based approach to resolving conflict with the help of a neutral third party is based on a different set of premises. We present it here schematically in its simplest form (Figure 1.3).

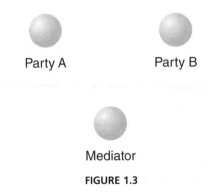

Party A   Party B

Mediator

FIGURE 1.3

In our approach, the parties and mediator may meet together with lawyers present or without them. Figure 1.3 represents our approach with all three participants of equal size and the mediator below the parties to symbolize that he or she does not play the role of judge (although placing all three on the same plane would more accurately reflect the spirit we are trying to capture). It also reflects that the responsibility of the parties is key. While other approaches to mediation and related forms of alternative dispute resolution vary explicitly and implicitly as to how much authority the mediator should have in the process, virtually all would agree that the third-party neutral has less authority in mediation than a judge has in the traditional system.

As we view it, the goal is to move beyond the right–wrong framework, where one view cancels out the other. Our goal is for the mediator and parties to *work together* so the understanding between the parties forms the basis for the decisions they will make.

How the Traditional Approach Influences the Alternative

When parties enter the world of mediation, they may think they are leaving the traditional adversarial system behind by replacing the judge with a mediator. But the adversarial system remains very much present in several significant respects. As we are fond of saying, you can take the parties out of the traditional system, but it can be much harder to take the traditional system out of the parties.

Understanding how the traditional system pervades the thinking of the parties and their counsel when they come to mediation can be critical to helping parties escape their *conflict trap*. It is a challenging task because the traditional approach to conflict is deeply embedded at a subjective level in the psyches of all the participants. It affects the way they think and feel about the conflict as well as how they approach its resolution.

Just as the parties are quick to view the mediator the way they would a judge, they also assume an attitude of blame, and of right versus wrong, toward one another. They readily rely on the law as the governing standard, as they would in court, and treat each other as adversaries as they would in a legal battle, largely because that is what they have internalized from the traditional way that conflict is approached in our culture.

It is in part the participants' experiences of traditional conflict settings, whether direct or vicarious, that lead them to impute to the mediator or other third party the type of authority that underlies the judge's role. But at a more basic level, society's traditional attitudes toward conflict carry the assumption that the fair and efficient resolution of differences requires the presence of a third party to decide for disputants, or at least to persuade or cajole. Indeed, the traditional way conflicts are dealt with is itself an expression of how individuals think and feel about conflict and how they want it to be dealt with.

And it is precisely that sense that has led different societies to place authority in the third-party neutral to say who is right and who is wrong, whether that neutral be judicial tribunal or village elder. Other than force, how else could a conflict be resolved when the parties strongly disagree, and each side thinks it is right or at least worthy of prevailing? Each party's belief that this is the only or inevitable approach to conflict is, in turn, reinforced by the parallel attitudes and actions held by its "adversary" who believes similarly.

That sense of how conflict must inevitably, and appropriately, be resolved is also present in and reinforced by the professionals. In what might be called the professionalization of conflict, parties often look to the experts—lawyers, judges, mediators—to resolve their dispute, just as Graziella and Ricardo turned to the judge and then to the mediator. And the lawyers and judges, and sometimes the mediators as well, see it as their role to do so. With those beliefs and expectations firmly in place, the *conflict trap* locks its vice.

That lock is particularly powerful because the participants are usually not aware of its presence and its impact. They carry it unconsciously as the exclusive way to reach a result. For the parties to entertain a different way to experience their conflict requires their realization that there may be more than one way. And if the internalization of the traditional approach is true not only for the combatants but also for the mediator or other third party, the challenge is all the more difficult. To help the disputants approach their conflict in a truly different way requires first that the mediator recognize that there is more than one way.

To best help the parties break out of the adversarial grip of the traditional approach to conflict, it is important to keep the focus on the *how* of the conflict rather than only on the substance. Two critical steps can release disputants from their conflict trap, as the mediator has started to do with Ricardo and Graziella.

1. The mediator helps the parties identify the ways they have taken on the traditional approach, the premises underlying that approach, and the ways the parties may have become trapped by working exclusively within that framework.

2. At the same time, the mediator introduces an alternative approach, with different premises, and the ways that this alternative may help the parties find a way out of their conflict.

After sitting down with Graziella and Ricardo, the mediator helped them identify how they were dealing (or failing to deal) with their conflict and the choice they faced about how they might want to do that differently. That choice held the promise of transforming their standoff of attack–defend—with a real or imagined appeal to some third party to decide for them—to a face-to-face dialogue where they seek to understand their own and each other's differing perspectives and make choices together about how to deal with their differences. When we return later to Standoff at the Ranch, we will see how keeping the focus on this basic choice about the *how* of conflict can make all the difference. In the following chapter of Radix and Argyle, we see how the dynamics of the *conflict trap* can play out when lawyers are added to the mix (and how their presence often exacerbates the conflict) as we visit the start of a mediation between two large corporations. We also see how the mediator can help the parties and their counsel begin to recognize the trap they have created for themselves and *work together* to release its hold.

Radix and Argyle: The Choice to Work Through Conflict Together

2

Sitting in the waiting room of a major law firm, I was still not sure just what I would say. Inside the large conference room were lawyers and executives from two major companies who had been locked in a multiyear, multimillion-dollar dispute. They were in the process of interviewing another mediator, whom I knew by reputation to be extremely effective. My task was to help those present understand the differences between the two of us, so they could make an intelligent choice. Could I do that in a way that was honest and reflected a different spirit in approaching their conflict? I didn't want to feel I had to sell them on my approach to mediation, or on me as a mediator.

When ushered into the room, I was surprised to find as many as 20 high-level executives of the two companies plus their lawyers seated around a large table. The moment I seated myself, one of the lawyers spoke:

Radix Lawyer: I'd like to get right down to what we're interested in. We have had a long series of disputes between our companies, and the one that we're in right now involves several hundred million dollars. The case is scheduled for trial in about six months. We'd like to mediate it if we can. So what we'd like to know from you is about your approach to mediation, particularly with respect to any differences between you and your principal competition, if I can call him that, Jim Black.

Mediator: I've never seen Jim mediate, but I do know him by reputation, and that reputation is impressive. Probably the most striking difference between us is that I prefer that the key decision makers and lawyers from both sides stay together in the same room with me throughout the mediation.

Radix Lawyer: You're right. That is a big difference. Why do you do that?

Mediator: Because in our approach to mediation, I don't make the decisions. The parties do. In order for your clients to be able to make decisions together, which I see as the goal of the process, I want them to have maximum control over the process and have access to as much information as possible to be able do that. That's not just control over the ultimate decisions— what a final resolution of their dispute will look like—but also how we will all go about getting there. For example, right now you are facing an important decision together, the choice of mediator. I wouldn't want to have separate meetings with each side where I might be saying different things to convince each of you to choose me.

Radix Lawyer: Noble thought, but I think there are a lot of problems with having us all in the same room together.

Mediator: I would expect that there are. We may be having one of them now. But there are also a lot of problems using the mediator as a sort of shuttle diplomat who goes back and forth between the parties. It's certainly a challenge to create a productive way of working together in the midst of a conflict, particularly when there's a history of animosity or even just sharp differences in each side's perception of what happened and what kind of solution makes sense. How you choose to face that challenge ultimately depends on why you might want to deal with your conflict through mediation.

Radix Lawyer: That's easy. We want to see if we can settle this case.

Radix Executive: Is it okay if I say something here?

Mediator: I would hope so.

Radix Executive: With all due respect to you lawyers, we have found ourselves in court with Argyle for most of the last 30 years. I think we'd all be better off if we didn't spend so much time fighting with each other. The changes in our industry are happening at lightning speed, and they are forcing us to change or be left behind. I'd really like to see if we can find a way to focus on that rather than spend so much time fending each other off. Depositions of five of our management team are scheduled within the next few weeks. The amount of time lost to litigation is enormous. Obviously, if that is what we have to do, we'll do it—particularly in this case where there is so much money at stake. But I'd like to think that we can do better than that.

Argyle Executive: Jerry, I'm really glad to hear that because I've been thinking the same thing. I'd like to be able to put this behind us and know that it's really over. Because what I know about this case is that there is so much at stake financially that we're not simply looking at going through a trial, which will be enormously time-consuming, but whoever loses will surely appeal. So we are all looking at years more of continuing litigation of this case, not to mention other cases to come.

Mediator: So one reason both of you are interested in mediating is to see if you can really put an end to the ongoing war.

■ ■ ■

The Active Participation of the Parties

The executives from Radix and Argyle had quickly jumped into the fray, which appeared to run counter to the lawyer-dominated approach that had marked the long history of their conflicts. The parties' active participation is central to our approach, and I welcomed their willingness to take the lead.

With Radix and Argyle, an endless stream of enmity and vilification, accusations and counteraccusations, and strategic maneuvering had kept the companies trapped in their conflict for years. At each juncture, the principals had turned the management of their disputes over to their lawyers and, in doing so, had kept themselves distant from the conflict and from one another and, ironically, had thereby kept their companies stuck.

Businesspeople are usually all too eager to turn legal disputes over to their lawyers. After all, that's what the lawyers are hired to do. And when lawyers become involved, they readily take over. If the two sides ever do sit down together to attempt to resolve the dispute, most executives are inclined to let their lawyers speak for them, and the lawyers, seeking to protect their clients, stay front and center. Adherence to these roles and the *implicit premises* and *assumptions* underlying them is one of the ways that the parties can become stuck in a *conflict trap* created by their reliance on their lawyers to deal with their dispute. We do not dispute the value that lawyers can have in serving their clients. In fact, in many disputes with legal issues, they are essential, and we would much prefer to have them in the room. However, reliance on aspects of the traditional way of seeing legal disputes often can keep the parties trapped in ways that limit their opportunities to work effectively together to resolve their conflict.

Here the goal was to find a way to help the parties identify how the assumptions they were making had them caught and, in doing so, help them escape their trap. When the lead executives from Radix and Argyle became active in the discussion, they may have made their counsel a bit nervous, but it was an important first step toward exiting their trap. They both recognized and acknowledged to one another the toll taken on both companies by 30 years of legal struggles, which would likely prove still more exacting in the future. In doing so, they indicated a desire to change the situation, and that motivation started to point to a way out.

In the understanding-based approach, we seek to place the parties front and center. It is *their* conflict, and it is they who ultimately know how best to resolve it. If the parties recognize that, they can begin to assume the *central role and responsibility* for the decisions they will need to make together. If they fail to recognize that fundamental responsibility, deferring instead to their lawyers, they are likely to remain trapped.

For many parties, simply entertaining *the possibility* that there may be an alternative to their mutually reinforcing adversarial stances can begin to point the way—particularly when they sense that the other may share the desire. We believe such impulses toward mutual recognition and the willingness to *work together* often lie under the surface. The possibility of finding a way that parties can together seek to honor these deeper impulses is for us fundamental. For the executives here, it was a telling moment.

Not surprisingly, the lawyers were not to be denied. Including them in the dialogue would prove crucial to supporting the parties' key role in resolving their dispute and keeping the trap from springing shut once again.

■ ■ ■

Mediator: What do you think about working together in the same room? Why would you want to do it? Why not?

Argyle Lawyer: Frankly, I don't think this case can settle unless both sides put their cards on the table, and we can do that more readily if we meet with you separately.

Mediator: I agree that putting your cards on the table might be essential to settling the case, but I would be concerned if I were the only one who had a full view of the table. If I meet separately with both sides and you each show me your cards and I'm bound to keep each side's secrets, what would you hope I would do with that information?

Argyle Lawyer: I would hope that you would know what to do with it. There are time-honored techniques that third parties have used successfully to settle cases on that basis.

Mediator: Such as turning up the heat on both sides to reach a deal.

Argyle Lawyer: That's one that can be effective.

Mediator: That puts a lot of power into the third party's hands. If you hire Jim Black as your mediator, that would probably be the way he would work. By both sides providing him with the information about your respective legal strategies, he's likely to get a pretty good take on where he thinks this case should settle. But by requiring him to keep that secret, you will have to trust him, without fully understanding the basis of his view, to persuade you and your counterparts to reach a mutually acceptable result. That is likely to feel rather coercive to both sides. To state it simply, I'd rather rely on the power of understanding than the power of coercion. That would include understanding your legal positions, but it would go beyond that.

Argyle Lawyer: What do you mean "beyond that"?

Mediator: I think it's important to look not only at your legal positions but also at the underlying business realities here and find out what is important to each company.

■ ■ ■

The Power of Understanding

The choice to rely on *understanding* rather than coercion is core to our approach, and we seek to make it explicit to disputants. When coercion is met with coercion, it keeps the parties locked in a struggle. *Understanding* can hold the key to escaping the cycle. We do not naively believe that all coercion can be eliminated. In a case like this, the very fact that the participants have recourse to the traditional legal system can itself prove coercive, as can other elements of the conflict.

But we do believe that motivated parties, whether inside mediation or on their own, can go far in increasing reliance on *understanding* and *their own choices* as the source of resolving conflict while lessening the use of persuasion and coercion. That effort starts with all participants, the principals and attorneys if present, recognizing the tendency to rely exclusively on appeals to coercive power—whether that is the power given to lawyers, to the law, or to a third-party neutral.

To help them work differently, the mediator introduced the executives and lawyers to another key concept—which we refer to as *the two conversations*. One way disputants get themselves into a conflict trap is by having an unexamined assumption that they must think in terms of *either* the legal reality *or* the business and personal reality—that one precludes rather than informs the other. Giving both conversations their due broadens understanding of the conflict and the possibilities for resolving it.

■ ■ ■

Argyle Lawyer: We have no intention of disregarding our legal position in this case. We have full confidence in going to trial and winning, if it comes to that.

Radix Lawyer: We've analyzed the law as well, and feel that our legal position is very strong. We're not afraid of testing that. We just thought that we could save a whole lot of time and money by making all of that clear—

Mediator: Both of you are fully prepared to rely on the law. And I would not expect either of you to disregard your legal—

Argyle Executive: —This is what has led us to this point. We can all see the lawyers disagree with each other, and that has characterized all of our discussions and left us stuck. I think you're right, Gary. We ought to be talking about the business reality here and avoid talking about the law. All that does is polarize us.

Mediator: So looking at the business reality is a priority for you.

Argyle Executive: From a business perspective, it makes a lot of sense to me.

Mediator: I would think so. But I also need to make clear that I am not suggesting ignoring the legal reality. It is a problem when the focus on the legal reality excludes the importance of the business reality. But it can also be a problem to leave out the legal reality, because it will always be lurking out there. If we can have a different type of conversation about the law, your understanding of the overall problem can be fuller if the law is not given too much power. You don't have to exclude either conversation. If you go this route, you can have your cake and eat it too. Indeed, you need to. And that may be a difference that characterizes my approach.

Argyle Executive: How so?

Mediator: Well, let me ask. In determining whether any result would be acceptable to your companies, I assume that you will be presenting a legal analysis of your strengths and risks to your boards of directors.

Argyle Executive: That's right. The size of this case is such that the legal result could actually affect the value of our stock. But that is between us and our board.

Mediator: Absolutely. You will ultimately decide within your organizations whether any deal reached here is acceptable, and that would certainly involve comparing it with the likely court result. The question is whether it would be valuable for you, the executives who are living the conflict and will have to live with the result of any resolution between you, to hear a more open and productive discussion from legal counsel than you have heard so far in order to educate you together about the law as it applies to your dispute.

Argyle Executive: Sure. I'd love to be able to hear more than our own lawyer's analysis of the situation. But it's not helpful to hear the Radix lawyer tell us that he has a sure winner.

Mediator: So you would find it interesting to have a discussion of the law where both sides are more open about what all the possibilities would be if you went to court.

Argyle Executive: Yes, if that were possible and it didn't just polarize us further. But you're suggesting that we talk about the business reality, and I don't want that to get lost.

Mediator: And what polarizes you is the expression of complete confidence of each lawyer that you'll win in court?

Argyle Executive: Yes.

Mediator: I think it's important that our goal when we talk about the law is for you business executives to get as clear a picture as possible, without going to court, of the likely legal outcomes—which would include both the strengths and risks on each side. When we have that discussion, the lawyers will take the lead to educate all of us. Then, we'll have a completely separate discussion about the business reality. In that discussion, each side will examine the underlying business reality, particularly with respect to what each side's priorities are that relate to this dispute. When we have that discussion, the executives from each side, who are the experts on that reality, would lead.

Argyle Executive: That's why I came here, to have that discussion. We have some fundamental concerns in common that we might be able to address even though we are and will continue to be in competition with each other. But the atmosphere gets spoiled when we talk about the law. Everyone gets on edge, and it makes it much harder to maintain constructive discussions.

Mediator: Right, that's the problem. Talking about the law, particularly with everybody together in the same room, often increases tension. But I want to make it clear that there are problems in not talking about the law. Ignoring the law gives it even more power, without our being able to come to terms with the impact it is having in the room. So for me the challenge is not whether to talk about the law but how to talk about it in ways that don't spoil the atmosphere, as you put it.

■ ■ ■

For the business executives, this dialogue was likely the first they had had with one another outside the law and lawyer-defined framework in which they had been enmeshed for years. It was able to take place in the manner it did when the restrictive and implicit premises about how they might talk together and who might talk were made clear to them. Engaging in a different way of *working together* based on an alternative set of premises and assumptions started to point the way out.

Sophisticated business executives can readily understand the polarizing and mutually reinforcing nature of each side's lawyers' "we can win this one" set of expectations. The problem was not just that the lawyers had always talked principally about the law, but rather *how* they had talked about the law and the impact of those discussions on the executives.

While the executives on both sides had likely had some sense of the dissonance from their respective counsel each asserting their confident legal pronouncements, they were at this meeting willing to say so in each other's presence and in the presence of their counsel. And that made all the difference.

Once acknowledged, the dissonance actually presented an opportunity to frame the challenge: *how* to have a conversation in which the parties are meaningfully educated about the law without being limited by the law. The executives seemed interested in exploring this different approach. In fact, they appeared eager. Not surprisingly, the lawyers again displayed some reluctance.

■ ■ ■

Argyle Lawyer: Hold it for just a moment. I am not about to have a discussion about the law where we lay out all of our trial strategy and educate the other side so that we leave ourselves weaker in court.

Mediator: Your concern is that if you don't reach an agreement here, you don't want to hurt yourself in court by having revealed something here that could reduce your chances of winning.

Argyle Lawyer: That's right. That's why I don't mind telling you about it in private if you keep it secret.

Mediator: And I should tell the other side that I have some information which I am not at liberty to disclose to them, but which they need to trust will reduce their chances in court and put pressure on them to adjust their sights?

Argyle Lawyer: Why not? It happens all the time.

Mediator: And do the same with you based on what they tell me in confidence about their trial strategy? Well, that's an option you could pursue with Jim Black. But I would not be inclined to go that route. I understand your concern. Indeed, I do not think you would be doing your job if you were not very sensitive to the risk of disclosing information in mediation that could come back to haunt you if you don't make a deal. What I would like you to weigh that against is the risk of not disclosing information that might change the other side's legal analysis, and therefore not making a deal in mediation. I don't think it would work well for you to disclose the information in caucus and keep it secret too—unless you are willing to have blind faith when I later tell you, based on what your counterpart has told me in confidence, that you will face real obstacles in court that you have not recognized and which I can't reveal.

Argyle Lawyer: So you are suggesting that we just trust you and for each of us to lay bare our legal strategy in front of the other. That sounds pretty risky to me, and I would have to so advise my client.

Mediator: I would expect you to. There are risks in having that discussion in a more open way than has likely gone on up to now. But you need to realize that there are also risks in not having it. In fact, it appears that you have all been living those risks for a very long time. I am not suggesting that you simply trust me and take what I am saying on faith. How open you will choose to be is one of the decisions that you will make together—and that will include executives and lawyers from both companies. And I would certainly assume that each side's counsel would be very wary of being open in such a discussion unless they knew that their openness would be matched by that of the other side. Otherwise, each side would have the understandable fear of being sandbagged, and would advise against participating.

Radix Lawyer: That's for sure.

Mediator: That is why we would first need to decide how we have that discussion and find a way of doing so that would make sense and be agreed to by both sides before we proceed. I would suggest that we design a process where the lawyers present both the strengths and risks of their legal cases for the purpose of educating the executives on each side. And at each step along the way, we would need to ensure that each side's honest assessment would be reciprocated by the same on the other side. After having that discussion about the law, we would then have a separate discussion of the business reality with the idea that we find out what is important to each side. Finally, we would try to create some ideas for increasing the economic pie for you to divide in ways that could help us bridge whatever gap there might be at the end of our legal analysis.

■ ■ ■

If the goal is to educate the parties about the law rather than threaten them with it, then it is essential that the lawyers reach some convergence about what would likely happen in court. That presents the lawyers with the challenge of discussing not just the strengths but also the risks of their cases, and of doing so in the presence of opposing counsel and opposing parties. This is not what lawyers generally do in the presence of the other side, but strong lawyers are certainly capable of doing so and readily see the good sense in doing so. And if they do, the executives will have the benefit of learning about the law while avoiding its polarizing impact as in the past.

For the lawyers to participate responsibly, there will need to be clear agreements about *how* to have that conversation if they are to act responsibly and be helpful to their clients. *Proceeding by agreement* is core to our work with parties in mediation. So is *mutuality of vulnerability*—going step by step while assuring each side's openness is reciprocated.

■ ■ ■

Radix Executive: This is all very interesting but it seems to be quite complicated and could take us a long time. Black told us that with his process, in a day or two, we'd be done. How long will yours take?

Mediator: Probably considerably longer. We would design the process together, including deciding what time parameters you want to work with. We would proceed by making small agreements about how we do this in order to reach the big agreement on a result. Right now the little agreement at issue is whether to use me as a mediator. If you choose me, our first order of business would be to decide together how to have those two conversations we just described and how much time to spend on each. Once you feel that you have sufficient understanding of both the legal and business realities, then the focus shifts to solutions: first by generating many ideas of possible options and then narrowing them down to something both sides feel is better for them than the legal alternative. That will take some time. I think it would be time well spent. You probably have a better sense than I how long it would take.

Radix Executive: You're right. It would take much longer than with Black. Can you tell me, in just a 20-second sound bite, why we should do that?

Mediator: Well, I don't know that you should. But if both companies are motivated to mediate, with Black you're likely to reach a solution rather efficiently, and it will likely be his solution. With me, you'll work harder and longer, particularly the executives, and you might not reach a solution. But if you do, you'll know that it's your solution.

Argyle Executive: And your role in making that work?

Mediator: To make sure you know what your choices are at every point in the process, and to help all of us establish a relationship where we bring the creativity of both lawyers and executives into the process. *If* you want to do that.

Argyle Executive: What I like about this is that we would have a lot of control over not just the outcome but how we got there.

Mediator: Shared with Radix, that's right. I think that is a major advantage. I also heard before that the relationship between your companies is of importance to both sides.

Radix Executive: I have to say that if we could turn around our relationship with each other, that could be of enormous value to both of us.

Argyle Executive: That may be so. But you need to be aware how deeply the adversarial relationship runs with us. Throughout our company, seeing Radix as the enemy has been a major way we motivate our staffs, and that goes back decades.

Radix Executive: No offense, but we have posters of your CEO that we use as dartboards for our staff.

Mediator: If you are both motivated to turn around that relationship, I think I can help. But you're going to need support and probably participation all throughout your organizations, and that might mean having both CEOs participate—if you think there's enough at stake here to warrant it.

Argyle Executive: They ought to be here. I'm not sure they would be willing to come.

Radix Executive: I think ours would come if he knew yours would.

■ ■ ■

There's a stark contrast between a generally accepted mediation approach where the mediator shuttles back and forth between the parties and their counsel and our model in which the parties, their counsel, and the mediator seek to *work together* throughout. The former puts a lot of power in the hands of the mediator, while in our approach we see that the *parties share the responsibility* for how the mediation will unfold. Some of the assumptions and values underlying each approach started to become clearer in this mediation.

Through the opening dialogue, these executives, and to some extent their lawyers, seem to understand how the dynamics *underlying their conflict* have contributed to years of unending strife between the companies—in effect, how they have been trapped in the conflict. And they have begun to see how a different way of approaching conflict might help them in finding a mutual way out.

Whether or not they will be able to turn their companies' relationship around, and together assume control for doing so, is at this point not self-evident. It will depend upon their motivation and willingness to do so. What is promising is their recognition of the mutually reinforcing conflict cultures within their companies, the possibility of changing them, and the potential value to both parties if they do. Their ability to work toward that shift in dealing with their conflict will surely affect the chances of working together in the future. And they know that.

■ ■ ■

Although I wanted them to decide to mediate with me, I was glad that they had an alternative that would be less demanding of their time and effort. I felt that if they decided to proceed with me as their mediator, knowing that it would entail a very different approach to dealing with their conflict, they would have achieved a significant step toward success. If the CEOs decided to come, then it would be far more likely that the process would be supported throughout both organizations and the possibility of not only creating but implementing ideas of cooperation between the companies that would make both of them better off financially would be much more realistic. Perhaps, even more important, their participation would be a signal within each company that it was time for the adversary culture to change.

I received a call from the Radix and Argyle lawyers the next week that both companies had decided to proceed and that the CEOs were prepared to participate. We spent the better part of six months in the mediation, meeting for two-day blocks, four times. Later we will return to how that work evolved.

Commentary: The Choice to Work Through Conflict Together

The first choice executives make in dealing with a business conflict with legal dimensions is *how* they will deal with it. The problem is that most parties do that reflexively, usually without much consideration of the different options they have and most often without any dialogue with one another about the choice. In fact, they may "make" a choice by *not* making it—they wait for their lawyers, they wait for each other, they wait for circumstances, or they wait until court proceedings seem to require a response. Deferring by each side readily contributes to, or even exacerbates, the dynamics of the conflict, but it can appear the sensible course at the time.

When locked in conflict, it may seem strange to think of sitting down with the other party and seriously asking: Just how do we want to deal with our conflict? But facing that critical question directly, and doing so together, can make all the difference. It was the question that the executives faced in Radix and Argyle as they sat down in the presence of each other and their lawyers. The mediator posed this critical choice—not just whether they wanted to mediate, but *how* and *why*.

Here, the purpose of the initial meeting was for the mediator to describe his approach to mediation and compare it with other approaches. But even if the parties had not raised the question of whether our approach to resolving conflict is *how* they might want to *work together* to resolve their conflict, we would ask the same question. It is integral to how we define mediation.

Mediation Definition: Mediation is a voluntary process in which the parties make decisions together based on their understanding of their own views, each other's, and the reality they face. The mediator works as a non-coercive neutral to help the parties negotiate an agreement that serves them better than their alternatives.

As we view it, the parties' intention to resolve their dispute gives the process its power. The choice about *how* they might *work together* will help bring that intent to the surface. Our goal from the start is to help parties understand this choice and, if they are interested in our approach, to make the choice with as full an understanding as possible about what it might offer them and what it would likely entail. That task was made easier by the lawyers' presence, on one hand, and the fact that the executives were also meeting with Jim Black, on the other. They came to better understand the different alternatives for dealing with their conflict: continuing on the course of preparing to go to court, or mediating either with Jim Black's approach or ours, which became evident as the dialogue in this initial meeting unfolded.

The lawyers' presence here also complicated the challenge. Their participation was perfectly justifiable. We do not believe it wise to eliminate lawyers or ignore the law. Both are critical to the protection of the parties, and, when included constructively, can prove invaluable to the proper resolution of disputes outside court. The problem arises when the lawyers' approaches to dealing with the conflict contribute to the ways the parties find themselves stuck, without the parties (or the lawyers) necessarily being aware of that impact, as appeared to be the case at the start of Radix and Argyle.

In order to help clarify the choices the mediator sought to pose for the executives and their counsel, we return here to a contrast of the traditional and the alternative approaches to conflict that we described in the first chapter. This time we include the lawyers.

The Traditional System (with Lawyers)

Within the traditional court-based adversarial approach to legal disputes, lawyers play a central role. Communication is customarily between the lawyers and their respective clients and directly between the lawyers as they negotiate on behalf of their clients. It is rarely directly between the parties as lawyers generally discourage their clients from dealing directly with each other, and clients are content to leave the legal problems and legal strategizing to their lawyers. In short, the lawyers speak for their clients.

The level of responsibility assumed by lawyers, judge, and parties is symbolized in Figure 2.1 by the judge appearing the largest and the lawyers, while smaller than the judge, still larger than their clients.

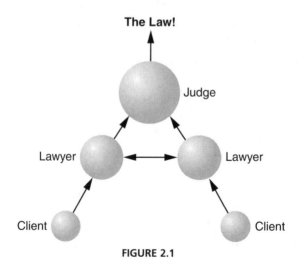

FIGURE 2.1

Lawyers' responsibility to speak for their clients is a known and accepted part of the traditional paradigm of legal representation as viewed by both lawyers and clients. It is an *implicit prem-*

ise rarely needing to be articulated. While there are clearly exceptions to this basic view, they are precisely that: exceptions to the
prevailing norm and practice.

Above it all is *the law,* or at least the lawyers and parties' perception of the law.

Lawyers make their judgments about how to proceed with
a view toward the legal rules and to their expectations regarding the judge who will apply the law to the facts. This, too, is an
implicit premise of the traditional system. These premises, and the
fact that they are usually kept implicit, can keep disputants firmly
trapped within their conflict without their being aware of the
nature or power of the premises or even that they are trapped.
The mediator's illuminating these premises can provide the key
to loosening the hold of the trap.

The Alternative (with Lawyers Present)

In business mediations, the lawyers' presence at the sessions is
more the norm than the exception, and we welcome their participation and the challenges it presents.

While the mediation alternative with lawyers present can
appear very different from the traditional, as we have schematically represented in Figure 2.2, how much it actually differs in

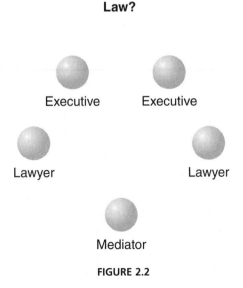

Law?

Executive   Executive

Lawyer   Lawyer

Mediator

FIGURE 2.2

practice depends in any given case on whether the lawyers, parties, and particularly the mediator will recognize and act on the potential of those differences. As seen in Radix and Argyle, the questions posed are: What is the role of the mediator? What is the role of the parties and their lawyers? And what is the role of the law?

While we have drawn the parties above the lawyers and mediator to symbolize their power and *responsibility* for deciding *how* they wish to resolve their dispute, the grip of the traditional court-based system does not necessarily disappear when the participants agree to seek resolution outside court. As we have noted, taking the parties (and their lawyers) out of the traditional system does not mean that the traditional system is out of the parties (and their lawyers). Particularly when lawyers play a central role, the potential for the parties to stay bound by the traditional legal framework—indeed trapped within it—is very strong, as the initial dialogue in the Radix and Argyle case quickly brought into focus.

The traditional model of dispute resolution is so familiar in our culture that most lawyers and disputants accept it without reflection, as appeared to have long been the case with the warring companies in Radix and Argyle. The point is not that parties should invariably dismiss the traditional framework in favor of some sort of mediative alternative. For many disputes, the model can make good sense, particularly when the dispute is clearly headed for court. Rather the point is that, particularly when trying to deal with their dispute outside court, disputants should not automatically accept the premises of the traditional framework in approaching their conflict.

But for the most part they do, and the unexamined acceptance by both lawyers and parties of these traditional norms readily reinforces the legally bound *conflict trap* while simultaneously keeping it hidden from view. Parties and their counsel who become aware of how this dynamic can take hold of their dispute, and take hold of them in the process, are armed with a laser-like tool that can enable them to choose a very different approach to dealing with one another, as the executives in the initial meeting in Radix and Argyle, and even their lawyers, quickly came to realize.

To ensure that the parties really do have the power to decide how to approach their conflict, it can prove essential that they understand how the legally bound traditional approach to conflict may be restricting them. If the parties are interested, the challenge will be how to have the benefit of the lawyers' participation and gain the knowledge of the relevant law *without* becoming ensnared once again in the limiting framework that so often attaches to relying on lawyers. Ensuring that the parties understood this possibility and this challenge was the mediator's focus at the start of Radix and Argyle.

For the practitioner who wishes to help the parties understand *how to work effectively together* to resolve their differences *without* becoming ensnared in the legally bound *conflict trap*, it helps to be aware of and sensitive to the reach of the traditional approach. In that regard, we look briefly here at both the evolving role of lawyers in alternative forms of conflict resolution and how the traditional norms of legal representation regularly affect the mediation setting.

The Evolving Form of Mediation with Lawyers Present

When the interest in applying mediation and other forms of alternative dispute resolution began to take hold in this country in the late 1970s, there was little recognition of the differences in the approaches taken by practitioners. Over the years, those differences have become clearer to both lawyers and disputants. Unfortunately, what the parties learn often gives them a restricted view of the power they can together assume for resolving their conflict. And when they are represented by counsel who themselves have had prior experience with mediation, as is now often the case, that experience can restrict their view of the possibilities.

Far more often than not in lawyers' prior mediation experience, the third-party neutral is seen as having great power in determining the outcome of the conflict. He or she sees it as the mediator's function to apply the legal standard much as a judge would, albeit in a nonbinding fashion. That is hardly surprising because the development of mediation has itself been strongly influenced by the role judges have traditionally played in judicial "settlement conferences." As any lawyer knows, prior to a trial, judges regularly meet separately with each side's lawyers, and sometimes with their clients, in an effort to encourage the two sides to settle. In that setting, many judges are known to cajole, twist arms, or otherwise use the persuasive power of their office to convince the parties to reach an agreement and avoid the costs, pressures, and risks of trial, applying the law to determine the outcome.

As mediation gained popularity, many mediators came from the ranks of these judges, carrying into their "new" work the norms and expectations from their settlement experience in court. The development of mediation was also enhanced by court-annexed mediation projects, many of which were themselves imprinted by the traditional judicial model. Other mediators and other approaches to mediation have frequently tended to adopt a similarly authoritative law-bound role for the mediator and for the mediation.

For example, many mediators start the process with an opening statement that sets out how the mediator works, followed by the recitation of ground rules that will govern. The way these rules are set out often feels to the parties that the power remains primarily in the hands of the professionals, with lawyers still talking for their clients. However, we do not start by laying down ground rules. Instead we explain our approach and the values behind it, as the mediator did in Radix and Argyle, so that the parties can decide what they want. If they choose the understanding-based model, we determine along with the parties and their counsel how best to proceed.

So too, many lawyers and mediators assume that it is the mediator's role to render a legal opinion or "neutral evaluation" that would guide the parties toward a settlement. We proceed differently, as the mediator set forth at the start of Radix and Argyle.

How the Traditional Norms of Legal Representation Affect the Mediation Setting

Many lawyers representing their clients in mediation are comfortable with a legally bound framework for mediation. It allows them to assume their traditional protective stance while avoiding the type of troubling questions about their role that quickly surface when the mediator poses an alternative. In order for them and their clients to proceed differently, it can prove critical to both the parties and their counsel to become aware of *how* the ways they have approached the conflict have limited their options for resolving it. The third-party neutral can help the parties and their counsel recognize *how* the prevailing attitudes and norms may have limited their options. We mention a few here.

- Mediation is usually preceded by an unsuccessful negotiation between the lawyers. When negotiating, lawyers are constantly looking over their shoulders with a view toward the governing law and the court that will decide the case—what is often referred to as "bargaining in the shadow of the law," a phrase coined by our colleague Bob Mnookin. In mediation, the courthouse continues to cast a broad shadow.

- Since the parties generally lack legal expertise and cannot be certain what will happen in court until it happens, they must defer to and rely on their lawyers' forecasts of what a judge or jury would do. In so doing, they fall within the grasp of one of the more powerful *implicit premises* that keep parties locked in conflict: that one should defer responsibility to one's lawyer. Once having deferred to lawyers about the law, it's not difficult for the parties to give up responsibility in other areas, in particular their personal responsibility for resolving their conflict.

- Once the conflict reaches the courts, each side quite naturally tries to convince the other, and the court, that it has the better case and will prevail. The lawyers tend to see the judicial alternatives from their respective adversarial perspectives, and each tends to exaggerate or emphasize the upside while discounting the downside of what might happen in court. *Trust your lawyer* can in this way lead to the different parties having often significantly divergent and inflated expectations of what would happen in court.

- With the courthouse as a backdrop, lawyers are often concerned that what is said or revealed in mediation could adversely affect what might happen in court if the

parties fail to reach a resolution. Professionally accultur-
ated to keep things close to their vest, lawyers caution
their clients not to reveal too much. Protecting against
the risk of being too open usually fails to take account of
the potential risk of being too closed to the exchange of
information needed to maximize the ability of the parties
to reach a sound settlement. The challenge is to find the
right balance.

- Focusing principally on the types of solutions a court would
  reach limits the thinking of both the parties and lawyers
  as to how they might resolve their conflict. If the mediation can move freely beyond that framework, a significant
  advantage is the potential for the parties and counsel to
  craft creative solutions that serve their interests far better
  than anything a judge could order. That openness would
  prove a huge difference in Radix and Argyle, as we will see
  when we revisit that case.

Establishing the Foundation for Working Together

When the mediator met with the executives and lawyers in Radix
and Argyle, he educated them about the understanding-based
approach not only by contrasting it with the way that Jim Black
might proceed, but also by bringing into focus how the parties
had felt about resolving their conflict and how the traditional
approach had limited their ability to deal with it. He did so through
an interactive dialogue with the executives and lawyers in which
he not only described our approach to mediation but also directly
applied it to the immediate questions and choices the parties
faced in that moment. In this way, the principles underlying our
approach can become alive in the room. The parties begin to recognize that the way they have approached their conflict may have
kept them trapped in it and that a different set of assumptions may
open the path toward resolution. If they are able to gain that recognition, they are in the position to make the choice to proceed
differently.

Once these executives began to see how the traditional protective stance of their lawyers had limited them, they immediately started to see other possibilities. Recognizing the power of the traditional approach and the hold it had on both companies provided the key to their working differently.

Whether the conflict is large or small, we devote the initial stage of mediation to *contracting*—clarifying our approach to the parties and their counsel and working with them to design a process that will make it work. Particularly in the context of mediation, a more open discussion can lead to a different way of working together, a fuller shared perception of the nature of the problem, and a wider range of possible solutions.

Given the importance we place on the parties' active participation and the importance of this dispute to both companies, the mediator recommended the CEOs be present if the parties were to choose this approach. Had the process continued without them, it would have meant mediating with representatives who lacked full responsibility. While acting through agents might appear efficient, it can actually result in keeping parties within their *conflict trap* by deflecting responsibility away from those with the knowledge and power to resolve the conflict.

When the executives and lawyers came back, it was with the Radix and Argyle CEOs present. That necessitated repeating much of the initial meeting so that the choice to mediate in this different way made sense to the CEOs and was supported by them. The mediator then spent much of the first two-day session contracting with them and their lawyers about how the mediation would proceed.

Contracting is the first of five stages in our approach to mediation. Those stages are:

1. Contracting
2. Defining the Problem
3. Working Through the Conflict
4. Developing and Evaluating Options
5. Reaching Agreement

This initial foray into the attitudes and assumptions under-lying the parties' and lawyers' stances toward one another and toward their conflict appears to have served these parties well. They began to clarify what it would take to mediate, the poten-tial benefits in doing so, and what might stand in their way. If in fact they have deepened their understanding and broadened their choices for *how* they might deal with their dispute and their business relationship, this frank dialogue about how they have approached their conflict will serve them well when they confront their substantive differences. We will see just how that came to pass when we return to Radix and Argyle.

A Holocaust Memoir: What It Takes to Mediate 3

The only indication of weakness was Mrs. Levi's walker, which she handled more like a weapon than an aid. So I was surprised she was accompanied by her middle-aged nephew, Adolfo, whom she claimed to need for moral support. This mediation was between Sara Levi and Patrick McAllister. Together they'd attempted to write a book. Her story. His writing. Patrick did not want Adolfo in the room. He found Mrs. Levi, as she insisted he call her, enough of a force on her own. "I don't want Adolfo to be part of this mediation," implored Patrick to me. "This is just between Mrs. Levi and me."

■ ■ ■

Proceeding by Agreement
Our work in mediation proceeds by agreement with the parties—actually by a series of agreements—about *how* we will be working together. The Holocaust Memoir case was unusual because Adolfo's presence in

the waiting room and Mrs. Levi's insistence that he join her immediately put us up against the first decision the parties needed to make: how to proceed, with whom, and under what conditions. Clearly the decision would not be the mediator's alone. The parties would need to decide, and the decision had to be acceptable to both of them as well as make sense to the mediator.

Reaching agreements about how the mediation will take place provides the foundation for all the work that follows. *Proceed by agreement* is one of our guiding concepts. The parties *deciding together* is essential to creating a real alternative to the traditional system.

Ground Agreements

In mediator's parlance, "ground rules" frame how the parties will work together on the substantive issues that brought them to mediation. We prefer not to rely heavily on the term "ground rules," as it suggests that the mediator will lay down and even enforce rules, as some mediators do. We prefer that initial understandings about *how* the mediation will proceed be full and clear *agreements* by the parties. To that end, we tend to think in terms of "ground agreements."

The distinction is important, because if from the start the parties assume *active responsibility* in helping to shape the mediation process, they are already making strides to assert themselves as active participants. If the mediator assumes immediate authority for setting rules, the parties will more readily look to him or her for the substantive solution as well, reinforcing a significant underpinning of the traditional *conflict trap*. When the *parties are themselves responsible*, they are relying on a significant resource for climbing out of their trap. *Working together*, they can help shape their own mediation.

The ground agreements in this case included who would be present. Other areas that typically need to be addressed are whether and how to have an open discussion about the risks as well as the strengths of each side's legal position, what information will be brought into the mediation and how it will brought in, whether the information generated and discussions between the parties might be kept confidential and thereby protected against use in the courtroom, and whether the parties want their interactions in the mediation to be shared with anyone. We would also probably address when and how long to meet, how the parties will communicate (inside and outside the mediation meetings), the role that attorneys might have (inside and outside the meetings), the responsibility of the parties for the mediator's fees, and so on.

One by one, we go through these issues about *how* to mediate until we reach agreements that make sense to both the parties and the mediator (agreements that may need to be revisited as the mediation evolves). Many mediators are skeptical of how much focus and time we give this initial phase, preferring to set out a series of ground rules at the start in an opening statement by the mediator and then move on to "substance." For us, the time we take in the contracting process is time well spent. (In this case it took the better part of two hours; in some cases it may take the better part of two days, as in the Radix and Argyle case.)

Whatever the issues about *how* the mediation will take place, the agreements that need to be reached to that end are not simply a preamble to the real work of the mediation but a critical and necessary part of that work. Authentically made, they give the process its integrity and its power. When rules are imposed on the process from the outside, as in court, or even by acquiescence to the ground rules posed by the mediator, the process can go forward, but it is without the motivation and commitment of the parties as the driving force. When the *parties decide themselves* for reasons that make sense to them, and that are consistent with the goals of both, the mediation can build from a common ground.

■ ■ ■

Once inside the mediation room, Mrs. Levi, who spoke with a heavy Italian accent, began: "I'm very upset with you, Patrick. I feel as if I have already lost. You've known my Adolfo for a long time. He's not against you. He's only here to support me. If I don't have him here, I don't think I'll be able to participate."

Patrick responded, focusing on me. "And if he is here, I think that I'll be at a disadvantage." And then, with a quick glance toward Sara, "You have someone to support you, but there's no one to support me."

Hearing them both speak so honestly and directly, I felt quite at ease, and out of that, began to speak to both. "I appreciate your forthrightness. It seems you disagree on how to begin the mediation."

Excitedly raising her hands above her head, Sara said, "Maybe this is all a mistake. I should have known better than to think we could work this out. That's the problem, Patrick. You just don't get it. You think we're here on an equal footing. We're not. My life is a wreck."

I intervened.

> *Mediator:* The two of you disagree about whether Adolfo should be here. So right now you are stalemated. Sara, you don't want to go forward without Adolfo's presence because you feel that you need his support in order to be on an equal footing. And Patrick, you don't want to go forward with Adolfo's participation because you feel it would place you at a disadvantage. So we need to find a solution to this problem to even begin. If you decide you want to take this first step toward mediating your differences, I suggest we try to understand what's really important to each of you, and maybe then we can find a solution that takes both of your views into account.
>
> *Sara:* Why don't you just decide for us because I don't know if we can work this out?
>
> *Mediator:* I don't either. But I don't want to be making decisions for the two of you. That's not what mediation is. The point is for you to make decisions together. And my role is to help both of you.
>
> *Patrick:* But if we can't even decide this, how can we possibly hope to resolve the big problems where we disagree even more strongly?
>
> *Mediator:* My guess is that if we try to find out what you each care about that has led to this disagreement about Adolfo's presence, we may touch some of the same territory that underlies your main disagreement. From my perspective, we need to find a way to go forward that makes sense to both of you. If we can't, then maybe mediation doesn't make sense for you.
>
> *Sara:* I am not interested in having a prolonged process where we have to spend a lot of time hashing out each little problem that comes up. Maybe I should go out and tell Adolfo to go home, and I'll try my best to make this work.

Mediator: That's a possible solution, but I think we might be able to do better.

Patrick: What do you mean? She's just said she'll agree to keeping Adolfo out. That's fine with me. How can we do better?

Mediator: The point is not that one of you simply gives in to what the other wants just because it's the easier course. If we go forward without Adolfo here, it could leave Sara feeling one down.

Patrick: But if we start with him here, then I'd feel one down.

Mediator: Right. My goal is to see if we can start with neither of you feeling one down.

Sara: But how can we do that?

Mediator: By finding out why you have each taken the position you have with respect to Adolfo's participation, and then seeing if we can find a solution that takes both of your reasons into account. It may be a bit uncomfortable for the two of you to live with this disagreement a bit longer and try to work through it, but if you're willing, we may have a more solid basis to move forward.

Sara: All right. Go ahead. But I have to tell you this doesn't feel good and meanwhile Adolfo gets to just cool his heels in the waiting room.

Mediator: Do you want me to check it out with him?

Sara: Yes. Yes. It's terrible to leave him there.

Patrick: It's all right with me.

■ ■ ■

It may seem easier for the mediator to accept Sara's acquiescence as a resolution of this issue, but that would have gone against the principles underlying our approach to mediation and missed an opportunity to secure the ground for the hard work that might follow. They would have settled on a way of proceeding that avoided what was important to at least one of the parties and, in doing so, left that party feeling at a disadvantage.

For us, *understanding* is more than uninformed acknowledgment. *Responsibility* is more than acquiescence. *Working together* is more than simply remaining in the same room. For mediation to proceed, the parties need to *make decisions together*. To do that, both parties need to be in a position to stand up for themselves and to gain the knowledge they need to make decisions. As mediators, we seek to ensure that each party has that ability or will gain the support needed to develop it. For Sara, to give in would not be a way out of the *conflict trap* but a surrender to it.

■ ■ ■

In the waiting room, Adolfo was pacing restlessly. "Maybe I should just go home," he said. "I didn't mean to make trouble." I told him we were trying to reach an agreement about his participation and asked him if he could hang in a little longer to see if they could decide this together, and he agreed.

■ ■ ■

The way a mediation begins is critical to its success. A primary goal of a mediator is to help the parties deal with each other on a relatively equal footing. In this case, an agreement about Adolfo's presence would support the mediation in two respects. First, Sara and Patrick would begin with a sense of being able to resolve a disagreement. Second, whatever the reasons, Adolfo's presence carried a lot of passion for both of them. If we could understand that better, it might unlock a key to the larger problem they wanted to resolve. I went back into the room not knowing if or how they could resolve Adolfo's participation, but knowing that if they could, we would probably have taken a major step forward.

■ ■ ■

Sara: Okay. I want to say why it's so important to me that he be here.

Mediator: Is it all right that Sara begins?

Patrick: Sure.

Sara (speaking to me): We've had several meetings between us already, Patrick and me. I've gone away from them feeling like I had lost my bearings. You must understand something. I am a child of the Holocaust. What I have experienced in my life has been unbearable. I am now well over 70 years old, and my life has been haunted since those terrible days. Adolfo is my rock, he's my lifeblood. He is the only person who can really understand me and bring me to myself. I lose track of what I am feeling and when I do, I don't know how to get back. And I don't want to do that here. Adolfo knows when this is happening with me, and he can help me find myself when I get lost.

Mediator: So the difficulty is that you keep getting lost in recounting that unbearable part of your life. And Adolfo helps you stay clear. Are you aware when you feel lost?

Sara: Only later. Adolfo sees it before it happens. He can see it coming.

Mediator: So you feel that his presence could support you to stay with yourself and not get caught up in reactions to what is happening outside you?

Sara: Exactly.

Mediator: And in your previous discussions what appear-ed to be a step forward during your conversations turned out in hindsight to be a step backward and you don't want that to happen again.

Sara: That's right. I want this to work, but I just don't know if I can do it.

■ ■ ■

I'm trying to see if I can understand Sara and confirm that I have understood her, by reflecting back what I have heard her say and affirming that I understand her view. We call this completing the *loop of understanding,* as we will develop further. Having gained some understanding of Sara's perspective, I can now turn to Patrick.

■ ■ ■

Patrick (speaking to me)*:* I would love to have the same thing for myself. But I have no Adolfo. You need to know a little about our situation. Mrs. Levi hired me to write a book with her about her Holocaust experiences, her teenage years. This book is about her, so having access to her is the key to the book. After each time we meet, I write up our session to incorporate it into the book. When I give the material to her to look at, she's disappointed, and we have these endless debates about what should be in the book. It's been frustrating for me to have these wrenching meetings with her. I feel as if we have made some progress and then she tells me afterward that she agreed to things she shouldn't have.

Mediator: So, from your perspective, having agreements that don't hold has made your job more difficult.

Patrick: Difficult is an understatement. Impossible is more like it. That is why I've quit the project. I just can't work under these conditions. This is a challenging project, and I've wanted to do it, but I have to have some consistent way of moving the book forward, so I need to have final say on the book. Mrs. Levi is too close to it. She can't tell the forest from the trees. She knows this. That's why she hired me in the first place.

Sara: It's easy for you to leave what you call the project. But for me, this "project" is my life. It's the only thing that I live for now. So you can walk away from it. I can't.

Mediator: Sara, I can feel your passion, and we will need to address that for this mediation to work. Right now I'm trying to understand what Patrick is saying and I'd like to respond to him so I can see what's at stake for him in this question of Adolfo's presence. Can you hold on?

Sara: All right, but I want to be sure to get back to this.

Mediator: I do too, but now I just want to see if I can understand what Patrick has just said. Patrick, with respect to the main problem, you have a solution in mind, which is for you to have final say on the book, and that comes from your desire to be able to make consistent progress. But with respect to Adolfo's presence and your being able to participate here, it seems that you have a somewhat different concern.

Patrick: I do. I feel like I keep getting pushed aside. It's hard enough to know that she is the only indispensable person to this. It is her story. It is her life. But I keep feeling as if there's no room for me to be part of this. So it's wonderful that she has Adolfo. I don't feel he is against me. But I don't want to be reduced to an object here as if this is only about money for me. I care about this book, too.

Mediator: Does that mean you don't see Adolfo's participation as a problem? You see his importance for Sara to be able to tell her story. The real problem for you is that it might make you feel smaller or marginalized in terms of your participation.

Patrick: That's right. It's hard enough to not be Jewish and to feel the distrust that Mrs. Levi has of non-Jews. But I understand that. I can live with it. I just don't want to become irrelevant.

Sara: You are hardly irrelevant. Don't you see that if Adolfo's here, I am less likely to get crazy when you and I are upset by each other? I know that is part of the process. If we are going to solve our problem, I know that Adolfo's presence will help me stay with myself. So if I say something is okay, I won't change my mind later, because I'll know that I stayed with myself when I decided.

Mediator: And how would you say you are doing with respect to feeling solid in this meeting so far?

Sara (starts to laugh): Pretty good. You're right. I am staying with myself. I'm not capitulating to Patrick. I'm not sure that I need Adolfo here to do that.

Mediator: From my perspective, that is critical to the success of this process. Adolfo's participation or nonparticipation is the surface issue. Underneath the question is whether you feel that you are staying with yourselves, not giving in, and being willing to face your differences and go through them. What impresses me so far is that you both seem to be willing to honestly say how you see things, knowing that there is a tension between you.

■ ■ ■

Going Beneath the Problem

After Sara and Patrick traded their respective stances on Adolfo, the challenge became to help them recognize and take into account what each cared about at a deeper level underlying their disagreement. The hard work of mediation often requires working toward that *deeper level of understanding*. When Sara and Patrick looked *beneath the surface*, their underlying concerns and aspirations became clearer and they realized what Adolfo's presence meant for each of them.

■ ■ ■

Patrick: I have a confession to make. I just understood for the first time why Adolfo's participation has bothered me so much. I am jealous that he is in this project, that you have his support, his companionship. I don't have someone supporting me. Not even you. I feel outside of the project. So I guess what I am saying is, "Go ahead. Have your Adolfo here, and I'll deal with my jealousy."

Mediator: And where would that leave you, Patrick? You said before that you would feel disadvantaged if Adolfo were in the room.

Patrick: When I heard Mrs. Levi say that she might not need to have him here, I realized that I would like her to have the support that he might bring her.

Mediator: And how would you get the support you need to make this work for you?

Patrick: I don't know. I'd like to think that I could do it for myself.

Mediator: Would it make any difference to you to clarify Adolfo's participation here?

Patrick: Yes, I don't want him to speak for her, and I don't want to be double-teamed.

Mediator: So if Sara wants to talk with him or he with her, that would be okay, but otherwise limit his participation?

Patrick: That's right.

Mediator: How about that, Sara?

Sara: Yes, that's fine. I just want him to stop me when he sees I'm losing myself, to take a break. But since we've been talking, I'm seeing it may be possible to work here without him. I'm feeling pretty good about this discussion. I don't want Patrick to feel one down, as you say.

Patrick: And, Mrs. Levi, I don't want you to lose yourself. I need you here to be able to make commitments that you can live up to. And if Adolfo might help with that, I need him here.

Sara: Why don't you call me Sara, Patrick?

■   ■   ■

We had spent almost three quarters of an hour to reach an agreement about proceeding. From my perspective we had made real progress, primarily because we now had a foundation for *working together* that felt solid. On the question posed by Adolfo's presence, both Sara and Patrick had expressed what was important to them *underneath the surface* of their initial positions. In reaching their agreement, both had shifted in important ways from where they began, and there was a fuller understanding in the room among us all.

The parties' *willingness and ability to assert themselves* and *make decisions for themselves* are central to what they need in order to go through the conflict, and we work actively to ensure its presence. Ironically, it turned out that Sara's willingness to set forth her view made Adolfo's presence less important to her. Through the dialogue, it had already become evident to her that she was able to stand up for what she cared about without "getting lost."

Now there was agreement between Sara and Patrick that Adolfo would be present and his role was to help Sara not lose herself. That she not lose herself was itself critical to their ability to work effectively together in mediation. Patrick had come to realize that it would be in his interest as well as Sara's for her to feel supported by Adolfo. And Sara had begun to see how she might support herself in the process whether Adolfo was present or not.

On an objective level, the result may have looked the same if Patrick had simply given in to Sara at the start, or if the mediator had come to that conclusion for them. At a subjective level, however, the parties now more fully understood what motivated the other as well as themselves. And those expressed motivations were consistent with, indeed supported, their going forward together.

They had made this first decision together with understanding and directness, and they knew that. They had, in fact, successfully mediated this initial difference that had arisen between them. In addition, what had arisen as the three of us worked to resolve this "procedural" disagreement might well foreshadow what we would need to deal with as we moved toward their substantive differences.

Would this ensure they would be successful in reaching an agreement on the dispute that had brought them here? No, but I felt more confident that because of this agreement, it would be more likely that the mediation would succeed. And we all had a clearer idea of at least the path to the solution and a shared sense that we could travel it together.

We then invited Adolfo to join us, clarified the understandings reached about his participation, and then proceeded with the other areas of contracting. We will return to the mediation of the substantive issues in the Holocaust Memoir case later in the book.

Commentary: What It Takes to Mediate

We have two central goals at the start of a mediation. First, we seek to put the parties in a position to determine whether they want to work with us to mediate their dispute; and, second, we begin to create the context for that work. The parties' clear choice to mediate is, of course, central to creating that context.

Contracting

Contracting is designed to provide the parties and their counsel, if they are present, with the understanding they need to decide whether to mediate in our way and, if so, to build the foundation to do so. There are four aspects to contracting:

1. Establish contact (engage the parties)
2. Explain the process
3. Clarify roles and responsibilities of participants (including intentions)
4. Negotiate ground rules

These are not necessarily four discrete phases. They are often quite interrelated as the work of the mediation begins. While what happened at the beginning of the Holocaust Memoir case seemed almost preliminary to any formal start to the mediation, the mediator and the parties were quickly in the midst of all four elements.

From the very beginning, the mediator seeks to *establish contact* or engage each of the parties. This can be done effectively by actively, authentically trying to understand them, and confirming that understanding. *Understanding* is, of course, central to our approach. The second and third phases in contracting—*explain the process* and *clarify roles and responsibilities*—are necessary so the parties can make informed choices about whether and how they want to mediate.

Making those choices together constitutes the fourth aspect of contracting—*negotiate ground rules.* With the mediator's help, Sara and Patrick negotiated an agreement on Adolfo's presence, which would later be followed by a number of other agreements about how they would work together. Each step proceeds by clear and informed agreements.

Making Conflict Acceptable

When we *explain the process* of mediation to the parties, we seek to engage with them in a dialogue rather than present a mini lecture, as many mediators do. The start of the conversation with Patrick and Sara, while unusual for its particular focus, illustrates how a constructive dialogue can emerge from the parties' initial concerns.

Disputants are often trapped within their conflict in ways they simply do not understand. Aspects of their *conflict trap* become evident as they begin to say what is on their minds. A central focus of our work is to change the parties' relationship to their conflict as the mediator did with Sara and Patrick's disagreement over Adolfo's presence, so that they can begin to move through it together.

From within the confines of the *conflict trap*, it can appear that persuading or prevailing, on the one hand, or giving in, on the other, may be necessary or inevitable ways to settle a disagreement. Another common way out is to let a third party decide, or simply to accept an unsatisfactory compromise. But each of these, as we view it, is a way in which the parties are avoiding their differences rather than dealing with them. Sara's giving in would not have been a way out of the trap but a surrender to it. But parties generally don't like conflict and a quick solution offers a ready relief from the tension they are feeling.

Which brings us to another of our guiding concepts—*allow tension.* In order for Sara and Patrick to move forward with the mediation in a constructive way, they will need to accept the discomfort that's part and parcel of having a disagreement. Ironically, often their refusal to accept the tension that comes from acknowledging their disagreement is what keeps them from moving through the conflict. Facing a disagreement is far better than avoiding it, denying it, or pushing it away and is an essential aspect of *working together* in mediation. In essence, parties need to be able clearly to disagree in order to to find a way to agree.

Criteria for Parties' Participation

In the understanding-based approach to mediation, *the parties make decisions together* that respect what is important to themselves and also to each other. Doing so can pose a real alternative to more coercive ways of resolving conflict. Much of the focus of the initial interaction in Sara and Patrick's case was on clarifying the roles and responsibilities of the parties. As developed earlier, parties' expectations of their roles in mediation are usually based on the way conflict is traditionally resolved in the legal system, where the lawyers are active and parties passive, and the judge decides. The understanding-based approach envisions a much more *active and responsible role for the parties.* The parties being *motivated, willing, and able* to draw on their inner resources makes it possible for them to *go through conflict together* in this way.

To assess whether our approach will work for the parties, we ascertain whether the parties each want to mediate their dispute. If so, what will it take for them to be able to do so? Are the parties going to be *responsible for decision making*, willing to *deal directly with each other* (in spite of the discomfort), and willing to *work toward mutual and acceptable decisions*?

These different capacities are neither assumed nor imposed by the mediator, whose task is to determine with the parties whether they are present. They are:

1. Motivation to mediate
2. Responsibility for decision making
3. Willingness to deal directly with other (including conflict)
4. Willingness to work toward mutually acceptable decisions

The first criterion, *motivation*, is the fuel that drives our process. To get through the challenging work of *going through conflict together*, the *parties' motivation*, rather than the mediator's power, will be key. If the parties come to mediation out of a sense of requirement or obligation—that someone else thought it was a good idea—that's not enough. If that appears to be the case, we ask whether there are personal or business reasons that make them want to work together in this context.

If one or both parties have no motivation to work through their conflict together, then there may well be an insufficient basis to mediate with us. On the other hand, their intention might not be clear to them, or they might have difficulty identifying or expressing it. That is usual and hardly constitutes an impediment. The question for us is whether an intention exists and can be tapped. However small or obscured from view the parties' *motivation*, *intention*, and *willingness* might be, we work hard to make them explicit.

So far, the mediator has not dealt explicitly with Sara and Patrick's motivation, but to collaborate and communicate are vitally important to both of them if Sara's story is to be told. Those motivations are important to the mediation as well. The question of Adolfo's presence demonstrated that each party could be *responsible for decision making*.

The third and fourth criteria—*the willingness to deal directly with each other* and *the willingness to work toward mutually acceptable decisions*—were clearly evident in our initial effort to resolve the question about Adolfo's possible participation. These last two are in dynamic tension with each other: the parties need to be able and willing to disagree *and* to agree.

Supporting Autonomy

We have succeeded in the first critical aspect of *working together.* The active participation of both parties means that they are *each* able to *make responsible decisions*. Each needs to be able and willing to realize and express what is important to him or her even in the face of tensions that so often accompany dealing with conflict. In order to engage in this dialogue with the parties, the mediator benefits from being able to keep a sensitive eye on what is happening within the parties and at the same time focusing on the objective dimensions of the problem they have come to resolve. Having this dual focus—on the inner and the outer—is an example of the value of the mediator maintaining *bifocal vision,* another of our key concepts. The parties need to be able to stand on their own. In Sara's case, she knew she needed the support of Adolfo and she got what she needed. This is indispensable to the integrity of the process. To this end, the mediator strives from the outset to *support the autonomy* of each party and in doing so can help assure that it will be possible to *honor their connection* as well.

This does not mean that only those disputants who are fully self aware and highly assertive are qualified for mediation. If that were the case, few might qualify, and those who did might be able to resolve their disputes without the presence of a third party. However, the parties need to discover their own priorities, express them, and stand by them. Our goal is that both parties are able to express themselves and that neither feels "one down." The resolution of the question of Adolfo's involvement posed that issue clearly.

Mediation as we practice it assumes that there is not a gross disparity in the parties' relative abilities to understand the situation and to stand up for themselves. It is the mediator's responsibility to help the parties recognize whether such an imbalance exists and to support them in addressing it. This is why the mediator cautioned against having Sara or Patrick "one down."

One of the reasons why parties to a conflict often hesitate to participate in mediation, particularly where lawyers will not be present, is that they are concerned they will not be able to protect themselves. In fact, a significant criticism of mediation is that parties who are unable to protect themselves can be taken advantage of in mediation. This concern is legitimate.

By raising the issue of possible power imbalances in the context of the mediation of Sara and Patrick, it may appear that this question is reduced to the mediator providing emotional support when there is a strong personal need. While it certainly may include such instances, and many issues parties face in mediation can have an emotional component for one or both, our goal of having a level playing field arises in varying contexts. Sometimes there are disparities in terms of financial or other information, sophistication in negotiation, structural disparities (between employer and employee, for example), or disparities of resources that need to be identified and potentially addressed. In each of these instances, we strive to establish a relatively level playing field for the decisions the parties will be making together. Imbalances in power can be a central issue in mediation.

Some participants need the support of others during the mediation (either in the meetings or outside) to understand what is important to them and to express it. Lawyers can often fulfill that role. An accountant's presence can prove crucial for some parties, a friend for others. With Sara, her belief that outside support would help her participate more fully led to her assuming greater *responsibility* even before Adolfo was present. The mediator attempts to have the parties clarify for themselves what they will need to participate fully. We are not "neutral" about that.

The Relation of the How *and the* What

In creating the context to mediate, we have focused on gaining the parties' agreement about *how* we will *work together.* Doing so follows from our goal of acting both respectfully and inclusively. If that were all, it would be sufficient reason, but there is additional value to agreeing about the *how* in getting to the *what*—the substance of the dispute.

This difference between the *how* and the *what* is a critical area where the mediator benefits from *bifocal vision.* Parties find it easier to reach agreements about the ways they will *work together* than about the substance of their dispute. By making agreements about the *how,* they are getting experience in making decisions together and gaining confidence in their ability to do so.

For Sara and Patrick, the substantive issue was about whether and in what manner they would continue to collaborate on the writing and publication of the Holocaust memoir. By first dealing with the issue of Adolfo's possible participation in a way that worked for them both, they gained practice in successfully making a mutual decision in an area that was not quite so charged as the substantive dispute. What transpired for Sara and Patrick about the *how* held promise for all that was to follow about the *what*. They had accepted that they had a disagreement, recognized and expressed what was important to them about the issue, and reached an agreement that not only validated what was important to each, but also took the other into account. They were learning to mediate.

In fact, they had already started to deal with some of the substantive issues underlying the dispute that had brought them to mediation—namely how their work on the book had broken down and what might be necessary to collaborate effectively to finish it. While this connection between the *how* and the *what* is not always so stark, we find it present more often than one might imagine.

Nature Preserve: The Loop of Understanding 4

The land had been in Kimberly's family for generations. It was an environmentalist's delight, with clear streams and ancient rocks, reasonably intact while much of the surrounding area had fallen victim to the ravages of development. Kimberly had worried that within the next generation or two, the huge increase in its value would tempt one of her heirs to sell it. So she had donated all 400 acres to a private environmental nonprofit group, which then created a subcommittee composed of friends and various conservation activists. Their charge was to ensure that the land remain undeveloped forever. Meanwhile, the forces for development eagerly awaited any sign of a crack in the phalanx of commitment.

The conflict at hand was an unexpected internal battle between some of Kimberly's friends on the board of directors who felt that the property shouldn't be touched in any way and the activists on the subcommittee who wanted the property opened up to the public so it could be enjoyed by many. By the time they decided to seek mediation, the relationship between the board and subcommittee had deteriorated to the point where several people were no longer speaking to one another. There was virtually no trust between the factions, and Kimberly was caught in the middle, doing her best to placate both sides. Finally, she had reached the point of exasperation.

■ ■ ■

My involvement began with a phone call from one of the board members whom I had barely known and hadn't seen for years. We had a brief discussion, which I advised the caller we should keep purposely brief since I strongly preferred to be communicating with both sides from the start. I suggested that we have a longer phone call with several key people on the board and subcommittee participating. Then we could talk about my approach to mediation and see how it fit their needs.

When I picked up the phone at the appointed hour, there was an awkward silence. I asked for a roll call. The phone line fairly crackled with hostility as eight participants announced themselves and their role in the organization. After describing how we might proceed if they were to mediate, I asked if anyone had questions. Deafening silence.

"Well, I have a question for you. Are you really interested in mediating?"

"We can barely talk to each other. Actually some of us don't talk to each other at all," Kimberly rasped.

"If you're not interested in talking to each other, then I might not be the right mediator for you, because I'll want to get everyone who is critical to participating in decision making to get together in one room for our discussions so that we can understand the different views and see if together you are willing to make decisions you need to make."

"The phone is hard enough," said Kimberly, "and in case you haven't noticed, we are not exactly all participating in that."

Given the difficulties of the phone call, I didn't expect to hear from Kimberly's group again, so I was surprised when they decided to set up another conference call to talk about how we might proceed.

"Who do you think ought to participate in the mediation?" I asked.

"We can't even agree about that. No one is willing to delegate decision-making authority to anyone else, so I guess everyone ought to be there," said Joe, an accountant.

"And how many people would that be?"

"About 30. Do you think you can handle that?"

I cringed, thinking of the challenge of working with 30 people who didn't trust each other together in the same room. But I said, "With your help, I think we can make it work."

After further discussion about mediation, agreement to provide me with some materials about how the organization functioned, and some background with respect to their difficulties, we scheduled a day together the following week. There were many issues to deal with but the main question was whether this group could work together in the future, and if they couldn't, what would happen next.

I arrived early on the appointed day to find the gate leading to the cabin where we were to meet locked, an ominous portent, but within a few minutes, the others began arriving and within a half hour, we were all seated rather uncomfortably in a large circle in a 200-year-old log cabin owned by a friendly nature conservancy.

All eyes turned. I spoke slowly, laying out some of the logistics of the day, feeling the enormous tension in the room. I ended by saying: "My goal is to see if I can help you make decisions together and for you to see if working with me in this way is something you want to do. To start, I'd like to hear briefly, from as many of you who are willing, your perceptions of where you stand and how you got there."

After about 30 seconds of silence, a tall, powerful-looking woman named Ellen spoke. "I'm a pretty impatient person, and I think it's only fair to say that I've just about had it with many of you. I joined this organization with the hope and the promise that I wouldn't be wasting my time, and I have found that I can't get anything done here. The committee just drags its feet. And, Kimberly, I don't think you really care about the public getting to enjoy the sanctuary."

I responded. "You sound frustrated with the way things have gone in this organization and your original hope of participating in something worth your time hasn't been met, particularly with respect to public access to the land. And you believe that Kimberly has had a lot to do with this. Is that right?"

"Not quite. It's not just Kimberly. It's all of her cronies as well. Either we do something to give people a chance to use this property or I'll go to the media and blow this thing wide open."

I responded. "So for you, the responsibility of shutting the public out extends beyond Kimberly, and your frustration runs so deep that you're considering ways of creating public pressure for there to be access, like going to the newspapers."

A short man named Harold, an attorney whom I judged to be in his early fifties, chimed in. "This is exactly why we're in so much trouble. Hotheads like you running around spouting off when you don't have a clue what's really happening with this preserve, its history, and Kimberly's vision. All you want to do is make a public show."

"Your frustration, Harold, is your feeling that members of the committee don't understand what's going on."

"I don't think Ellen gives a damn about having accurate information, nor does she give a damn what most of the people here really think."

"So you'd like her to care about what the others of you think as well as care about having the real story? Do I have that right?"

"Actually, I've pretty much given up on that."

"So it's something you may have wanted, but it no longer seems likely. Do I have it right, now?"

"Unfortunately."

Another person was heard from, a gray-bearded man named John, a retired naturalist. "The issue here doesn't have a damn thing to do with the people in this room. I've lived in this watershed for over 70 years, and what you need to know is that The Preserve is the heart of a fragile ecosystem that could easily be destroyed by having it overrun by hikers, bikers, and campers. There are many rare plants and animals that would disappear if we open it to whomever wants to come."

"That is the excuse that's used to keep everyone out," Ellen chimed in. "By that logic no one will ever be able to use that land, and then what good is it if no one can enjoy it or learn from it?"

"For John, the critical issue is taking into account the fragility of the ecosystem so that the animals and plants can continue to be protected. And, Ellen, you believe it's crucial to allow public access to The Preserve."

Kimberly joined in now, in a frustrated voice: "What you're missing once again, Ellen, is how easy it would be to ruin the land so that no one would enjoy it. Maybe you just want to turn it into a housing project for your developer buddies."

"So your fear, Kimberly, is that The Preserve could end up being developed?" I asked.

"Absolutely. When I donated this property to this organization and created this committee, I never dreamed that we would end up having the enemy in our midst. I'll be damned if I'm going to stand by and watch this land go down the tubes. I gave up millions of dollars in order to preserve it, and the only development that will ever take place will be over my dead body."

Phil, an engineer in his late thirties, jumped in. "The problem, Kimberly, is that it looks like you're just trying to take advantage of the tax breaks you got by donating the property and having nothing else change. We have a public trust here that we have to serve. Change is part of life, and you better get used to it. You can't control this land now. It's not yours anymore."

As I had done with the others, I made sure I understood what Phil had just said.

"Your perspective, Phil, is that The Preserve needs to go through a change since it's no longer in Kimberly's family, and that the needs of a wider circle of people ought to be taken into account to chart the future direction."

"That's right. It's got to be opened up."

"So bring in the bulldozers, boys. We need more housing here," taunted Sam, owner of a local fruit orchard and Kimberly's friend.

"I think I understand the central issue now," I said to the group. "Let me see if I can frame it in a way that you all would agree captures it."

■ ■ ■

Framing the Issue

I was looking for a frame to define the issue between them that would help in their working through their conflict together. It is critical that the frame be broad enough to hold everyone's point of view without one canceling out any other. Each party needed to see their perspective fitting within the frame.

If the issue was described in a one-sided way or in a manner that left out any particular point of view—such as how the environment would be protected—that would put a significant number of the people on the defensive, and I would lose my position as a neutral. If I described the issue too generally, such as whether the organization should survive, it would not be specific enough to frame the context of their disagreement. I gave it a try.

■ ■ ■

"The question is what kind of access, if any, ought to be provided to The Preserve and what kind of protection ought to be provided for the environment. Is that right?"

"Not quite," said Jane, a soft-spoken businesswoman in her fifties. "I think that the basic issue is what kind of access ought to be provided. I'd really like to know from everyone in this room where you stand with that. There've been lots of accusations and innuendoes but we've never had a discussion where everyone revealed specifically where they stand."

"Bravo!" replied Ellen. "I'd like to have it out once and for all to see if my suspicions are correct that significant numbers in this group just want to keep the status quo and are blocking every plan for access because they don't want any."

"Do others agree that it would be valuable to have that discussion about what kind of access ought to be provided?" I asked.

Several people nodded their heads, but Sam, his face reddening, said, "No, it's imperative we protect the environment. Access is the secondary issue."

"So including the protection of the land needs to be part of the frame for you in this discussion. The question is what kind of access ought to be provided that will also protect the environment."

Sam softened slightly. "You got it."

We had reached an agreement about the issue, one in which each party in the room could find a place. And even though the agreement was only about defining the disagreement, it was a significant step in the right direction. It not only established that this group was capable of agreeing at least on the issue they faced, but it also demonstrated how our mediation proceeds, moving forward with everyone's assent.

The tension in the room had not disappeared. In fact, in some ways it was stronger, because we had actually articulated a difficult problem. Now that we had defined it, part of my job would be to hold all of the participants to the task of working on it. Our challenge would be to agree on a solution that satisfied everyone. We would have to do that together, without my doing all of the work of understanding the different views by myself.

"Then let's give everyone a chance to say where they stand with respect to access and protection. Let me suggest that everyone make an effort to do this concisely. If each person took five minutes, it would still take us two and a half hours for everyone to speak. I'd also like to suggest a system for how we proceed. Has anyone noticed what I've been doing since we began the meeting?"

"You seem to be agreeing with everything anyone says," Ellen said sharply.

"No, he hasn't," Phil interrupted. "I've been watching you carefully. You haven't said that anyone is right, and you haven't given us your opinion. But you have lowered the temperature a little."

"And how have I done that?"

"By repeating back to each person what they said," Phil replied.

"Not exactly," said Jane. "I think he's been showing people that he understands what they're saying without making anyone right or wrong."

"That's what I've been trying to do. I call it 'the loop of understanding.' 'Looping' means demonstrating my understanding of what someone else is saying in my own words, but to their satisfaction."

"I think this 'looping' is very effective," Jane said, "because I know that when I spoke, after you did that, and I saw that you understood what I said, I felt a little more relaxed. I hope you'll keep doing that, because I think it slows things down and helps calm the atmosphere."

"I will. My hope is that we can work to create a context in which I try to understand what is important to each of you and that in doing so, you also understand more clearly what is important for yourselves. There is also the possibility that you'll be a little more open to understanding each other."

"That sounds nice," interjected Ellen, "but where does it leave us? We seem to see the goals here very, very differently, and that hasn't changed a bit."

■ ■ ■

It's Okay to Disagree

Like Ellen, many people think that if they disagree with one another, they'll quickly reach an impasse. There is good reason to be fearful of disagreement. Most of us have been stopped in our tracks by conflict at one time or another. We have learned to form strategies to avoid it. Some people try to dominate the other, while some give in or give up rather than disagree. Others, including some mediators, seek shortcut solutions that too often bury the problem, leaving ill feeling and the possibility the conflict will resurface later. These strategies may avoid the unpleasantness and dissonance that usually accompany disagreement but at a cost.

In our approach to mediation, expressing disagreement is a positive and critical step forward. Disagreement is often accompanied by strong feeling. If we can disagree clearly, we can identify the problem that needs to be solved. If disagreement is implicit and stays hidden, then we are shooting in the dark. Expressing conflict, particularly with strong feeling, can be the gateway to understanding the basis of the problem and the seed of the solution.

Part of the mediator's job is in fact to encourage the participants to disagree and to make the room safe enough for the parties to do so. This means that the mediator must be comfortable with having the disagreement out in the open. The dissonance that accompanies disagreement is no fun. Yet, if it's valued as a positive step, over time a mediator can become more comfortable with intense conflict. Parties are encouraged to disagree, with the understanding that its expression can move the mediation forward. Once understood and accepted, clear disagreement can provide the basis for moving together toward agreement.

For that to happen, the disagreement needs to be met by the mediator's understanding of the different views.

■ ■ ■

"Yes, it appears that you may see things very differently, and it also appears that there may be serious disagreements among you. I think we need to first understand where you disagree. Then let's see if you're willing to work toward ways to agree."

"And do you think there's a chance?" Ellen continued.

"Sure, or you all wouldn't have made the effort to be here together. You all obviously care about The Preserve, even if you view aspects of its use in different ways. I think we'll all be better able to judge how good your chances are when we understand more clearly your differences."

■ ■ ■

Validating Differing Views

To my mind, we had made a lot of progress. Many people in the room had expressed their views with a fair degree of clarity and passion. I had worked hard to demonstrate my understanding of their views without trying to change them. It was of primary importance that the people who were speaking knew that at least one other person in the room understood their perspective. Further, if the people who disagreed with each other saw that I understood their point of view *and* that I also understood others whom they believed to be absolutely wrong, it was possible that they might come to a significant realization: that other points of view could simultaneously exist with their own, without canceling one another out.

While it was too soon to acknowledge this any more fully, the perspective that I had as a mediator—that there was value in all of the differing views—might, at a later point, help them reach a similar understanding of how their differences could coexist. In effect, if I could do it, maybe they could too, with my support. If I could not, but rather saw it, as did they, as a question of which view cancelled out the others, then we would together fall prey to the same trap that had them stuck in their stalemate, which had by this point had degenerated into name-calling.

The first meeting came to an end with a discussion of how we would proceed. We agreed to meet a couple of weeks later.

Commentary: The Loop of Understanding

Developing understanding systematically, authentically, and compassionately is core to our approach to mediation and the *loop of understanding* is central to that effort. *Looping* is a technique that helps focus the dialogue and develop understanding throughout the mediation. Although the approach is similar to and borrows much from what others refer to as *active* or *reflective listening*, looping captures a fuller sense of the challenge. There are four steps to the mediator's loop:

1. Understand each party
2. Express that understanding
3. Seek confirmation from the parties that they feel understood by the mediator
4. Receive that confirmation.

This last step is crucial. Confirmation completes the loop.

Looping from the Start

The mediator's looping from the beginning of the Nature Preserve case shows just how central a role looping plays in our approach. With *understanding as central to the parties finding a way through conflict together*, the purpose of looping is not to convince or contradict, not to take exception, nor explain away. It is to understand.

Our recommendation for looping from the start applies to the mediator's looping the parties, *not* to suggesting that the parties loop each other. Many mediators, drawn by the desire to increase understanding, will turn to the parties early on and ask: What did you understand the other to say? Our advice, generally, is *not yet.* People are much more willing and able to understand one another when they feel understood themselves. To put it another way, believing yourself to be misunderstood is not a good place from which to try to understand another. Parties in conflict are often mired in misunderstood feelings. By establishing some understanding at the start (from the mediator of the parties), the mediator begins to help break the cycle of misunderstanding.

The mediator:

1. Gives each party the experience of being understood;
2. Shows each that the other's view, which often seems incomprehensible, can be understood at least by the mediator;
3. Restates each party's view in a way that may be easier for the other to hear; and
4. Models the art of looping.

People ensnared in a *conflict trap* tend to want to defend their position, to blame the other, to try to convince a third party that they are right and the other wrong. The mode is one of defense, persuasion, and coercion.

When conflict takes that form, as is usually the case, misunderstanding prevails. The more the parties feel blamed or vilified by the other, the more they feel misunderstood. The more they feel misunderstood, the more they tend to blame and vilify. The cycle is well known and yet it may feel as inevitable as it is restricting. Looping from the beginning can help soften conflict's powerful hold and suggest a possible way out.

Already this is much more than many mediators (and others) will do in an effort to listen. More often, people make a sincere effort to understand by paying silent attention, nodding agreement, or uttering the catch-all, "I understand what you are saying." These are not bad, but expressing specific understanding goes further. It demonstrates understanding. It does not demonstrate agreement.

Understanding Is Not the Same as Agreeing

Understanding as differentiated from agreement is a fairly subtle point and not just because understanding may resemble agreement. In Nature Preserve, the mediator is seeking agreement from each party that he correctly understands his or her position while not saying that he agrees that the property must be preserved or that increased access would threaten preservation or that preservation should yield to greater access. He is simply validating that these are the differing views.

But, at first, it can feel like agreement to many parties, as it did for Ellen. As a result, even this initial effort can become fairly heated, with a share of the heat directed at the mediator. If the parties think understanding means agreeing, looping can all too easily reinforce their *conflict trap*, and the mediator can get caught inside as well. In explaining looping, therefore, the mediator needs to make very clear that understanding is not the same as agreeing.

To guard against parties mistaking understanding for agreement, and jeopardizing their neutrality, some mediators prefer to reserve any outward demonstration of understanding for private meetings, caucuses, where they meet separately with the different parties. For us, understanding each party in the presence of the other does not compromise mediator neutrality. It establishes and validates it.

Looping from the Inside Out

To really understand looping is to recognize that it is more than just a useful skill and that it has an inner life. In that inner life the essential spirit of looping is grounded.

The mediator must truly want to understand the parties in dispute. The mediator needs to listen from the heart when each person is speaking and must make the effort to understand how each experiences the situation, particularly when they are hard to understand or their views easy to criticize. That inner desire to understand is key.

Focusing too much on looping's outer skill, on getting the words right, on learning to rephrase or reframe (which are important skills to learn), can miss the essential point, which is to truly and intentionally understand.

When one party is speaking, the mediator is listening—seeking to understand. When the mediator responds, it's with a genuine desire to communicate his or her understanding. Actually, better said, it is to inquire whether he or she understands. Seeking confirmation is also heartfelt, and the parties' response to "have I understood?" is critical, letting the mediator know whether he or she and the parties are connecting. For looping to truly serve its purpose, each step needs to be grounded in the authentic desire to understand the other, and the mediator and the parties need to know whether they are being successful in that effort.

If the inner desire is lacking, methodically covering each of the four steps (understand parties, express understanding, ask for confirmation, receive confirmation) may well be inadequate. The goal must be to have both the inside and outside processes working together.

The Point Is Not to "Get It Right"

Looping does much more than accurately reflect what the speaker has said. The significance for the party is not that someone can accurately repeat what he or she just said. The significance is that the party can *feel* the mediator trying to understand and feels understood. In our mediation training programs, we often say, to participants' surprise, "You know you're successful when the party says to the mediator that he did not understand her." Why? Because it demonstrates that the party is taking seriously the mediator's effort to understand. When that happens, it can become clear that the two are engaged in a sincere effort to move toward understanding. So at the start of the Nature Preserve case, when Ellen and then Harold indicated that the mediator did not understand or did not understand fully, that was a success. The effort to understand was shared.

The willingness to affirm that understanding has *not* happened does not come easily. It takes a fairly assertive party and a fairly open mediator for the two of them to acknowledge when the mediator does not seem to understand. When the mediator asks whether he or she has correctly understood what the party has said, the answer may be a half nod or "hm-hm," which an impatient or insecure mediator might take as validation and move on.

But people respond that way for a number of reasons. We are all so used to being not listened to and not understood, particularly in a conflict-ridden situation, that any glimmer of someone hearing can be a welcome relief. Also, the norms of social and professional contexts can make it hard for many parties to say at the start anything that might appear to challenge the mediator's expertise and accuracy. Conversely, a party may be anxious to get on with their story and may experience looping as an interruption of that chance. The sensitive mediator is alert to the half nod, and asks: "What am I missing?"

Helpful Hints for Looping

First, set the context for what the parties and the mediator will be doing together at each point in the mediation. Doing so creates a focus for the dialogue that follows. The mediator did this at the beginning of Nature Preserve when he sought to make clear that the initial task was simply to get a brief sense of the differing perspectives.

"My goal is to see if I can help you make decisions together and to see whether working with me in this way is something you want to do. To do that, I'd like to hear briefly, from as many as you who are willing, your perceptions of where you stand and how you got there."

The focus of that invitation, plus the realization that 30 other people might want to say something, kept the opening remarks brief and targeted on how each saw the challenge before them.

Without clarity, looping may lead you far astray. Later, the agreed-upon task might be to understand the different perspectives in greater depth and at greater length, and the mediator can emphasize that. Then the looping itself might be fuller and include questions that could open an inquiry rather than summarize a point of view. So, it is important to make the intent clear and seek agreement to the task.

Second, taking a crash course on memory expansion isn't needed in order to loop effectively. If a party tends to speak at such length that it makes it difficult to remember what he or she has said, it would be appropriate, indeed respectful, to say: "Let me stop you for a moment to see if I understand you so far." The point of looping is understanding, not testing memory. Looping in segments can be easier for the mediator and often for the speaker as well.

Third, remember the importance of *trying to understand.* When the mediator listens with both head and heart, it is easier to remember. Asking for clarification will be both easy and appropriate.

Barriers to Looping

Barriers to looping can emerge, even for an experienced mediator. Here are some common experiences that await almost any mediator who uses looping to bring greater understanding to the room.

Trying to Change a Party's Mind

It's hard to keep the focus only on understanding. The urge is to demonstrate a little understanding in order to get to the real work. "I think what you're trying to say is that preserving the integrity of the property is really important. Right?" And then the mediator moves to "the real agenda"—perhaps trying to soften or alter the party's point of view: "But of course there are other considerations that are also valid. . . ."

We term this use of the loop of understanding "tricky looping." Tricky looping is for a purpose other than simply understanding.

Trying to Solve the Problem

Another tricky loop is when the mediator tries to solve the problem for the parties. "I think what you are trying to say is that preserving the integrity of the property is really important. Right? Have you considered the following ways to do that?" This tendency is so common that most approaches to mediation contend that solving the problem *is* the point. Forget about the looping. But trying to solve the problem can be a formidable barrier to understanding. The mediator is looping, but her mind is on what is coming next. It's almost irresistible, particularly for lawyers trying to work as mediators. After all, isn't the goal to help people come together and solve the problem?

That makes sense. But for us the question is *how* to solve the problem and *who* is solving it. Looping effectively, as we see it, *is just trying to understand.* To help people solve their conflict, we believe in starting with just understanding. It's paradoxical, but to move forward into the future means first simply accepting where things are in the present.

A tension exists between understanding the parties and solving the problem and also between accepting the reality of the present and moving into the future. Tensions are normal in situations of conflict. The mediator needs to learn to allow tensions and to navigate through them, not to try to make them disappear, which occurs when looking for solutions and jumping over the present.

The barriers posed by using looping to attempt to change minds or set up a solution for the problem are relatively easy to catch, but only if as mediator you are paying attention to yourself. When in the course of listening, the mediator hears an inner voice say, "But doesn't he realize that . . ." or "I see a way out of that," a barrier is in the making. Those are not bad impulses. They are quite natural and will likely be helpful at some point. But not yet.

Judgments

Conflict is replete with judgments, and judgments are a common barrier to successful looping. Ellen accused Kimberly of not caring about the public, while Kimberly accused Ellen of wanting to turn the land into a housing project. Phil believed Kimberly was taking advantage of tax breaks, and Harold called Ellen a hothead. Accusation, retort, counter-retort in a hail of judgments. And those are just the ones that the parties were willing to say.

If the parties are going to speak together in an atmosphere designed to foster understanding—which is our aspiration— something has to happen about the level of judgments and their impact on any possibility of understanding. But the first hurdle is mediator judgments. And while these might be somewhat gentler than the electric interaction between the two camps at Nature Preserve, they are no less pernicious in their ability to undermine the mediator's attempt to understand the parties.

It would be easy for any mediator to have his or her own judgments about the parties in Nature Preserve. Maybe Kimberly was unrealistic, or Phil a bully; Ellen too abrasive or Harold too arrogant. Judgments like these are the norm. They're a source of information, though skewed. But the problem is that such judgments also put others in a box—they protect us from having to deal with the difficulty and complexity of the other's point of view. And when we put others in a box, we usually end up cut off from them.

Even knowing this, it's easy to side with one party against the other. Sometimes, the judgment is a reaction to the individual: "I hate selfish people." "She reminds me of. . . ." Mediators as well as other professionals know well how many times they have complained about parties, lawyers, colleagues, adversaries, and others whose conduct is irritating. Sometimes the judgment affects the viability of the mediation: "I just don't see how this is going to go anywhere with his attitude so fixed." Unfortunately, judgments have the effect of creating a barrier to the effort at understanding. Even hidden judgments can be felt, an unspoken sting.

What to do? Some mediator colleagues say "Caucus!" Once separated, the parties would surely cool down. And it's much easier to focus on each party without having to referee a war of verbal assaults. The parties may keep their judgments about each other, but apart they're less able to inflict or suffer judgment-fueled abuse.

But for us, mediation includes the challenge of finding a way out of being judgmental. For that to happen, the mediator needs to lead. If we can overcome the restricting power of our own judgments, it does not guarantee that we can help the parties do the same. But without the genuine effort to lessen the impact of our own judgments, we will be much less able to assist the others. To deal with how judgments obstruct understanding, it helps to be aware of the judgment when it happens or recognize it upon reflection. Otherwise, without awareness, the mediator may think the reaction is appropriate and remain prisoner to the judgment. To overcome the barrier of judgment, the mediator needs to want to understand the other more than protect the "rightness" of his or her judgment. Otherwise, understanding is the loser.

The Clarity That Comes from Understanding

In our description of looping, we have focused principally on it as a skill, and explained the vital significance it has in our approach to mediation. The mediator's efforts initiate the search for understanding that is too often lacking when people are in conflict. It's how we break the cycle of misunderstanding that feeds the traditional *conflict trap*. Another simple yet fundamental benefit to looping is how it can create clarity about the substance of the conflict.

The initial dialogue between the various participants involved in the work of the Nature Preserve culminated in defining the issue that they needed to address, and doing so to everyone's satisfaction. People in conflict are often confused about or disagree about the nature of their substantive disagreement. Defining the disagreement in a way that makes sense to all parties, and includes their differing perspectives, can be a critical step in moving the mediation forward.

Defining the problem is the second of our five stages of mediation, and getting clear about the disagreement is an essential part of that task. With the disagreement defined, looping shifts to helping the parties move through their conflict, including understanding the realities and ramifications of the dispute. In this mediation, coming to understand these realities and ramifications was crucial to the outcome.

The Nature Preserve Conclusion

I looked forward to our next meeting, seeing it as an opportunity for the parties to understand more deeply both their own views on the key issues that divided them as well as understanding the other's perspectives. Also they would need to understand more about the realities in which their dispute existed, including the alternatives open to the parties if mediation were not successful. In fact, central to how we define the mediation is that the task of the mediator is to help the parties negotiate an agreement that serves them better than their alternatives.

When parties come to mediation, it is invariably because they have not been able to successfully negotiate a resolution of their dispute on their own and neither has the unilateral power to follow the course of his or her choosing. The alternatives, such as going to court, are usually sufficiently onerous in terms of time, cost, or emotional toll to provide a strong incentive to try to work out a mutually agreeable resolution through mediation. The second meeting on The Preserve quickly exposed a very different reality.

■ ■ ■

When we sat down in the room, the group agreed, with some reluctance on the part of the subcommittee members, that it would be valuable to clarify what would happen if they were not able to reach an agreement. This became the principal focus of the meeting. Before long it was reasonably clear that under the charter of The Preserve, the board had the ultimate power to reject a subcommittee's recommendation and decide as it saw fit. That meant that the group whose priority was protecting the environment was, in fact, in control of decision making.

With the recognition of the board's authority for decision making, I noticed some surprised looks, particularly among the board members who hadn't realized before that they had this power to "resolve" the problem on their own. It was also fairly clear that there were significant downsides to going this route. Any hope of working things out together in a way that addressed the concerns of both sides would likely be lost. The interests advocated by the subcommittee for more open use would not be realized, and the people advocating for more open use of The Preserve might well become disaffected and even leave the organization. The rift could have negative consequences for the reputation of the board and The Preserve itself. When the meeting ended, it was not clear that this path would serve the board well. But their power to go that route was clear to the members and to the subcommittee as well.

As they all left the room after that second meeting, I was not sure whether with this new understanding, the board members would even choose to continue in the mediation. I did not have to wait long to find out. Kimberly called me several days later and explained somewhat haltingly that when the board met after our session, it decided to reject the subcommittee's recommendations for access, and also to abolish the subcommittee.

"I'm really sorry," she said with much feeling, "that we couldn't hang in there long enough to be able to find some solution that would work for everyone. But it was clear to the members that the highest priority of The Preserve was preservation, and nothing would change that. In fact, to be frank, most of the board really hoped the subcommittee members who did not support their environmental stance would ultimately resign."

I offered the possibility of one more meeting if the parties wished, and she said she'd let me know. But my sense was that the mediation was over. And, in fact, it was.

■ ■ ■

I had to confront my own reactions to this development. I felt regret that the mediation had not moved forward. Was it a failure? I wondered. Had I failed as a mediator? I never feel great when a mediation does not result in an agreement. Yet I also know that the primary *responsibility* for the result rests *with the parties*. Mediation is voluntary. Indeed, its power comes from that.

I felt badly for the subcommittee members who had "lost." Their views were honestly held and ran deep. And I imagined there could well be some long-term negative consequences for the "winners." While they may have thought they had done the right thing, they might have to confront the same or similar issues on another day without having learned much about working through differences.

I thought I had lived up to my commitment as a mediator to do the best I could to help them find a way of *working together*. But what about my commitment to helping *parties understand*? This result was a lost opportunity, at least in my mind, for the parties to better understand themselves, each other, and what they might accomplish together for The Preserve. But in this case, the understanding of the external governance reality trumped. I didn't much like it, but, like the subcommittee members, I too had to accept this reality.

Deepening Understanding

Part 2

The San Francisco Symphony: Tapping the Impulse to Work Together

5

Tapping the parties' deeper motivations for *working through their conflict together* can make all the difference in the quality and success of a mediation.

■ ■ ■

Several years ago, I was asked to be part of a team headed by Robert Mnookin, Williston Professor of Law, Harvard Law School, with Joel Cutcher-Gershenfeld, member of the faculty at the Massachusetts Institute of Technology and part of Harvard's Program on Negotiation, to mediate a dispute at the San Francisco Symphony Orchestra. The prior contract negotiation had failed and the resulting strike had proven disastrous for everyone. While an agreement had eventually been reached, the toll on the board, management, and players had been heavy; and when I became involved several years later, the wounds had not really healed. Everyone was wary, as well as fearful that if the upcoming contract negotiation failed, another strike could jeopardize the very future of the Symphony. With this in mind, representatives of the players, management, and the board agreed that they needed outside help to deal more effectively with each other if the new contract negotiation had any chance of succeeding.

My colleagues and I met with representatives from these three groups, and together we designed a process intended to teach *all* the parties, not just the representatives, three critical skills of interest-based negotiation. The first major component is communication, particularly looping. The second is learning to go underneath the problem—under the respective positions to the interests at stake in the negotiation. The third is how to develop mandates from each constituency that would give their representatives clear direction but sufficient flexibility to be responsive to one another.

The board, players, and management were very clear about what they did *not* want, which was a repeat of the ways they had dealt with conflict in the past that had led to the debacle of the strike. What was less clear was what they did want. In most mediations parties simply want the conflict and the cost and pain associated with it to end. In short, they want to avoid, stop, or limit the negative impact of the conflict. They want it to go away. The idea that the conflict itself might have value, or that there might be value in their going through it together, would not be readily apparent, to say the least.

From our perspective, however, the success of this mediation would depend largely on the willingness of the groups to find a new way of working through their differences together. And this would require identifying and validating *why* they might want to work together.

■ ■ ■

We believe the impulse *to work through conflict together* is a natural part of the human condition. It may be nascent, buried, or blocked; and it certainly receives little support in our society. But we proceed in each mediation from our sense that it is present, waiting to be tapped and given room for expression. The parties' motivation is the fuel that drives the process. It provides the indispensable, elusive *why* parties might want to mediate. For many, entertaining the possibility that there may be an alterna-

tive to their mutually reinforcing adversarial stances can begin to
point the way out of the *conflict trap*, especially if they sense that
the other side may share the desire to find that way.

■ ■ ■

The *why* here was buried beneath a dynamic of tensions that were,
in large measure, a carryover of what had happened in the previous
negotiations but also were fueled anew as the time approached to
negotiate again. For example, management felt that not appearing
sufficiently hard-nosed might allow the players to gain the upper
hand. Many of the players had a reciprocal feeling toward management. In addition, there were tensions not only between the different
sides but also among the participants within each side.

With all these cross-currents, ascertaining and tapping the different parties' motivations for *working together* seemed at first daunt-
ing, but with the players it appeared overwhelming. They numbered
more than 100 musicians. They were loosely organized, divided into
different groupings within the orchestra, and had a number of differing perspectives on the dispute.

Most parties come to mediation with some ambivalence, and
that proved to be true for many in the orchestra community. Some
felt they could not be too cautious, given what had happened only a
short time earlier. Others, for the same reason, felt it was important
to take a bold approach. Were such tensions to persist, it could be
hard for the players to do better than look for the lowest common
denominator amongst them, and that would surely make the process
much less likely to succeed.

■ ■ ■

Tapping Motivation

In our model of mediation, we recognize that ambivalence is part
of the reality from which the parties often start. Ambivalence
may exist between different participants who are on one side of
the dispute, as in this case, or for one party and not the other.
Persistent ambivalence, while natural, can lead to half-hearted
or uneven participation that only reinforces ambivalence in the
other. Recognizing and understanding ambivalence is the begin-

ning of the solution. One way through ambivalence is to tap the motivation of the parties to work things out with one another.

Knowing the problem that ongoing ambivalence can create, the mediator may be tempted to use his or her own motivation to urge the parties forward, in effect supplying the energy to keep their ambivalence from stopping the process. The parties are then dragged along by the power of the mediator's commitment rather than their own. We prefer to find a way to stimulate the parties' interest in participating so the mediation will run off *their* steam rather than ours. We do that by engaging the parties in a dialogue to help them identify and express the deeper motivations that may lie *under the conflict.* In a mediation with two parties, this is a relatively easy task, at least logistically. Our challenge here was how to do it with 100 people at the same time.

■ ■ ■

Initially, I had a series of meetings with the players to elicit the mix of motivations likely present. While we usually don't like to meet separately and confidentially with each side (caucusing), it was clear that sitting down with the orchestra members would be necessary. This was because of the sheer number of musicians, the difficulties that had arisen among them in the past negotiation, and simmering tensions that had persisted, as well as the fact that they needed to select and give direction to a much smaller number of their group who would represent them in the later meetings with management. Addressing the issues among the participants on one side of a dispute before they meet with the parties on the other side is one of the few circumstances where we do think it makes sense to caucus.

In order for the players to openly explore the differences between them, it was important to a good number that they know that the conversations would not be reported back to management. While I was uncomfortable with that, I agreed. I took some solace in the fact that, given the number of players at the meetings, it was quite likely that management would indeed learn what had been discussed, and the players knew that as well. We made some progress at these meetings, but ambivalence was ever present, and I had the feeling we were not really getting to the heart of the matter. Something was missing. Something within them or between them was absent from the dialogue.

■ ■ ■

I recalled an exercise that Jack and I use when teaching mediation to large groups of lawyers and other professionals that stresses the central importance of building on the motivations of both parties and mediators. In those seminars, we divide the group into pairs and ask them to take turns talking about their motivation to help people in conflict, while the other "loops" the response. We believe that the mediator's motivation is as essential as that of the parties in working in this model.

Bingo! I realized that might hold the key in this case: put looping into action to get to what was missing with the players.

■ ■ ■

Once conceived, the exercise was relatively simple. At the next meeting, I asked the orchestra members to divide into pairs and have the following structured dialogue: Taking turns, they were to ask one another to identify their motivations for being part of the orchestra, to loop what they heard from the other, and then to talk about what they had learned.

With many people talking simultaneously, the room was quickly abuzz, and soon, even though I could not hear the content of any one exchange, I was touched by a feeling of the "reality" of the conversations permeating the room. I felt honored to be in the presence of a kind of deep connection that seemed to rise out of their dialogue. I sensed that the same might be true for at least some of the musicians. I didn't have to wait long to find out I was right.

When they finished, we came back together as a large group, and I asked them what the experience had been like.

> *Jane* (a violinist): This was a fascinating exercise for me. I've been playing alongside Phil for the last 15 years, and we've talked about a number of things, but until now, we never talked about why we love doing what we do. Hearing him say what he did was really no surprise, because I could feel a lot of what he said in his playing, but actually confirming what was unspoken between us all of these years was wonderful.

George (another string player)*:* I hadn't really thought about this question, and when I did, I realized how much I had just taken this for granted and how essential a part of my identity is wrapped up in being part of the orchestra.

Mediator: Can you say what it is that is so important to you?

George: All of us have been such high achievers. To be able to play at this level, we've been competing and succeeding almost all of our lives, and the pressure has been enormous. Just to have the opportunity to play with others who are at similar levels of proficiency is really a great achievement. This may surprise you, but when I play the violin, I am one of many people playing at the same time, and I cannot hear myself play. I don't know if you can imagine what that's like.

Mediator: Having reached this level in your playing where you have always stood out, it might be somewhat of a shock not to even be able to single yourself out when you are playing.

George: That's right.

Mediator: What does that mean for you in being part of this group?

George: I can hardly say. On the one hand, to know that together we are creating some of the most beautiful music in the world is an incredible pleasure. But it also makes me aware how much I depend upon everyone else here to be able to do this together.

It went on like this for a while, with one then another member of the orchestra sharing what drew them to music and to their work with each other. The tensions present before had not entirely disappeared, but they eased as people began to articulate the powerful and common reasons why this musical group meant so much to them.

At one level, what had transpired was very simple. People who shared a similar interest and had worked together over the years were talking with each other about what they had in common and what drew them to their work. At another level, it felt quite profound, artists reaching deeply within themselves for what was most meaningful to them, for what drew them to create something sublime through the collective artistic expression of music. Simple or profound, I knew it could make a significant difference in the work we would be doing.

What we all knew, in a way that struck a resonant chord through-out the room, was the depth of emotional investment that a very large number of the players felt for their work together. Knowing that the fate of the Symphony rested at least partially on their shoulders, this deep sense of caring would be critical in helping us find a way past the ambivalence, which there would surely be, when we reached our points of crisis in the negotiations, as inevitably we would.

Particularly significant for me, we all recognized that I had not put those motivations into the minds and hearts of the players by sugges-tion or plea. The exercise had simply created a context for them to express their deeper intentions to each other and affirm each other's experiences. They now had invaluable common points of reference that we could draw upon when we reached difficult moments.

We hadn't begun to solve the problems within the players' group or those between players and management. Yet this reference point recognized by a significant number of the players could both join them together and support the effort it would take to work collabora-tively with a group of colleagues, many of whom still held each other responsible for the previous failure.

There was not total uniformity among the players. This was an assemblage of strong, committed individuals with a range of diverse views they were not afraid to express. Some had not joined the meet-ing. Others who were present were less than enthusiastic. And a small number just plain disagreed with the group as a whole. But despite these very real differences, the exercise had tapped something that was true at some level for the whole group. That helped create a con-text for moving forward. However, we needed to work to make these gains concrete and operational.

■ ■ ■

In the previous negotiation, the negotiating committee had seen its job as trying to please all of the players, which presented a serious obsta-cle to the success of that process. The consequence of this dynamic was that a small minority had the potential to, in effect, hijack the will of the entire group. We therefore had to help the players' rep-resentatives take the pulse of the orchestra as a whole and find a direction that worked for the most members. They would not have to be stopped cold by objections from a very small group. Although a consensus would have been ideal, strong support from a majority of the players was sufficient to determine the direction for the representatives. In order to help the players deal with their differences, we worked with the representatives to create questionnaires to identify issues that were a priority for the greatest number. Then, meeting with the orchestra to share and discuss the results, the representatives learned what those priorities were. By contrast, in previous negotiations players' representatives had entered the process with a list of several dozen unprioritized issues.

Under the new system, the representatives had a dialogue with the players both in writing and in person that gave them a clear sense of direction, but with sufficient flexibility that they were not locked into nonnegotiable demands. The representatives understood what the primary issues were to the players as a whole.

■ ■ ■

Building on Motivations

The looping exercise about their motivations for being part of the orchestra would continue to prove essential in creating a context for the work as we proceeded. That exchange, which had probably lasted no more than a half hour, had made explicit what had been implicit. They all now knew how widespread and strong that sense of shared commitment was. They were all a part of the same community despite sometimes sharp substantive differences. Their shared commitment to support each other extended to the Symphony as a whole.

■ ■ ■

We also worked with management, as we had with the players, to tap their motivations for working together to settle their conflict. The group was much smaller, and the dialogue not so structured. But the goal was the same: to examine under the conflict dynamic to the deeper reasons they were drawn to work in the Symphony.

Here, too, I had expected ambivalence, particularly given that management was still smarting from the days of the strike and fearful of a repeat of those troubled times. While this might appear to be a traditional labor dispute, with management at odds with labor, management had a strong desire to work with the players as partners.

This created a dilemma for management. While management knew it was vital to be able to work effectively with the players, there was a concern that the players could overreach if management appeared to be too receptive. In particular, they felt that the real financial constraints of limited resources as well as how they would be seen by other orchestras made it necessary to disclose only limited information about their situation to the players.

It soon became clear that every choice carried risks. Disclosing information that the players had not been privy to could open the door to being taken advantage of. Playing their cards close to the vest, however, virtually assured that the players would assume that management had greater resources than it did. This, in turn, would increase the players' suspicion, leaving everyone stuck in an all-too-familiar *conflict trap*. It was also clear that if the relationship between management and players did not change, the entire enterprise was at risk.

As mediators, our goal was to support management and the players to work through their conflict together. Since the disaster of the previous conflict, virtually everyone shared a motivation to find a way through this one together. That motivation resonated with management and with the board members as well, and they were willing to express it. Once articulated, it became explicit among them and created a new ground for moving forward.

To create more understanding about conflict and how the different participants from the Symphony might have very different, but understandable, perspectives on their common problems, we conducted a series of weekend workshops on core negotiation and mediation skills for many of the musicians' representatives and other players, including some of the skeptics, as well as management and the board. In particular, they learned how to communicate with one another with an emphasis on understanding rather than persuasion and how to *look under* individual positions to find what was important to all parties. If we could elicit both sides' deeper interests, these could form the basis of a cooperative search for mutually viable solutions.

In order to give the participants some perspective, we used simulations from problems other than orchestral, and we assigned roles to the participants that would give them a different frame of reference. Players had management or board roles; management had player or board roles, and the board had management or player roles.

A significant by-product of the role-play was the real interest in one another that developed among the players, board, and management. The players were pleased that the board members cared enough about getting to know them to spend their weekends on these exercises. The board members were pleased to find out who the players were, apart from their musical skills. Management connected with both the players and the board, without being caught in the middle. From these experiences was born a growing sense of commonality.

One breakthrough occurred during a training session, when one of the people from management pulled me aside.

> *Management:* I am trying my damnedest to change my negotiating style, because I know that I engender fear in people, and that's not what I want to be happening here. Do you have any advice for me?
>
> *Me:* I can see that you're trying to present yourself in a different way than before, but what's more important is whether the others believe the change is genuine. My advice would be to be as transparent as you can allow yourself to be. For instance, can you say to the players what you just told me?
>
> *Management:* I think that would be hard.
>
> *Me:* Maybe it would be somewhat easier, although still challenging, if you simply told the player reps that you want feedback from them.
>
> *Management:* Good idea. I can do that.

By the time we came to address the substantive issues in the mediation, *working together* began to pay off concretely. Management and the players' representatives were fully ready to find a way through the conflict together.

■　■　■

From management, the choice to translate new-found understanding into action came quickly. They initiated a meeting with the players' representatives and provided unprecedented amounts of financial information. The impact on the players was immediate and enormous.

First, it gave the players confidence that this would not be business as usual on the part of management. Second, the players now saw the negotiations as a shared problem. As a result, we all decided to create committees composed of players and management to investigate further information, particularly with respect to what was happening with other orchestras in the country, again moving them closer to working together in a new way. The problem had become a shared one, and so was the motivation to go through it together.

For their part, the players realized that they had to deal fairly and responsibly with management in making contract demands. They ultimately chose six different issues as priorities for the orchestra as a whole, including traditional ones such as pensions, health coverage, and touring conditions. They also chose something that had been an issue for several of the players for a significant period of time but had never enjoyed sufficient backing to make it to the negotiating table. It had to do with the configuration of the orchestra and the pieces most frequently chosen for performances, which created a central role for the string players, who were a significant minority of the orchestra. As a result, the string players bore a particular burden, resulting in a succession of repetitive stress injuries to several of them.

While this previously had been a central concern just for those players injured or at risk for injury, it now became an issue backed by the whole. That all players were willing to support this issue in negotiating with management rested in no small part on the shared sense of their common commitment affirmed back in the looping exercise.

Mutual recognition and support moved the entire orchestra toward a kind of harmony that solidified their unity in a powerful way. When it came to the actual negotiations with management, management understood and appreciated the significance of this issue's priority.

The other critical issue arose toward the very end of the mediation. The legal entity of the orchestra had always been defined as management only. While this may have appeared on the surface to be a technical issue, it had been felt by the orchestra as a source of separation and tension that was one of the undercurrents in the previous negotiations. There was a legal "us" and a legal "them" that each side could point to and reinforce when the inevitable differences in their points of view arose. The issue was largely ignored but it was always there.

At the final stage of the mediation, after a surprisingly short three days, an unprecedented six-year contract was agreed on. The longest previous contract had been for three years. Everyone coalesced around a significant piece of the agreement that signaled just how deep a shift had taken place. They all understood now that creating music together at the high level they had attained required recognizing and honoring their shared commitment. From this point on, the San Francisco Symphony would belong not only to management but to the players as well.

The preamble of the new collective bargaining agreement that resulted from this process stated:

> It is recognized and acknowledged that the "San Francisco Symphony" encompasses the Musicians of the San Francisco Symphony, Administrative Staff, and the Board of Governors. It is also recognized that the San Francisco Symphony has a Youth Orchestra, a Symphony Chorus, a Volunteer Council, and that other volunteers and professionals work for and are committed to the San Francisco Symphony Organization."

Commentary: The Underlying Motivation to Work Together to Resolve the Conflict

The Symphony mediation was so poignant precisely because the orchestra was collective in its aspiration to honor the highest in the human spirit through music. The mediation allowed that fundamental and soaring motivation they all shared to be vitally present as they addressed the schisms that had taken such a toll in the past. As we view it, many in conflict have a deep desire to find a way through their conflict in which they can be true to themselves *and* also honor the other, if only it were possible.

One of the most difficult aspects of conflict—in addition to the losses and injuries that the parties are fighting about—is the fact that simply being in conflict can rob us of our basic "I–you" regard. In the effort to resolve a conflict, the best that is usually hoped for by the parties, as well as the professionals supporting them, is that they reach a satisfactory accord—each getting enough of what they are seeking to stop the fight without either being taken advantage of by the other. As mediators, we seek that as well. But we also hold out the prospect of something more that not only respects each party but also touches and honors an underlying connection between them.

What made it possible to tap the deeper intention that ran through the orchestra was in significant part the mediator's belief that the possibility was there. Without that belief, a mediation is more likely limited to tradeoffs and compromises. With the belief, the sky is the limit. While an ultimate deal may still involve tradeoffs, tapping the parties' deeper motivations and connections can dramatically affect both the substance of the agreement reached and the meaning it has for the parties. Of course parties in conflict may not choose that course. But the possibility is always there—the hope of finding a way together in which the participants can be true to themselves and yet honor each other.

In the understanding-based approach, the principle of *working together* with the parties has this dual focus: supporting their autonomy while also honoring their connection. Ordinarily, we pride ourselves on our separateness and distinctness. We cherish autonomy. In conflict, tensions turn our natural and vitally important sense of separateness and autonomy into alienation, fear, and aggression. We become reactive to one another, fear being taken advantage of, and stand ready to fight and defend ourselves.

In traditional dispute resolution, where a judge has the responsibility for deciding the outcome, choosing between competing arguments keeps the parties locked in their struggle, reactive to one another in the effort to win over the third party. So, too, does the mediator who takes significant responsibility for fashioning the solution and does not allow a full exploration of what is really at stake for the parties.

Mediation holds the possibility and challenge of honoring the autonomy of each party, but without the destructive pattern of attack–defend–counterattack. Making the parties responsible for resolving their dispute is one way to support and respect their individuality. So, too, is the mediator's effort to understand each of the parties differing views. When the mediator seeks, through looping, to affirm each party's distinct perspective on the conflict, the parties have the opportunity to clarify for themselves what matters to them most *underlying their conflict.*

Working together with the parties need not stop with validating the parties' autonomy. We also seek to honor their connection. After understanding the parties' separate views, the mediator can support them in seeking to understand each other, if they are willing to do so *and* if they do not lose their separate perspectives in the process.

In conflict situations, any sense of our interconnectedness may seem nonexistent. Even entertaining the notion can feel threatening as we are impelled to run from any identification with someone we experience as a threat. But the ability to experience interconnectedness with one whose views seem so opposing and threatening can be as rewarding and deeply validating as it seems unreal and impossible.

A central motivation for us in working with conflict is the recognition that whether it is in the family or the neighborhood, in business or between businesses, between groups and between peoples, there is an underlying human connection. And there always exists even in the face of conflict the possibility and challenge of recognizing and seeking to honor that connection. We believe that underlying connection is within us as is the motivation to reach for it. Tapping that motivation can make all the difference.

It may seem paradoxical, and the experience may often be one of dissonance, but in the understanding-based approach, autonomy is fullest in the context of connection, and connection is most honored when it allows and supports autonomy. The mediation principle of *working together* gives the possibility of both. The Symphony mediation lived that paradox.

Standoff at the Ranch: About Right and Wrong | 6

I have rarely, if ever, experienced the contrast between mediation and judicial decision-making with such starkness as that morning when summoned to see Graziella and Ricardo arguing their case to a somewhat surprised local judge on the grounds outside the Ranch.

Both parties were powerful presences. It was clear that sharing the power to resolve their conflict together would be far preferable to giving that power away to somebody else. But for them to be able to *work together*, they would need to get out of the right-wrong *conflict trap* in which they were so firmly entrenched.

People who feel as badly treated by one another as Graziella and Ricardo did often expect to convince me that they are right and the other wrong. And I often find that I do have reactions that move me to one side or the other, even though my commitment as a mediator is to hold a reality that includes both. To help them escape that trap, I have to be sure not to get drawn into it myself.

95

■　■　■

Once we sat down to speak, the history of the siblings' conflict began to come out. Graziella and Ricardo had inherited the property that they had grown up on in the form of two parcels—she receiving the parcel on which the inn was now situated and he the land on which the farm was principally located. Graziella's primary commitment was to the inn while Ricardo's was principally to the growth of the organic farm and to his dream of establishing a bird sanctuary on the land. Originally, they had cooperated well in developing both the inn and the farm. Tensions grew with time, however, and they had had a series of gradually escalating fights over a period of eight years. When I met them, they had lost most of the trust they had enjoyed growing up. They now either avoided one another when they could or attacked one another when they had to have contact.

In preparation for the mediation, Ricardo had put together a written history of a series of problems that he wanted to discuss, along with different papers documenting a number of points. Graziella was not interested in reading or even having me read what she called his "endless series of complaints, always distorting every problem." She preferred to just talk rather than "drag out all of the letters and e-mails, which just end up confusing everything."

One highly charged issue seemed to be at the root of many of their disputes. At the time they inherited the two pieces of land that made up The Ranch, both were aware of a disparity in their parcels' values, in spite of the fact that they were of relatively equal size. Reflecting the good will between them, Graziella had agreed to pay Ricardo the equivalent of about $200,000 to make up the difference. Because Graziella was then under some financial pressure, they had decided that Graziella would make periodic payments whenever she was able at no interest. By the time we met, close to 10 years had passed and Graziella had paid down "the loan," as they termed it, with a remaining balance equivalent to about $25,000.

We agreed to start with them clarifying for me how they both saw this issue. Ricardo had prepared a detailed chart comparing the amounts he received from Graziella with what he would have gotten if he had charged annual interest of 5 percent and 10 percent, representing interest rates that Graziella had actually paid to friends and the bank for other loans she had taken out during that period of time. When she saw Ricardo's charts, Graziella was outraged.

> *Graziella:* So now we're starting with your charts again, which you say will help clarify. But once again what you're trying to do is change the agreement we made.
>
> *Ricardo:* I'm not trying to change the agreement. Let's just go through the analysis.
>
> *Graziella:* I'm not interested in going through the analysis. This is stupid.
>
> *Ricardo:* Gary, help us. She is quick with numbers. I have to get it down on paper to understand it. My calculations are that if we figured on the basis of only a modest rate of interest, the original $200,000 would be almost doubled.

They went back and forth in rapid-fire exchanges, getting more and more upset. I did my best to follow what they were saying, and show some understanding to each of them through looping. It became clear to me that they were each missing something in what the other was saying that, if understood, could potentially make a significant difference.

■ ■ ■

Differing Perspectives

Parties in conflict stand ready to plead their case to anyone. From their respective perspectives, each seeks to protect one's self, family, business, assets, or whatever else they value. Given the suffering experienced or anticipated, they assume that the other's intention is to cause them harm. From the perspective of the other, the picture is reversed. The mediator's appreciation of this fundamental dynamic that so often underlies conflict can prove enormously helpful.

■ ■ ■

> *Mediator:* As I listen to you, I think the two of you are missing something important here. You each feel that you are right,

the other is wrong, and that, in fact, you have been wronged by the other.

Ricardo: I only know what happened.

Mediator: What I think you are missing is something very basic in what the other is saying. As a result, you feel maligned and misunderstood. The more you feel misunderstood, the more frustrated and upset you get with the other. The more upset you get, the less you understand. And so it goes on and on. I want to slow this down a bit and see if I correctly understand what you are each saying. If I can understand each of you, maybe you'll better understand both yourselves and each other as well. OK?

Ricardo: I think I'm being very clear.

Mediator: Is that a yes?

Ricardo: Sure.

Graziella: Yes. Go ahead.

Mediator: Graziella, if I understand correctly, you are afraid that Ricardo is seeking to renegotiate the terms of the loan because he's not happy with the division, and this is his way of indirectly getting what he can't get directly. Is that right?

Graziella: More or less. I'm not going to revisit the deal we made. I agreed to equalize the division between us in good faith, and I've made every effort to pay Ricardo back as quickly as I have been able. Whenever I've had extra money, I've given it to him. He knows this.

Mediator: You have worked to pay back the loan in a timely way, which itself arose from a good-faith effort to equalize the way the two of you inherited the land.

Graziella: Yes.

Mediator: Ricardo, what I understand from you is that you are *neither* trying to change the original agreement, *nor* the terms for paying back the difference. Through the charts, you are trying to point out to Graziella how generous the terms for repayment of the loan were and how that has saved her money over time, even compared to the deals she made with her friends.

Ricardo: Exactly. And she won't even bother to look at the charts. I passed up a lot of opportunities to make investments with that money that would have been very profitable to me.

Mediator: So the point of all the charts and this conversation is not to change anything at all. What you really want is for Graziella to see your very real effort at generosity to her.

Ricardo: This is what you do for family.

Mediator: So you feel good about having made this financial sacrifice because of your family relationship?

Ricardo: I don't view it as a sacrifice.

Graziella: I've been generous to Ricardo, too. Initially he'd abandoned his land right after the division. I was left all alone to deal with developers who threatened to take it away. Later Ricardo realized that the land had value, and then it was there for him.

Mediator: So you too feel that you did things for Ricardo that you would like him to recognize.

Graziella: Of course. Wouldn't anybody?

Mediator: So what you both want is some acknowledgement from the other of what you have done to help each other.

Graziella turned toward Ricardo and asked in disbelief: You're not trying to change the division?

Ricardo: No. Not now and not before.

Graziella: You're not asking for interest?

Ricardo: I never did and I never will.

They paused, and the three of us sat in silence. The moment was emotionally powerful. The history of the difficulties between them prevented them from seeing that the original generosity of spirit on both their parts was still intact. They were stunned. Later, we were able to draw upon this moment when it came time to deal with another part of their dispute.

■ ■ ■

The Dilemma of Intentions and Impacts

What had happened between Graziella and Ricardo was in one sense very simple, but a challenge they had not been able to contemplate, let alone undertake, for years. Without abandoning how they themselves experienced their own intentions and goals, each of them suddenly grasped how the other saw it. And their differing perspectives no longer needed to cancel out one another.

If we look carefully at this dynamic, we find it flows from our existence as separate human beings. Stated succinctly:

We tend to judge ourselves by our intentions.

We judge others by the impact of their actions on us.

Our own intentions usually seem justifiable and well-meaning. But if the impact of the other's actions proves hurtful to us, *those* intentions must be malevolent. When both parties are attributing the best to their own motives and the worst to the other's, the slide into conflict is as normal as it is precipitous. This is a way that conflict can readily trap us.

To challenge the hold conflict can have over people, it is critical to find a way out of this dynamic. Otherwise the parties' negative judgments of one another will block any authentic understanding. One way out is to help the parties recognize that they are seeing things, and each other, from different subjective vantage points. Separating parties' reactions and clarifying that they are experiencing the conflict from different points of viewing can often hold the key to finding a way out of their trap. What had just transpired between Graziella and Ricardo was to prove crucial as we looked at the issues that they identified as core to the divisions that had developed between them.

When Graziella and Ricardo were both able to see the intention behind the others' words and actions, the impact was immediate and transforming. They were eager to visit the other elements of their conflict from their new vantage points, which we proceeded to do in detail and depth over the next three days.

■ ■ ■

Essentially, the two of them were running a family business, or actually two businesses—the inn and the farm. While each business stood on its own, the farm of fruit trees, vegetables and flowers, and sanctuary for birds provided a lush environment for guests at the inn to meander through. The guests became customers for the farm.

Graziella and Ricardo drew the same monthly compensation but differed, often dramatically, on what was important, what needed safeguarding. While their running disputes had distinctive elements, they often had a similar tension at the core. Ricardo was deeply committed to the development of a bird sanctuary and felt that Graziella failed to recognize that as well as the importance of their natural surroundings and what it took to make it flourish; Graziella felt that Ricardo failed to appreciate the exigencies of the financial and legal constraints in which both ventures operated.

One of the most serious difficulties stemmed from an incident that had occurred two years ago. When they began to talk about it, I immediately understood why the scene I had witnessed the day before with the bus and bird's nest had taken on such epic proportions.

In the previous event, there had been a change in the law regarding ingress and egress for fire trucks and emergency vehicles at places of lodging. This required that the inn submit detailed maps showing any such routes, their dimensions, gradations, and surfaces. Ricardo was convinced that two of the property's gravel roads would amply meet the requirements, but was concerned that a survey would not properly convey the roads' full operable widths. If this were the case, the town would require further widening, with resultant destruction of the vegetation along the boundaries.

Graziella hired a surveyor to map the property and these specific routes and informed Ricardo. The surveyor sent his assistant, unannounced, to do some preliminary work the day before the scheduled appointment. Neither Ricardo nor Graziella were on the property at the time. They found out from their employees what had happened only after the fact.

In an effort to plot the exact location of the roads, the surveyor decided to use the charted boundary line between their properties as an existing point of reference. But in trying to do so, the assistant confused the boundary line with a pristine walkway that ran roughly parallel to it, but totally separate from the access roads at issue.

That walkway had contained many rare and fragile young plants that provided a perfect nesting area for one particular species of bird and were therefore highly prized by Ricardo. It had taken him and his foreman, Carlos, two years of repeated efforts before they were able to succeed in having one particular species of that flowering plant take root, one originally indigenous to the area that had been a nesting area for one species of bird when Graziella and Ricardo had been growing up, but that had become almost extinct with the general development and resulting erosion occurring over the years. For Ricardo, these reestablished plants would provide a crowning aesthetic touch to the bird sanctuary and the ambiance he wanted to create for visitors to the inn.

While working on the path, the surveyor's assistant inadvertently destroyed a significant portion of these young plants and any nesting areas they could provide. When Ricardo saw the destruction, he was devastated. He immediately called Graziella and became so enraged in talking with her that she hung up on him and refused to respond to his further efforts to contact her.

While the siblings were on a much better footing after having cleared matters up about "the loan," when Ricardo started to talk about this two-year-old event, his voice shook.

> *Ricardo:* She wouldn't answer any of my e-mails or phone calls. I assumed that she instructed the surveyor to damage the property because she was angry with me on another matter at the time.
>
> *Mediator:* You took her silence as confirmation that she intended to do you harm?
>
> *Ricardo:* Of course. Otherwise, we could have talked about it.
>
> *Graziella:* Talk about it? The way Ricardo talks is to attack and abuse me. I won't put up with it.
>
> *Ricardo:* What was I supposed to do, congratulate you for destroying my work and what it meant for making this a true bird sanctuary?
>
> *Mediator:* I think we're experiencing a similar communication problem to the payment adjustment you made for the land.
>
> *Ricardo:* What do you mean?
>
> *Mediator:* I imagine that Graziella felt badly about the surveyor's mistake.
>
> *Graziella:* Of course. I had no idea he would be so careless. I had given him very clear instructions about the boundary, but he sent someone else to do the actual work on the day before it was scheduled.
>
> *Mediator:* So you never intended to harm those new plants or intrude on the nesting area?
>
> *Graziella:* Of course not. Why would I do that?
>
> *Mediator:* And when Ricardo called you, it sounds like that was very upsetting to you.

Graziella: He yelled at me. He even said that he hated me.

Mediator: So your withdrawal from him was an effort to protect yourself.

Graziella: I had to draw the line.

Mediator: It sounds like you were frightened.

Graziella: I felt like crumbling.

Mediator: Ricardo, for you, it must have been horrible to find out about this destruction.

Ricardo: I had tended these plants for months and months, and had been dreaming for years before about their taking root again at the ranch and the birds once again nesting there. I knew she knew how much they meant to me.

Mediator: And in the telephone call, you were really upset.

Ricardo: I was.

Mediator: What did you want from her?

Ricardo: I wanted her to know how badly I felt.

Mediator: The reactions of both of you in this situation seem understandable to me. You were devastated and expressed it angrily to Graziella. Graziella, you felt you had to protect yourself and withdrew from your brother. And, Ricardo, you took that as a sign that Graziella didn't care about or support your commitment to the sanctuary.

Ricardo: I see what you are saying. I find this very helpful.

Mediator: How so?

Ricardo: When you help clarify what is behind Graziella's actions, I feel more open to her.

Graziella: That's true for me too with Ricardo. I, too, care for how you want to protect the different birds—not as much as you do, but I do.

Mediator: From where I'm sitting, it looks to me as if each of you is doing something quite similar. This happens a lot in conflict, especially when trust is disappearing. You are quick to jump to conclusions about the other. You each judge yourselves by what you know to be your good intentions. But you judge each other by how the other's actions affect you.

Again, a moment of quiet, and then Graziella and Ricardo both started to laugh.

Mediator: What just happened?

Graziella: You're right. I was just thinking about what happened with the bus and its impact on the bird sanctuary.

Mediator: What was that?

Graziella: I was angry with Ricardo because I *"knew"* that he was trying to villainize me in the community.

Ricardo: And I was angry with Graziella because I *"knew"* that she had instructed the bus driver to disregard the sanctuary.

Mediator: And you each also knew that when it came to your own actions, *your* intentions were much more benign.

Graziella: I was trying to find a way for the bus to park without interfering with traffic. I had no idea that this might cause any damage. If I had, I would never have done it.

Ricardo: And I was just trying to protect the bird sanctuary.

Mediator: What is it like for you each to have this clarified?

Graziella: I'm afraid that much of how I have been seeing Ricardo I have been dreaming up, or at least exaggerating, which I now see fed my distrust.

Ricardo: Same with me. It has been hard to think that my sister might be trying to get me. Now I see her more like I used to know her.

This was another key moment in the mediation, because it allowed Ricardo and Graziella to see each other in a light that felt truer and made more sense to them.

■ ■ ■

Differing Perspectives

Differing perspectives can stand next to one another without one canceling out the other. Differing truths, seen as absolute, cannot. Educating the parties to see conflict as a question of differing perspectives rather than singular truths can prove a critical step. A fundamental shift can occur which allows a way out of their *conflict trap*. That shift was beginning to take place with Graziella and Ricardo.

When they were able to quell the flames of conflict for a moment, they could see that what they each wanted was very much the same, and they were able to rediscover their mutual desire to affirm their underlying connection. That is certainly not always the case with parties in conflict. But by separating parties' reactions and clarifying their different points of view, a way out of their trap may begin to open.

From this point on, they quickly turned their attention to a number of critical decisions that they had been stuck over for years. These included among others: renegotiating a loan from the bank, deciding on the location of an auxiliary parking area, agreeing to a tour package that had been proposed by a travel agency in the country's second largest city, updating furnishings at the inn, and purchasing new equipment for the farm.

Commentary: About Right and Wrong

The Standoff

In the case of Ricardo and Graziella, we had the classic standoff, illustrated in Figure 6.1.

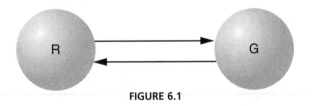

FIGURE 6.1

Each party stands ready to convince the other, a judge, or anyone who will listen of the essential rightness of their view. Given the harm suffered or threatened, "the other" and their actions are to be condemned. Each may well want to be understood by the other. But they are not interested in understanding. Rather, it is persuade–defend–attack. "I'm right! You're wrong!" Neither is understood, and neither feels understood.

If they try to go from standoff to solutions, the result is that one gives in to the other, or they settle for a frustrating compromise or a "resolution" imposed from the outside.

What we seek in the understanding-based approach is a way for the parties to make decisions together not by coercion or persuasion but by understanding and agreement. When it works, we can create a basis of understanding from which the parties can fashion mutually agreeable solutions (see Figure 6.2).

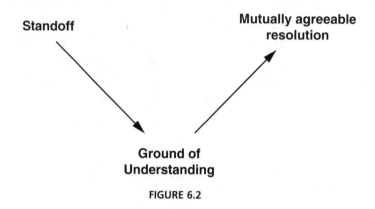

Standoff

Mutually agreeable resolution

Ground of Understanding

FIGURE 6.2

If a decision based on *understanding* is the goal, the mediator can make a crucial difference. The challenge posed by the right-wrong *conflict trap* is how to help the parties escape the trap and pursue a different way to face their conflict.

The Right-Wrong Trap

In conflict, the instinct to defend why we are right and the other wrong is as old as it is pervasive. Both sides stress the rightness of their position, look for weaknesses in their counterpart's presentation, and turn to others who might see it their way for reinforcement and solace. Repeating the pattern over and over, they become hopelessly mired. The dynamic takes on a life of its own. Feelings of violation and anger, the desire for retribution, and the hope for vindication keep the enmity raging.

This right-wrong mode of self-justification is as popular as it is seemingly inevitable, emotionally captivating at the same time it breeds frustration. Courtroom dramas hone this basic paradigm to a social art while judge, jury, and the public sit as arbiters. It is ever present in news reports, talk shows, and television crime dramas, all of which attest to the enormous pull the paradigm has on individuals and cultures and to its central place in social discourse.

Arguing about who is right and who is wrong usually does not lead to a solution. Rather, focusing on blame obscures possibilities for resolution. The right-wrong framework is simply too shallow and confining. To be able to work through to a mutually satisfying resolution, parties need to enlarge their view of the problem and let go of the belief that 100 percent of the responsibility for the problem rests with the other.

Despite the enormous presence and power of the dynamic, in very few conflicts is one side totally right and the other completely wrong. The truth is, as with Graziella and Ricardo, each side has a different perspective on the shared problem, in which they each tend to justify how they have acted and what they seek. But from inside the trap, they don't readily see or feel that.

Once they realize they are trapped by their conflict, a significant number of parties can be supported in moving beyond that frame and recognize that each side's view need not negate the other's.

Pointing the Way Out

Helping parties find the way through together is an essential and regular part of our work. The first step is to support the parties in understanding how their right-wrong framework has them trapped. That is exactly what the mediator did with Graziella and Ricardo when he sought to understand each of their views and pointed out how their reactions to one another led to their missing the import of what the other was saying. The mediator can show that their differing perspectives, no matter how strongly held, need not cancel out one another. Looping holds the key. It is almost always helpful to know that someone else understands how profoundly you are "right," and what underlies the strength of your convictions. Once you believe you are truly understood, you can begin to free yourself from having to fight for your position. Without that belief, you have to hold on tighter, and you feel alone. As mediators, we can provide that understanding to each party.

We seek to understand not only the parties' differing positions, but also what lies *underneath their conflict.* Because it is often at these deeper levels that feelings of fear, anger, confusion, betrayal, victimization, vindication, and the like reside that fuel the right-wrong frame that accompanies conflict and obscures any nascent aspiration to relate differently. To move beyond the confines of that trap, these powerful underlying forces are best acknowledged, expressed, and understood.

In order to help develop this ground for resolving a dispute, the mediator needs to acknowledge the goal of understanding all parties. That is not always easy because mediators are themselves not immune from taking sides and getting caught in the *conflict trap*. Accepting that the parties can both be "right" can create an inner challenge for the mediator as we find ourselves siding with one party or the other. If as mediator you are caught within the trap yourself, you first need to make your own escape before you can help others.

Bubbles of Understanding

To affirm and assure that we will be there for both parties with their differing and strongly held views, we seek to allow room inside ourselves for the parties and their separate views. To help us work in this way, we think metaphorically of filling "bubbles of understanding."

As mediators, we imagine that we have inside ourselves two empty spaces, what we metaphorically call "bubbles," one for each party (Figure 6.3).

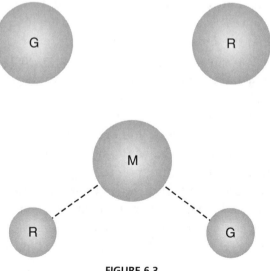

FIGURE 6.3

The point is to for the mediator to put aside his or her own life for the moment, and the judgments he or she may have formed about the parties and their conflict, and find a balanced and open place to connect with each party, despite their differing views.

The Mediator's Understanding of the Parties

As each party speaks in the other's presence, and the mediator seeks to understand that party, the "bubble" we have of that person starts to fill up with information and impressions. While seeking to understand one party and do so deeply, we remain aware of the presence of the other and the "bubble" for the other.

The parties come in, of course, with their own understandings of themselves and each other. In effect, they hold "bubbles" both of self and of other. That understanding may well be distorted by the defensive postures they have assumed in the conflict. When the mediator loops Ricardo, seeking to assure him that he is understood, the pressure is off Ricardo to respond to or defend against Graziella, and he may be able to develop a fuller "bubble" of his own views (Figure 6.4).

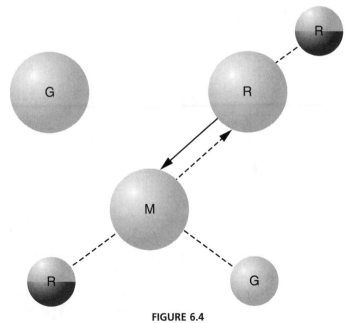

FIGURE 6.4
Note: Solid line is assertion. Non-solid line (dashes) is understanding.

Similarly, the mediator turns to Graziella with the same goal: that with his understanding of her, she feels understood, and begins to have a fuller understanding of her own views.

It can be an extremely dissonant feeling for a mediator when the second bubble begins to fill, especially if the parties' differing perspectives are extreme. As each party describes himself or herself as right and the other as wrong, the mediator may feel, as do the parties, that one perspective must necessarily cancel out the other. If the effort is to understand both, the mediator needs to hold the "bubbles" of each party, without deciding who is "right" or "wrong." We have come to learn to welcome and embrace that dissonance, because it is a sign that we are exactly where we need to be, standing in the middle without choosing one's view over the other's (Figure 6.5).

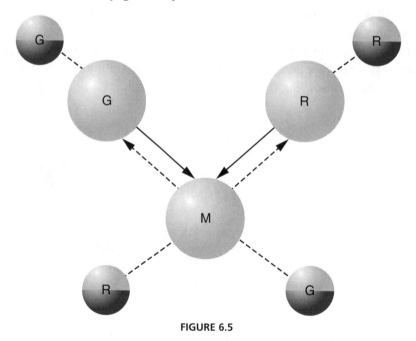

FIGURE 6.5

If all this work resulted only in the parties understanding themselves more fully and feeling understood by the mediator, it would be time well spent, because it opens the door for the parties to make responsible decisions based on an appreciation by each of their own view. Without that understanding, mediation's goal for parties to make informed decisions is compromised. But there is another possibility and another opportunity here.

Helping the Parties Understand Each Other

By speaking separately to each party while in the presence of the other, and by giving each a chance to explain their view without having to defend themselves, we are taking the pressure off of them to have to understand each other before they've had an opportunity to express themselves. It is a lot to ask of either party to a conflict to try to understand the other before they have had a chance to be heard and understood themselves. Once each party realizes that the mediator appears to have understood not just their perspective but also the other's, they may be open to the possibility that their views need not negate one another. Put simply, we are more willing and able to understand others when we feel understood ourselves.

The mediator's attitude is very important. He or she needs to be receptive to all parties, in this way providing the understanding that each craved but was unwilling, and often incapable, of giving the other. By starting with the mediator understanding the parties, we take the pressure off the parties to understand each other.

The parties, of course, have bubbles not only of themselves but also of one another (Figure 6.6).

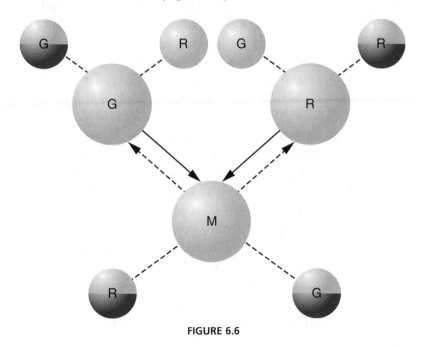

FIGURE 6.6

Gabriella's and Ricardo's views of one another at the start of our interactions were filled with misimpressions and distortions. As they defended themselves against their perceptions of one another, hurling accusations back and forth, the gap in perceptions grew. But when both were understood by the mediator, the situation changed. As each observed the mediator's dialogue with the other, without the pressure to defend themselves, they began to develop a somewhat clearer understanding of one another's perspective.

Just as the mediator experiences dissonance when trying to hold the differing perspectives of both parties, the same may be true for the parties, only more so. Until now, they felt their truths had canceled out those of the other, because surely only one of them could be right. But when the mediator understands them both, it often raises a fundamental question for each: How can the mediator, who understands me, also understand the other if only one of us is right? In that question lies the paradox of conflict's right-wrong framework.

This is a critical moment in many mediations, at least those where the mediator meets together with all parties as we do in the understanding-based approach. If the mediator endeavors to understand each party in the presence of the other, the possibility exists that they too might make the effort to understand each other without choosing between their differing perspectives.

When this opportunity is ripe, we ask the parties if they are each willing to make the effort. It's important to represent mutual understanding as *a possibility* the parties are free to choose. It is not indispensable to a successful mediation for the parties to understand each at an emotional as well as a cognitive level. But if they do, the mediation has an entirely different feel.

Part of the mediator's job is to assure parties that if either feels that the effort to understand the other is undermining their understanding of themselves, it is a step backward rather than forward. Giving up one's own view is too high a price to pay for mutual understanding. Neither party should give up what is important to himself or herself, but rather simply allow room for both views in the mediation. We therefore make the critical distinction here between agreeing and understanding.

If they are willing and able, they can begin to establish a connection of understanding between one another. The mediator then becomes a looping coach, helping them in the effort to understand their differing perspectives.

When this goes well, we are all working from a full base of understanding the differing perspectives in the room, what we call "mediative consciousness." This can be the gateway to joint problem-solving that is different than if the mediator is the only person in the room with an understanding of the whole.

The Standoff Ends

The standoff eases, and ultimately can end, when the parties can both express their individual views *and* be open to understanding the views of the other (Figure 6.7).

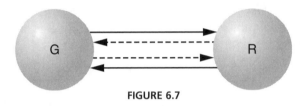

FIGURE 6.7

They are then in the best position to understand and resolve their differences with the support of the mediator. And if they fully understand and want to take on the challenge, when similar tensions arise in the future, they may be able to achieve resolution on their own.

■ ■ ■

That was the case in my final meetings with Graziella and Ricardo. After they realized what was behind one another's behavior, they were increasingly able to do much of the work themselves. I supported them in doing so, making sure that they understood themselves and each other and occasionally helping them stay on track by targeting the dynamic between them when they threatened to be drawn back into their all-too-familiar *conflict trap*.

As we reached the end of our several days of meetings together, Ricardo turned to me.

> *Ricardo:* This has been so helpful, but what are we going to do when you leave?
>
> *Mediator:* Good question. One of my major goals as mediator is to put myself out of business.

Graziella: Good. You're fired.

Mediator: Thank you. It will be up to you now to deal with problems that come up in the future in a new way.

Ricardo: You really think we can so easily do that?

Mediator: No. It will take a lot of work.

Ricardo: I know we can't just bring you back whenever we have a problem. But really, how will we do that?

Mediator: You need to learn how to mediate without a mediator. The first thing is to recognize what I've brought to your conversations and figure out how to do the same yourselves.

Graziella: The most important thing you have done has been to create safety for us so that we can really talk to each other. And a respect for both of us.

Ricardo: I think we now have a better sense of where we were each coming from.

Mediator: So you must remind yourselves of that in some way to be able to do it on your own.

Ricardo: We'll put a third chair in the room to remind us.

As we parted, I hoped that they would be able to deal with each other without my help, but I wasn't sure they could. Six months later, my apprehensions were greatly allayed by a report from my friend who had referred the case to me. He sent me a note that read in part "I visited Graziella and Ricardo and they are referring to the mediation as 'the miracle.' More important, they both feel a profound commitment to stay with the change."

A Holocaust Memoir: Helping the Parties Deepen Their Understanding 7

Sara Levi and Patrick had come to mediation after becoming stuck in their joint effort to write a book recounting what Sara endured in the Holocaust only to find themselves at an immediate impasse over whether Sara could be joined in the mediation by her nephew, Adolfo. Sara believed she needed Adolfo to help keep her from "losing herself" if she were to address the question of talking openly with Patrick about those horror-filled years that affected her so deeply. Once Patrick understood her fear, he realized that it was important for both he and Sara to have Adolfo present. That they reached agreement on this largely procedural issue of Adolfo's presence augured well for their ability to address their underlying differences.

After Adolfo joined us, we moved through the contracting process and then reached agreement about the areas that constituted the substance of their dispute.

Three main issues divided them: the terms of Patrick's compensation; the related dispute about the amount of

115

time Patrick had devoted and would continue to devote to the project and whether he would take on outside work; and most central, the substantive differences between them about the content of the book.

When Sara and Patrick started their work together, they anticipated that the project would take about one year. They agreed to meet periodically for Sara to relate parts of her story to Patrick. He would then draft a section of the book based on their dialogue and e-mail it to her for comments or edits. Patrick agreed to make this project his top priority. At designated intervals, Patrick would receive agreed-upon payments for his work.

From Sara's perspective, things had come apart when Patrick failed to give the work the priority they had agreed upon. She thought that he was slow to respond to her comments and edits. She believed he had been taking on other competing projects despite his avowed commitment to the primacy of this one. To make matters worse, Patrick was demanding more money or a share of the royalties.

For Patrick, the problems between them had developed because Sara was always partial in recounting any aspect of her story, requiring Patrick repeatedly to revisit a sequence, delaying the process further. He felt she was slow in responding to his comments and edits, leaving him hanging. So he had taken on some small projects that needed his attention, and these seemed to come at exactly the moment when Sara was ready to proceed. If he had to put off other work, he wanted additional compensation for the amount of time he found himself investing in this project.

We spent considerable time together, as I sought to understand and loop back what was important to each of them. In doing so, I gained a fuller appreciation of their differing perspectives, and they even showed some understanding of each other's point of view. I then worked with each of them to identify, in a few phrases, words that captured what was important to each underlying the dispute, what I termed "their interests."

■ ■ ■

Interests and Needs

In Chapter 6, we focused on *how* the mediator seeks to understand each party and in doing so can help them understand themselves and each other. Here we focus on the content of that understanding—*what* is important to the parties underlying their conflict.

When we seek to understand the parties, we *go underneath* the concrete level of their positions to a second level—of *needs and interests.* This deeper level embodies the reasons *why* the parties seek the ends they do—in other words, what has led them to their different views. At this more subjective level, parties can usually identify several elements that underlie the concrete level of their positions, and we have an opportunity to expand the possibilities for solutions beyond simply either/or or compromise.

It is by asking *why* that we understand the parties' most essential needs and interests. We articulate this level as we work to understand the parties and, at some point in the mediation, work with them to identify their specific respective interests, presenting them side by side on flip charts.

When the parties see the problem in terms of their interests, they can begin to hold somewhat less rigidly to their concrete positions and imagine that there might be more than one possible solution. When the parties see not only their own interests but also the other's interests charted alongside, it gives them a deeper and expanded understanding of the dispute. When we later come back up to the concrete level to solve the problem, this will translate to possibilities that might work for both.

■ ■ ■

With Sara and Patrick, their interests became fairly clear with significant overlap between them. I was optimistic for our crafting a mutually acceptable solution.

Sara	Patrick
Get the story out	Get the story out
Work collaboratively together	Work collaboratively together
Keep the book a priority	Proceed expeditiously
Deal with pressure created by painful recollections	Maintain income flow

But even after exploring their interests and needs in considerable depth, we all had the sense that we were circling around the heart of the matter. They both agreed that they continually got stuck about the substance of the book: that what they called "the real story" wasn't being told. If they couldn't clarify that, they both felt the project could not go forward, and the other issues would become moot. In the midst of this dialogue about the book's content, they reached a vital insight into their conflict.

■   ■   ■

Level of Meaning

Underlying many conflicts is a deeper level of meaning that is not touched or examined in most conflicts. And while it might not be necessary for the resolution of the problem, this deeper understanding offers an opportunity that, if made explicit and discussed, can change the parties' relationship and elicit a range of possible outcomes.

Ironically, the dispute itself invites this kind of introspection, which can prove vital to the parties and their ability to reach an accord. Conflict has a way of bringing out the worst and best in people, either of which can raise fundamental questions about ourselves and our relationship with one another. Including the level of meaning as part of the discourse over the dispute can therefore be deeply validating for parties. Whether or not the level of meaning is talked about explicitly, simply knowing that it may be operating inside the parties can deepen the mediator's understanding of the problem.

This level of conversation, as with everything else in mediation, takes place in the context of the dispute that brought the parties to mediation. We do not seek to have a discussion about the meaning of life or push people beyond what is right for them. What we seek and hope for is to provide the parties the opportunity to resolve their conflict at the fullest level they wish. As with everything else in our style of mediation, it is the parties' choice whether the level of meaning is made explicit in the room, and we *proceed by agreement.* Sara and Patrick agreed that there was a deeper level to explore.

■   ■   ■

Mediator: You each have said that we haven't touched on something essential here. Is this the right time?

Sara: Yes. There has been something missing I need to talk about. An important story about the Holocaust has not been told. It has to do with what I and others experienced as teenagers in Italy during the occupation by the Nazis. There was a breaking of my heart which will never be healed. Until this story is told, and others know what really happened, my life will be incomplete. When I found Patrick, I felt I had met someone who could help me tell this story the way it needs to be told, who could do justice to the horror. I hope you will excuse me if I become emotional about this time because for me, even though this happened more than 50 years ago, it is as vivid in my mind as if it had happened yesterday.

Mediator: It's fine. (Patrick was silent and attentive.)

Sara: It is so horrible for me to revisit these memories, I can hardly bear to think of them, but I know that I can't die in peace unless I know this story has been made available to the world. Of course, so much has happened in my life since. I grew up, married, could never even think of having children, so I became a successful accountant, burying myself in my work. But what happened then remains at the core of my life, the horror of it, the survival through that time of atrocity. What Patrick represented, still represents, is someone from the outside, not a Jew, who could craft that story for others.

When she reached that point, Sara's body began to shake and she sobbed.

Sara: I don't know how much longer I will live. In some ways I have not had a real life since that time, but if I know that others understand what happened, I can then die in peace.

Patrick: I know this. Your story is important. I have tried to do justice to it. I don't know what the problem is.

Sara: There's something that I haven't been able to convey to you, and I'm not sure I understand it myself, but when I read what you have written there is something missing.

Patrick: I desperately want to know what that is. I have tried so hard to capture the essence of what happened to you.

Sara: But you haven't. It's still missing.

Patrick: But if you can't communicate what that is to me, how can you expect me to be able to write it?

Sara: You're right. This is what is so frustrating to me, but I think that I should just let it go. I don't know. . . .

Mediator: Is this a place that can be dangerous for you, in terms of what you said your fear is? Are you in danger of "losing yourself" now? (Adolfo nodded his head vigorously.)

Sara: Yes, thank you. This could happen. It is what has happened before. We reach this point, and I know there is something more. I can't say what, and then I feel lost.

Mediator: Can you stay with this moment, not knowing what's there to see, if we can help you reach a new point? Does it feel all right to continue?

Patrick: This is what I need from you, Sara.

■ ■ ■

When the inquiry deepens, the mediator helps the parties realize and articulate what *underlies* their differing views as well as what they might need from each other to deepen their understanding. To support the parties moving deeper, the mediator's attitude is crucial. The mediator should be supportive without being coercive, encourage without being directive. The parties need to be respected in their efforts to deepen their communication, without feeling pressured to go beyond their limits.

■ ■ ■

Sara: I find myself getting very angry. I don't know who I'm angrier with, Patrick or myself.

Mediator: This must be very frustrating for you, to have a sense of something more that you can't quite reach in yourself.

Sara: Yes. It is. Adolfo, what do you think? Am I crazy?

Adolfo: You haven't said what is so frustrating for you with Patrick.

Sara: You're right. There are some things I am afraid to say because I don't want you to abandon this project, Patrick. In some ways I see you as my lifeline. I need you to find the words for me.

Adolfo: But you need to tell him more about what bothers you first.

Sara: But I don't want you to give up, Patrick.

Patrick: I don't want to give up. Tell me whatever you can.

Mediator: This seems to be where you have gotten stuck before. Sara, are you afraid to say something you think could be upsetting to Patrick?

Sara: Yes.

Mediator: By telling Patrick you're worried about alienating him, that could jeopardize the project. By not telling him, you're withholding something that could be vital to the project and that you feel is missing. If that's true, either way you risk losing the project.

Sara: Thank you for saying that. That is absolutely true.

■ ■ ■

When this inquiry goes well, the parties may speak directly with one another, with the mediator coming in as needed in the effort to support their inquiry. In mediations where the parties are trying to preserve the continuation of their working and/or personal relationship, as was the case with Sara and Patrick, they may move quite naturally from what they need from each other in the mediation to what they may need from each other in their future relationship if they are to resolve their conflict.

■ ■ ■

Mediator: So what makes sense to you to do, Sara?

Sara: I'd like to be able to tell you my frustration, Patrick.

Mediator: Is there anything that Patrick could do that could help here?

Sara: Please try to not take this personally, Patrick.

Patrick: I agree that this is the only way to move forward. Otherwise, we are sunk, because I don't have your trust. So please tell me.

Sara: I don't know if I can say this right. It seems to me that you see this as a story just about my life. It's true that we are going back into my teenage years. But my life is not important.

By just focusing on me, you diminish the importance of what happened to everyone else who suffered. What I worry about is that my suffering will be seen to be *only my* suffering. I am afraid that we will be mocked because you don't understand this. But how could you? You didn't go through it. This is just another writing project for you. And not only that, you aren't even a Jew; so how could you begin to understand it? I like you very much, and I am very disappointed that we can't seem to get beyond this point. You keep wanting to go further into my experience as if that were all there is.

Mediator: You're afraid that the important truth of your experience, not *just* your experience, won't be at the center of the book. You don't think Patrick can understand this because he didn't experience the devastation himself. And since he isn't Jewish, he cannot relate to it in a way that is real.

Sara: Right.

Mediator: Is there more you would like Patrick to understand?

Sara: Yes, but it all comes back to this.

Mediator: What's your perspective, Patrick?

Patrick: I don't feel trusted. I feel as if I'm dismissed because I'm not a Jew.

Mediator: What would you want Sara to understand that she doesn't?

Patrick: That I know this isn't just a story about her. It's much bigger than that. But the particulars of her experience can open people to the bigger picture. I've been touched by this story not because it's just about her.

Mediator: What touches you?

Patrick: It's true that I'm not a Jew. And I have never suffered in my life like you, Sara. But this project has given me a glimpse of the devastation and hopelessness that were part of that time that defined your life. It has gone right to my core, and I think it will change me forever.

Sara (begins to cry)*:* I've never heard you say that before, Patrick.

Patrick: I didn't think that it was my place to. But why else would I put myself through this torture? The project has started and stopped a dozen times. I know those days when you can't face what happened, when you're overwhelmed by the power of what you went through. I have put my life on hold for it because I know how profound this story is. You're right, it's not just your story. In some strange way that I can't possibly explain, it's become part of me as well. And the challenge is how to reach the universal truth for others through the particular of what happened to you.

Mediator: What's it like for you to hear that, Sara?

Sara was extremely emotional and couldn't speak. She took a break, leaving the room with Adolfo for a few minutes. When they returned, she was still flushed but ready to continue.

Sara: I have been carrying the whole burden of knowing that the project is important. I didn't realize that it is important for you, too, Patrick. This is a great relief. Adolfo told me that he has known this about Patrick from the beginning, but until now I couldn't see it.

Patrick: I'm glad you do.

They were both silent for a long moment. I then turned to Sara.

Mediator: Sara, what is the significance of knowing this now—that the project is this important to Patrick?

Sara: I think I can have more confidence that the book will touch more people than I thought. I didn't want the book to be just about me or just for Holocaust survivors or even just for Jews. I do think there is still some tension between us about how much the book should be about me, but now we have a different basis for working together. I feel greatly relieved and heartened.

Mediator: How about you, Patrick?

Patrick: Sure, it's a relief to know that I am more trusted here. But I need something from you Sara. I want to devote myself to this project and bring it to an end as soon as I can. To do that, your participation is obviously indispensable. I want to be able to count on your being available.

Mediator: So feeling a renewed sense of trust from Sara is very important and you seem ready to move forward to complete the book. "Devoted" in fact to doing so. What you need from Sara is to know you can count on her.

Patrick: Exactly.

Sara: You know that as much as I want to continue, there are some days when I just can't bear to look back, when I don't feel as if I have the strength. There is a great cost to me each time I revisit that time and face more about what happened to me, my family, my friends. So it's true that you have called me sometimes and I have felt unnerved, incapable of talking to you. Even knowing that you will call or we will meet at times fills me with dread. Yet I know that I am trying to liberate myself, or at least lighten my load a little by sharing this story.

Patrick: I know that and I respect your difficulty. But without you, the project stops. Without your consistent participation, I have to go to other projects. Not because I want to, but I have no other choice. And then, of course, whatever momentum we've established in moving forward is stopped, and when we do resume, it's like starting all over.

Sara: And I know that I could not find someone else to do this project in a way that would work for me.

Mediator: So you each know that you need each other. What is it like to know that?

Sara: For me, I feel encouraged to know how deeply this touches Patrick. I feel supported.

Patrick: I'm glad to know she needs me as much as I need her. I've thought she was trying to get rid of me.

Sara: I did think of that when you disappeared into other projects or I thought you were trying to make the story too small. But I understand better today why you are the right choice for me, for the project.

Patrick: That helps me a lot. We will need to find some way to deal with those times when you are not up to working on this.

Mediator: Sara, can you understand why Patrick can't move forward without you and the consequence of that for him?

Sara: Yes. I wish I could control my reactions, but I can't. It helps to know that Patrick understands that.

We had arrived at a point where the tension between the two of them had eased considerably, mostly as a result of their efforts to reach deep inside and express what was truly important to them, and then to try to understand each other.

■ ■ ■

Parties Understanding What Is Important to Each Other

Understanding each other can be a critical part of the mediation, as it represents an opportunity for both parties to broaden their understanding of the dispute. For Sara and Patrick, it proved essential that they be able to understand each other at a deeper level if they were to resume work together on the project. They had each been able to stand in the shoes of the other, to emotionally as well as intellectually appreciate what was going on in the other's mind and heart.

Not everyone who comes to mediation has the same capacity or interest that Sara and Patrick had in undertaking such an effort. While mediators often have the impulse to have the parties understand each other, the mediator must not coerce the parties into doing so. Actually this step can backfire if, in making the effort to understand the other, a party loses their own sense of what is important to them. This had been a very real danger for Sara and was one of the reasons that Adolfo's presence was so helpful. In any event, before the parties understand each other, a basis must be established for both parties to express what is most important to them underlying the dispute. With this basis established, the next step is possible. Otherwise we run the risk of a result that reflects what is important to one party at the expense of the other.

In some cases, efforts can be made that fall short of full mutual understanding but that are nonetheless helpful, and sometimes lead to further understanding. Some of those steps include the following:

1. After the parties have each told their version of the events that occurred, often they may have questions for each other. The mediator can give them each an opportunity to ask each other questions. Those questions need to be genuine, not accusatory.

2. Another possible in-between step is to ask both parties to identify what they would find most valuable for the other person to understand. This allows each to think more about not just what the other should understand but why.

For Sara and Patrick, the depth of their commitment provided the motivation to understand what was most important to each of them underlying their work together on the book, and their effort to do so proved essential for both.

■ ■ ■

Sara and Patrick then discussed a realistic schedule for meetings to complete the project. Patrick said that if they were able to adhere even roughly to that schedule, he could go back to his original commitment and would not need to change the arrangement for compensation. Sara was reassured.

At last, I asked Adolfo if he had anything to say. He addressed Patrick, hoping his participation had been all right, and Patrick responded that it had been "very all right." Then he asked Sara if she wanted him to tell her when he thought she was holding something back from the story, and she said yes.

■ ■ ■

By *working through their conflict together*, Sara and Patrick created a new basis to build trust with one another. And they had done that without Sara losing her bearings. Adolfo's participation in the mediation had been crucial, but not because of anything he said. His presence supported Sara as we had expected. What was surprising was how much his presence also supported Patrick.

Commentary: Understanding the Levels of Conflict

Einstein's words—"You can't solve a conflict at the level at which people experience it"—resonate for us. We work with the parties not just to help them communicate better but also to *understand the deeper dimensions underlying their dispute*, where elements vitally important to each may lie hidden.

Conflict's Inner Life

Conflict has an inner life, although the terms on which it presents itself usually keep the parties and the back and forth between them focused on externals—who did what to whom and what the parties want in terms of money or action from one another. We challenge conflict's singular focus on the outside by working with the parties to include what is important to them *underneath* the surface, which can often provide what is critical to helping them resolve their differences.

Part of *what lies underneath* has already surfaced in terms of the emotions and attitudes that accompany conflict and keep the parties trapped—the anger, resentment, frustration, or feelings of hopelessness; the exclusive reliance on right and wrong; the yielding of responsibility to the lawyers or the law. Identifying, recognizing, and addressing these inner patterns can begin to loosen the conflict's hold and open to other emotions, impulses, and motivations that are also under the surface, such as hope, connection, and the desire for mutual understanding and resolution.

Levels of Conflict

We find it valuable to distinguish three levels of conflict. The *concrete level* involving objective realities such as money, possessions, and specific actions is where most parties in conflict tend to focus. Negotiations usually begin with the parties making concrete demands and taking concrete, usually mutually exclusive, positions.

From positions to a solution, the shortest distance would seem to be a straight line (Figure 7.1).

Positions ⟶ **Solutions**

FIGURE 7.1

If neither party can successfully convince the other to give in or to give up a position, they likely move toward some kind of compromise between their positions which, at best, might lead to a sense of grudging acceptance by both. A common saying among lawyers is that the test of a good agreement is whether each party is equally dissatisfied. We think that by going beneath the level of positions, we can reach for something more.

Developing Interests and Needs

Rather than going directly from positions to solutions, we invite the parties to go *underneath the problem*, one of our core principles, to identify the level of *interests and needs*. Once the mediator and parties have reached a common understanding of their interests and needs and charted them side by side for all to see, the parties can then go back up to the concrete level of solutions from this *deeper ground of understanding* what is important to both *underlying* their differences.

Thus there is a dynamic interaction between these two levels (Figure 7.2). We think of this diagrammatically as a "V."

Concrete positions   **Solutions**

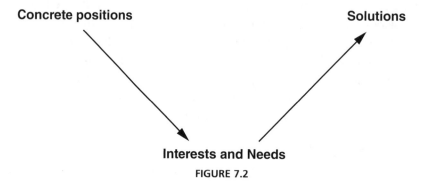

Interests and Needs

FIGURE 7.2

How to Help the Parties Identify Their Interests and Needs

Put simply, we take turns asking one party and then the other why they have adopted their positions. The point is not to challenge or change the party's position, but to simply explore the parties' motivations that underlie their positions. The focus is on the *why*, not the *what*. In fact, we call this "following the *why trail*." If later the parties conclude that their underlying interests are met equally well or even better by a different concrete option, they will change their position on their own. Here the focus is on the underlying *why*.

As mediators we seek to identify with each party, trying to experience the conflict as each party does, putting ourselves in the shoes of one and then the other (metaphorically filling up our bubble of each). We ask what lies beneath a position, we loop what the parties say in response (including the content and the emotion), and we explore further.

If a party seems stuck in exploring beneath, we can use our attempt at empathetic connection with that party and how he or she experiences the conflict to offer a suggestion. We might say, "I imagine if I were you that it might be important to me that . . . ," and then suggest the underlying reason why we might take that position. This last we do very lightly, not trying to convince the party to accept our formulation, but rather simply to stimulate the inquiry at the *underlying* level of interests and needs. The task is to find the party's underlying reasons, not to substitute ours.

How to Frame Interests

Framing interests is a key function in mediation. It has two primary purposes: first, to serve as a foundation for the creation of possible solutions, and, second, to be able to test those options in order to find out which solutions have the best chance of meeting the underlying concerns of both sides.

Using charts to record the key words that capture the primary interests of both parties helps to keep everyone focused on the task of framing the interests in a way that moves the mediation forward. To work effectively toward this end, the interests need to be understood and articulated in a form that helps point to possible options for resolving all or a part of the dispute. To do so, the mediator and the party whose interests are being charted need to agree on the particular frame to give to the interests. No interest is recorded on the chart unless both the mediator and the party whose interest is identified agree.

More an art than a science, framing interests is in effect a negotiation between the mediator and the party whose interests are being articulated. The goal is to work with each party to find the right words that capture each interest that the party has *underlying the dispute* in a manner that will be useful when we later come to developing and evaluating options for resolving all or a part of the dispute. We find four criteria central in so framing the parties' interests: that they

1. Are significant to the party (have emotional resonance)
2. Point toward multiple options (not too specific)
3. Are tangible/graspable (not too general)
4. Describe a present or future benefit (rather than a cost to the other party)

First, the particular words used need to resonate with the party whose interest is being identified. Toward this end, if the words come from the parties themselves, this is quite likely. However, since the framing task involves the mediator's active participation, the mediator may find it necessary or useful to suggest words or a phrase that describe the interest. Even if those words seem accurate to the mediator, they make it to the list only if that party agrees that those particular words accurately capture the interest.

Second, it is critical to frame an interest with sufficient generality that it not describe a position or solution rather than an interest. The test is whether in an agreement there is more than one solution that might express the interest. If not, then you have found a position masquerading as an interest, and the framing will need to occur in a more general way.

If, on the other hand, the party has framed the interest too narrowly, questions from the mediator that delve beneath the level of solution may be necessary before the interest can be charted. We often do that by asking the party who has framed the interest too narrowly what will be accomplished for the party by that "interest."

Third, it is important that an interest be framed in a way that points to particular directions in thinking about and testing solutions. That means that the interest shouldn't be framed so broadly that, while true, it will not be useful in terms of formulating possible solutions. For example, if a party frames his or her interest as "being successful," that concept is so broad as to be of little use in moving the process forward.

Finally, the last criterion is that the interest be framed in a way that is positive for one party rather than negative for the other. Here the mediator's job is to help reframe an interest that has been described as something negative to a positive, forward-looking direction for the party whose interest is described.

Focusing on the importance of framing interests positively presents another challenge to conflict's ready terms. Without it, parties could easily state their interests by blaming the other party or insisting that that they act differently; and the effort to clarify interests could lead to yet another round of attack and counterattack. One of Sara's interests as charted, for example, was to "deal with pressure created by painful recollections" while one of Patrick's was to "proceed expeditiously." One can imagine the discord created if either or both parties formulated these interests in terms of stopping the other from doing something. Asking the parties to try to understand and express each other's interests if framed negatively can lead to the parties becoming more deeply enmeshed in conflict's trap.

For the mediator to help the parties frame their interests in constructive ways is not simply an exercise in being a skilled wordsmith. The challenge is for the mediator to form an empathetic connection with each party, trying to help the party articulate the desires, hopes, and needs that lie *under the conflict.*

We use these criteria in framing the needs and interests for both parties on a sheet of paper divided down the middle to provide everyone in the room with a definition of the challenge in creating and then testing solutions.

Understanding the parties' interests in helping resolve their disputes is hardly unique to our understanding-based approach. Indeed, it is a mainstay of what is termed "interest-based negotiation," and a central theme in Roger Fisher's and William Ury's groundbreaking *Getting to Yes.* Where we likely differ from many mediators is that we work hard with the parties to help them find and articulate what is important to them, rather than the mediator concluding it for them, and we stress the importance of including the emotional significance to the parties more than many mediators might.

Our approach also acknowledges a third level of Meaning or Life Direction. It is by asking *why* yet again that we invite understanding with the parties at this deeper level. Including this level can bring clarity and personal depth when we return to the level of interests and then to options (Figure 7.3).

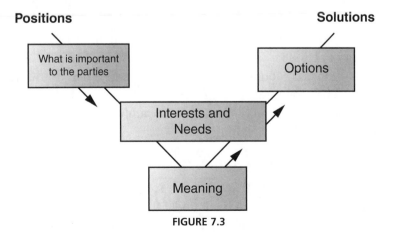

FIGURE 7.3

The Level of Meaning

Conflict has a way of "getting to us" as little else does. For many who come to mediation, the dispute has been consuming and has permeated every aspect of their lives, sometimes creating a personal crisis. People can find a dispute so unnerving that they begin to ask fundamental questions about their lives. Opening to that level and doing so together can make a crucial difference for the parties and for their relationship with each other.

That certainly proved the case for Sara and Patrick in coming to a deeper level of understanding that allowed them to *work together* in ways that honored each and the connection between them. It can also be true for institutions and the people within them, as with the musicians in the Symphony about the meaning of their work together or in Radix and Argyle, which we will return to later.

Whether this level of meaning will be explored is a function of three different questions: First, is the mediator personally open to this level of strong feeling, pain, fear, disappointment, hope, or longing that can accompany this deeper exploration? Second, are the parties capable of and willing to entertain this kind of conversation and the feelings that may come up? The very depth and strength of the conflict itself often pressures the parties to go to this level. Finally, does the atmosphere in the room feel safe enough for the parties to engage in this quality of inquiry? If the mediator is not open, the parties not willing, or the atmosphere not sufficiently safe, it would not make sense to inquire at this level.

While we cannot be certain whether touching this level with Sara and Patrick in each other's presence was necessary to reach the solution they found, it surely made a difference in the quality of their work together in the mediation, how they both felt about the resolution they achieved, and possibly in their carrying out their agreements in finishing the book.

Pointing Toward Options

Whatever level of depth we reach in our work with the parties, we must ultimately come back up to the level of options and solutions to give any agreements a clear and concrete form.

When the parties see the problem in terms of what is essential to them, they can begin to hold somewhat less rigidly to their concrete positions and imagine more than one possible solution. When they also see what is important to the other, with the interests charted side by side, it gives them a deeper and expanded understanding of the dispute. This will translate to more possibilities that might work for both.

Challenges in Working Together

Part 3

The Publishing Case: Bringing in the Law

8

When lawyers are in the room, we pursue an approach that does not keep them and their clients trapped in the legal right–wrong back-and-forth that mimics an argument in court: each lawyer trying to persuade a neutral third party or the other side that they should prevail. The "legal conversation" not only can inform the parties about the relevance of the law in their case but it also can help them decide how significant the legal reality is, as compared to their personal and business priorities.

■ ■ ■

This mediation started with a call from Rob, the lawyer for Rick, owner, president, and CEO of a small publishing house, BookPro. Rob told me that his client was in a dispute with a writer, Charlene, whom they had under contract and who was represented by counsel, Carl. I told Rob that I'd prefer to talk with both lawyers at the same time with the permission of their respective clients. Rob had anticipated my request and, with Carl's agreement and their clients' permission, we scheduled a conference call for later that day. Carl, who seemed guarded and skeptical, introduced himself as representing Charlene, "who had published with BookPro and who had been under contract but was no longer." Rob quickly countered that the contract was fully in force. It was apparent that the status of the contractual arrangement between BookPro and Charlene was central to their dispute.

The lawyers explained that they and their clients had participated in several previous efforts to resolve a long-simmering dispute that had taken a sharp turn toward litigation in the prior month. They believed it might be worth making one more try to see whether they could avoid trial. I briefly explained my approach to mediation—that we would work together with all the parties to the conflict in one room. I further asked the two attorneys to prepare short memoranda that described how they saw the dispute, to send copies to me, to exchange them with each other, and to share them with their clients.

The memoranda provided some background. BookPro had published three of Charlene's books as part of a series conceived by her. Their relationship was initially satisfactory, but when sales fell off on the third book, Charlene wanted to approach a larger publisher to continue the series, and she believed that she had the freedom to do so. But Rick thought BookPro had a right of first refusal on all future books in the series, according to the contract with Charlene. The lawyers took diametrically opposite legal positions on this key issue, and I imagined each had informed his client that they would likely prevail in court.

The nervous banter among the four people in the room came to an abrupt halt when I said, "Let's start." After the lawyers reviewed their previous efforts at settling the dispute, I asked why they thought those efforts had been unsuccessful. I was met with short, clipped answers. Each side blamed the other for its intransigence. I had very little idea where they had gotten stuck, other than in the blame game.

We talked generally about the mediation process. No one was particularly hopeful, but all wanted to see whether they could reach an agreement. We also agreed upon several ground rules, spending a significant amount of time talking about confidentiality, since a court hearing was already scheduled. I then suggested how we might proceed through *two conversations*.

■ ■ ■

The Two Conversations

The role of law in the traditional system is clear, as the principal guide for judges in making and justifying decisions, but its place in mediation is very much in question. Whether dealt with explicitly or not, the law influences and sometimes even directs the action.

When legal action has already been considered or threatened, as in the Publishing case, it is highly likely that the parties and their lawyers are comparing what might happen in the mediation with what would likely happen in court. The question isn't whether the law is involved but how to deal with the law's involvement.

Some mediators urge parties to leave the law (and their lawyers, too) at the door before entering the mediation. These mediators believe that including the law is like bringing an elephant into the room. The power and authority of the law will inevitably dominate, making it impossible for the parties to focus on their business and personal interests. In essence, these mediators keep quiet about the legal assessments they are surely making, and collude in the pretense that there are no elephants for miles.

At the other end of the spectrum are mediators, many of them former judges, who weigh in with their opinion of what the legal outcome would be in court, and urge the parties to reach a settlement that reflects that opinion. This often works to resolve conflict in court, so why not in mediation? Or they may, by meeting separately with the parties and their counsel in confidential caucuses, point out the dangers in each side's legal strategy in an effort to move each closer to the other's position. In this approach, the elephant is triumphant.

Understanding-based mediation seeks to include both the legal reality and the business/personal reality. Recognizing that these two realities may at times be in tension, we want to give each its proper due. The law is part of the picture. The parties must determine with counsel from their lawyers how much the law will affect the decisions they make in mediation. In effect, we hope to cut the elephant down to size, making it no bigger or smaller than the parties want it to be.

In order to properly integrate the law into the mediation, the participants must understand that there are two realities: the legal reality and the business and/or personal reality. They may be interrelated, but they are not the same. To help the parties understand this concept, we suggest the need for *two conversations,* and we seek to structure the mediation in a way that will include both.

■　■　■

Mediator: I think it might be helpful if we could clarify the legal reality before we move on to understanding the business reality. If that makes sense to you, I would ask each lawyer to talk about what might happen if this case were to go to court, both in terms of the strengths of your case and the risks.

Rick: Why do you want to do that? That's where we've been stuck before.

Rick's voice betrayed a sense of impatience, drawing several silent nods around the room.

Mediator: Fair question. We don't have to, but I'd like you to know why I think it could be valuable.

Carl: There aren't many statements Rick has made that I agree with, but here I would have to say that Rick is entirely correct. We have been through mediation before, and we spent a tremendous amount of time talking about the law and all that did was polarize us. We'd like this to be productive, and I don't think it will be if we get into our legal postures and start shooting at each other again.

■　■　■

I had barely begun the mediation and had not yet created relationships with anybody in the room, and here they were agreed that my first suggestion made no sense. I could feel the tension rising in me, and I felt a strong impulse to defend what I thought was a good idea.

We've seen similar dynamics in mediation before. Parties with lawyers frequently come into mediation wanting to put aside the law to see whether they can cut a deal with the other side that makes business sense. That is an impulse that we want to support, but we also know that parties, particularly when represented by lawyers, cannot just throw the law away.

For Rick and Charlene, their lawyers' assessments of the probable outcome if they went to court likely provided different yardsticks to measure whether a mediated result based on their business reality would be acceptable. If you don't talk about the law at all, it doesn't go away. Indeed, silently and unseen, it might prevent the participants in the mediation from thinking more creatively about a solution. Paradoxically, giving the law its place in the mediation may keep it from looming so large.

We also differentiate between the role the parties will have in the mediation and the role of their lawyers. Otherwise, the lawyers may easily dominate. The lawyers would take the lead in the legal conversation, *conversation one*. The parties, experts in the business and personal reality, would lead *conversation two*. If we didn't talk about the law at all, the lawyers might feel compelled to participate throughout the mediation in a way that could infringe on their clients' active participation and keep the legal realities mixed up with the business realities.

For these reasons we suggest having the conversation about the law first, so we can size up the elephant and know what damage it might do.

But having the legal conversation is not my decision alone, and I had acknowledged that it was Rick, not his lawyer, who had expressed impatience with any discussion of the law. And although Charlene's lawyer had responded, she didn't appear to be intimidated by the presence of Rick's lawyer. I decided to explain to the group why I felt a discussion of the law might help the mediation. Carl had given me an opening by saying that each prior effort had polarized them.

■ ■ ■

Mediator: Given your prior experience in attempting to discuss the law, your reluctance to talk about it makes sense. But maybe your previous problems stemmed from how you approached the discussion.

Rick: What do you mean? Rob made it abundantly clear that Charlene hasn't lived up to the promises she made in our contract. Then Carl attacked me and we were off and running. It was not only unproductive, it poisoned the atmosphere.

Mediator: So your lawyer set out his view that Charlene had not fulfilled the contract, Carl retorted, and you ended up feeling attacked by him. Bottom line, no good came out of talking about the law, and it may even have made it harder for you, Charlene, and the attorneys to deal productively with one another.

Rick: That's exactly right.

Mediator: If you decide to talk about the law here, we would need to clarify what we hope to accomplish. I hope that with each lawyer talking about not only your legal strengths, but also the risks you face going to court, we might be able to create fuller understanding and perhaps more convergence than you have now about what would happen. If we can do that, you'll be in a position to find better business solutions than you could pursuing litigation.

Rob (to Mediator): It's pretty clear to me that we aren't going to get anywhere talking about the law. We have precious little time to see whether we can make this work, and I don't want to waste it by spinning our wheels. Besides, we already went through the legal aspects.

Carl: Rob, we didn't talk about risks. But I also don't think it would be the best use of our time here to talk about the law. We have a lot of work to do to resolve this outside of court, and I'd like to get to it.

Mediator: So both lawyers think it's not a good idea to talk further about the law. How about you, Rick and Charlene? Would you find it useful?

Charlene: I'm willing to put it off for now. But it might make sense later, particularly if the lawyers are going to talk about risks.

Rick: I already gave my view.

I could see that I would be bucking the tide to try to go further now. The two sides would likely stay polarized if we were to begin the legal conversation at this point. So we agreed to revisit it later in the mediation.

■ ■ ■

As the mediation progressed, the following history emerged: Charlene had spent a year trying to market an idea she had for a book titled *The Adventure of Parenting*. Thirty publishers had rejected her proposal before she approached BookPro, Rick's fairly new publishing company. Rick offered Charlene a small advance, which she jumped at.

The book became very successful, resulting in a second book focused more specifically on the child's first years: *The Adventure of Parenting—From Years One to Three*. At the time the second book was published, Rick and Charlene envisioned a series on parenting, using a similar format to the first two books and covering the remainder of the growing-up years in two- to three-year increments. At the time of the mediation, three books had been published, all of them very successful, with more in the works.

But sales of the latest book had fallen off. Charlene blamed this on the failure of Rick and BookPro to put sufficient resources into marketing. Rick claimed the cause was a slumping economy and significant changes in the publishing industry. Meanwhile, a large publisher approached Charlene with an offer to publish the remaining books in the series for a large advance and a promise to heavily market and promote the books.

We made progress in the mediation, but one issue remained intractable. Rick had entered into a contract with Charlene that he felt gave him the right of first refusal on all her future books on the growing-up years. Charlene wanted to be sure that she had an out if she felt that Rick wasn't putting in a sufficient marketing effort to adequately publicize the books, particularly given the interest of the other publisher.

We were beginning to explore the question of the business/personal reality for Charlene and Rick when Carl spoke to Rick.

> *Carl:* Rick, you have to understand that you cannot lock Charlene into an exclusive with you for all books she publishes in the future, even if it's a continuation of the series that you've already published. Indentured servitude violates the Constitution.

Rob: That's not correct, Carl, and you know it. There is a clear commitment, spelled out in the contract for the first book and each subsequent one, that BookPro will publish the books in the series.

Mediator: This sounds to me like the beginning of a discussion about the law. Is that something you want to be doing?

Carl: I think it's necessary that they have a realistic view about this issue if we're going to make any kind of workable agreement, but I don't need to go any further with it right now.

Mediator: How about you, Rob?

Rob: No, I just need to be sure that everyone realizes that Carl is wrong.

Mediator: From my perspective you're both being very clear, but you are taking opposite views of the law. I want to say again that I think that it could be a valuable discussion for us to talk about the law, especially if both lawyers will talk about both the strengths and the risks of your legal positions.

Charlene: I think if we don't do that, we're just going to beat around the bush.

Rick: But we need to find a better way than before.

■ ■ ■

Here we were again, but with one big difference. Now the parties were motivated to have the conversation about the law. They hadn't been ready to have the lawyers talk about the law for fear that it would quickly degenerate as in the past. But now the failure to have a separate discussion about the law was impeding their efforts to continue the other conversation about their business and personal interests.

We return here to an essential point: the value in the mediator's maintaining *bifocal vision*, a focus on both the content and the dynamic, on the *what* and the *how* of the conflict. In so doing, I was able to hear the content of the legal point that Carl was making and also to see how Carl's raising the point in the middle of the conversation about Rick's and Charlene's personal and business interests impeded that conversation without adding any legal clarity. Both parties were quick to acknowledge that unless the conversation about the law could be different than in the past, they were likely to remain polarized.

■ ■ ■

Mediator: To achieve a fuller understanding, both of your lawyers have to be willing to talk not only of the strengths of your legal positions but also about the risks that you each face.

Carl: I'm willing to talk about risks, but I think you should know that there is very little risk to us in litigating.

Rob: Our downside risk is also pretty low.

Mediator: Both of your lawyers are working hard and are good at protecting you. But neither of them is saying that you don't face any risks in litigating. I think it makes sense for us to ask each of them to clarify your legal strengths, and then talk about risks.

■ ■ ■

The Strengths of Each Side's Legal Position

The point here is obvious for most lawyers, particularly if they are looking at the mediation from the outside. Since our goal is for the parties to have as full a picture as they can, they need to understand both the strengths and risks of each side's legal position. And lawyers are going to be more comfortable sharing their side's risks if they have first been able to explicate their strengths. When we return to the dialogue, my challenge is to keep the focus on increasing the parties' understanding of the law and how it affects the parties *working together.*

■ ■ ■

With everyone in agreement, the legal conversation commenced when Carl invited Rob to begin.

Rob: Our position is clear. The contract for the first book had the standard clause giving Rick the right of first refusal on Charlene's next book. The next contract, the one for the second book, has an addendum that gives Rick the right to publish all remaining books that Charlene writes in the series, spelling out the terms of the compensation, the royalty percentages, etc. The addendum states: "All future titles to be published by author as part of the *Parenting* series shall be published by publisher. The provisions of the agreement (earlier agreement) shall apply to all titles listed in the series." Our position is that Charlene is committed under the second contract for BookPro to be able to publish the entire series. If Charlene wants to write a book on some other subject, she can pick her own publisher. And this is fair because Rick has made a huge marketing investment in the series. That's why he's entitled to be able to rely on this negotiated commitment.

Mediator: So you have two different arguments you would present to the court. The first is based on the terms of the contract, and the second is based on fairness. Your argument under the contract for the second book is that Charlene agreed to let BookPro publish all books relating to the parenting series. Second, if I understand you correctly, you would argue that Rick relied on that agreement and made marketing investments that he otherwise would not have made. Is that right?

Rob: Yes. But it would be sufficient to prove that the wording of the contract unambiguously spells out Rick's right to publish future books under the same terms as the second contract.

Mediator: So you are satisfied that you would only have to prove that the language of the contract was clear enough to describe any other books in the series for the court to decide in your favor. The fact that Rick invested so heavily in marketing would only help to incline the court toward holding Charlene to the contract.

Rob: Not really.

Mediator: What am I missing?

Rob: Rick's out-of-pocket marketing investment is evidence that the contract was unambiguous.

Mediator: So his marketing investment not only supports the argument that it would be unfair to release Charlene from the contract, but it also proves that the only possible interpretation of the contract is that Charlene is locked in to the whole series being published by Rick.

Rob: Right.

Carl: When you read the second contract, it is not at all clear what all of the terms would be for future books in the series, so at the very least that is an ambiguity, which would be construed against the drafter of the contract, namely Rick. The original contract provided that BookPro had a right of first negotiation for Charlene's next "book-length manuscript." This right, as originally granted to BookPro, was limited to a right of first negotiation *for one more book.* If Rick elected not to publish the next book, or the parties could not reach an agreement on terms within a short time period, Charlene was free under their original contract to take any of her subsequent works to any other publisher. At the same time the parties executed their second agreement, they also executed a Contract Addendum stating: "the provisions of the earlier agreement with respect to the work apply to all titles listed in the series." This contract addendum did not incorporate all of the provisions of the second agreement. That's so because later in the same agreement, there is a clause that provides BookPro with first negotiation/ first refusal rights—not a perpetual option over anything that Charlene might write in the future. If they had meant to lock Charlene in to all of the terms of the other agreement, they would not have added that clause.

Mediator: Your position is that the addendum only sets out an intention to publish the remainder of the series, but because a first negotiation/first refusal right was included, an ambiguity was created by having both clauses as part of the addendum. And as you see it, the ambiguity then means that Charlene is not locked into BookPro publishing the remainder of the series.

Carl: Right, especially since Rick drafted the contract.

Mediator: You're referring to the law that the court will resolve any ambiguity against the drafter of the contract. The fact that Rick drafted the contract means that a judge would decide against him.

Carl: Yes. Besides, even if a court did conclude that there is a valid contract, it's unconstitutional. Slavery was abolished more than a century and a quarter ago.

Mediator: So, the essence of your argument is that a court would decide not to uphold the contract either because it's not definite enough to be a binding commitment, or because of a public policy against locking people into deals that would be too restrictive of their freedom.

Carl: We would also argue that the marketing investment by BookPro was paltry, especially when compared with the other publisher's offer.

Mediator: By comparing Rick's marketing investment with the offer by the other publisher, you would show that Rick hadn't made himself vulnerable in his commitment to the series.

Carl: Not exactly. We would be able to obliterate any sympathy that a court might feel for Rick since his marketing investment wasn't significant.

Mediator: Once a judge understood that the marketing investment was comparatively small, the judge would not be inclined to favor Rick.

Carl: Particularly when the basic freedom to publish is at stake.

Mediator: I think it could be useful for the sake of clarity if each of you could restate the essence of each other's legal argument.

■ ■ ■

Asking the Lawyers to Loop Each Other's Arguments

Up until now, I have been inviting the lawyers to expand on their legal positions, and then by looping their arguments back to them, I've confirmed that I have understood what they have said. This has not only helped clarify my understanding, it has helped assure the lawyers that at least the mediator understands their arguments.

My looping the lawyers has served other purposes. It has slowed down the legal back-and-forth, allowing the lawyers to hear more of each other's arguments and the parties to gain a fuller understanding of the two positions. Asking the lawyers to demonstrate that they have understood each other, in effect to "loop" each other, goes further. Usually, when lawyers hear their counterparts present the arguments for the other side, they are mentally preparing their counterarguments—understanding the other's position only to the extent that they need to counter it. This has an impact on their clients since it subtly, or not so subtly, says: "You need not really listen to the other lawyer since we are right, and if it goes to court we will ultimately prevail."

Now the lawyers are being asked to do something that in many ways may feel counterintuitive for them, although they likely realize the sense of it: to allow the full picture to come out in a way that their clients can begin to understand. And for the clients, hearing their own lawyer articulate the other side's legal argument can be an eye-opener. They may even begin to examine their belief in the soundness of their legal position as articulated by their lawyer. At a minimum, the lawyers' doing this task is a significant step toward the goal of *building a basis of understanding* in the room, where everyone comprehends not only his or her own perspective but the other side's as well. After a little further exploration of the task and its purpose, the lawyers agreed.

■ ■ ■

Rob: Carl thinks he can prove that the contract is vague and, because of that, Charlene is free to publish the remainder of the series with whomever she wants.

Mediator: Does he have it, Carl?

Carl: Yes.

Rob: That did not apply to agreements by adults who knew what they were getting into.

Mediator: I know that you disagree with Carl's argument, but right now I think it could be helpful if you just show that you understand it.

Rob: I understand it all right. It just doesn't apply here.

Mediator: And what would you argue, Rob, if you were Charlene's lawyer?

Rob: I would argue that you cannot force a person to work for another. That since this series represented Charlene's major work commitment, it virtually amounted to an employment situation that prevented the employee from quitting.

Mediator: Does he get it, Carl?

Carl: Yes.

Mediator: What's Rob's essential argument?

Carl: That the second contract committed Charlene only to publish the remainder of the series through Rick, and that if there was any ambiguity about the specifics, the previous contract should be used as the model.

Mediator: Is that right?

Rob: As far as it goes. What tips the scales in our favor, if there is any question in a judge's mind, is that Rick's marketing investment was made relying on that commitment.

Carl: Yes, but it was an insignificant sum compared to what was already on the table from another publisher.

Mediator: That's your argument. What's his?

Carl: That for the size of the company, Rick's investment was greater than it would have been had he not believed he would be publishing the remainder of the series.

Every good lawyer knows the arguments of opposing counsel. The ease with which each lawyer could imagine himself the lawyer for the other side was likely not lost on the parties: the arguments of their trusted advocates were at least in part a product of which side they had been hired to represent. We were ready to examine each side's risks in going to court.

■ ■ ■

The Risks of Each Side's Legal Position

Strong lawyers usually want their clients to know the risks of their case as well as its strengths. But they are not usually called upon to articulate those risks in the presence of the other side. The mediator can show them the value of doing so.

■ ■ ■

Carl: I don't see much by way of risk.

Mediator: Perhaps not. My experience is that there is almost always some risk, however small, and lawyers know that, although it may not be the norm to reveal it to your counterpart. And if you lawyers simply trade your best arguments and counterarguments back and forth, it will leave you where you've been until now, with your clients having less than the full picture, and the atmosphere sullied. The whole point of doing this is to get past the exclusively adversarial exchanges and give your clients a more realistic sense of the likely outcomes that could occur in court.

Let me make a suggestion that may make this exercise a little easier if you're willing to do it. I'd like each of you, Carl and Rob, to imagine that you've gone to court, presented your case, and disaster has struck. The court has ruled against you. Now your task is to explain to your client how this could have happened. If you are each willing, let's go back and forth, each of you sharing a possible risk.

■ ■ ■

I have stated the task in terms that both lawyers can relate to and that they cannot pretend could never happen. And the clients listening to this suggestion are likely aware that for at least one of them, the imagined dialogue could become a reality.

I have suggested that the lawyers take turns sharing their possible risks. This seems important to us here, where it was not when the lawyers were setting forth the strength of their cases. What we are striving for is *mutuality of vulnerability*. If Rob began by sharing all the risks his client faced, and then Carl refused to match Rob with the same seriousness of purpose, then Rob could find himself and his client hanging out to dry. *Mutuality of vulnerability*—"I'll share a little if you share a little"—helps ensure that will not happen and gives the process a chance to build toward a shared openness.

■ ■ ■

> *Rob:* Since there's very little likelihood that I'll find myself in that position, I don't mind doing it.
>
> *Carl:* I'm willing, too, but you need to understand that we have nowhere to go but up. If we go to court and a judge doesn't buy our argument, and that is possible, we're no worse off than we are now. We're locked into a deal we don't like.
>
> *Mediator:* You're talking now about the practical consequences of such a result, which I would also like us to explore, but I'd first like us to talk about the legal risks.
>
> *Carl:* Fine. So understanding that we aren't risking a more negative situation than we're in now, even if we lose, I'm willing to say that, of course, there is some risk that we could lose.
>
> *Mediator:* And how could that happen?
>
> *Carl:* We could run into a conservative judge who wants to protect business interests and doesn't really give a damn about the Constitution's regard for individual rights.
>
> *Mediator:* How could the judge justify that?
>
> *Carl:* If a judge found that the contract was clear and didn't violate the 13th Amendment, then Charlene could be faced with having to publish the remainder of the series through BookPro, or give up the series. I don't think that would happen, but it could.
>
> *Mediator:* How could it happen?

Carl: The judge could resolve the contract's ambiguity by falling back on the terms of the second contract, even though that would be unfair to Charlene.

Mediator: If the judge felt sympathetic to BookPro as a small publisher, you could run this risk?

Carl: Yes, but it's a small one.

Mediator: Could that happen if a judge looked at the size of BookPro's marketing investment in Charlene, compared to other books Rick has published, against what the large publisher was offering?

Carl: That's possible.

Mediator: How about you, Rob? What's the risk Rick is running?

Rob: If a judge were convinced that the books would do better with a larger publisher, that might tilt the scales in Charlene's favor.

Mediator: And the size of BookPro's marketing investment could be considered insufficient. . . ?

Rob: I don't think that would happen. But if you're asking whether it could, it could.

Mediator: Good. Carl, what else might incline a judge to rule for Rick?

Carl: A judge might think that Charlene's freedom to write about subjects other than parenting didn't represent a significant restriction on her work as a writer.

Mediator: That she still had the freedom to write in other areas. Rob, what else could happen that would lead a judge to release Charlene?

Rob: I guess if a judge were a libertarian, he or she could let Charlene off the hook.

Mediator: A judge more inclined toward a free-market approach might find enough ambiguity in the contract to release Charlene.

Rob: It's possible.

■ ■ ■

Something very interesting had happened in the room. The lawyers were not revealing their innermost secrets or fears. They were simply acknowledging realities that were possible. They might not have used these exact words with their clients before, but they had very likely acknowledged that no case is ironclad. So when Rick and Charlene heard the risks articulated by their lawyers, while they probably found it somewhat unnerving, they likely were not shocked.

But what was likely startling for each of the parties, and perhaps also a relief, was to hear the other lawyer, who had projected only the utmost confidence in the infallibility of his legal prospects, reveal chinks in his armor, and not so small. As they spoke, one could imagine the reality they were describing actually coming to pass. There was a palpable softening in the room.

Educating the Parties

The fundamental goal of discussing the law is the education of the clients. At this point I have demonstrated understanding of the points the lawyers have made, and the lawyers have shown that they understand each other's arguments. But it is not clear how much the clients have taken in, and what questions they might have. Ensuring the *parties' understanding* of the legal reality is the central point of the whole exercise.

■ ■ ■

Mediator: Charlene and Rick, do either of you have any questions about the risks we've just described? The purpose of this conversation about the law is to educate you about the legal realities of your case. So if you have anything you want clarified, please ask.

Charlene: Why didn't, or doesn't, Rick put more resources into marketing the series? It would have put him in a better position legally. More than that, it would have avoided this whole problem.

Rick: Can I show you how much we did put in? I've put together a comparison of our marketing investments in the parenting series with what we put out for other books.

Mediator: You both seem anxious to talk about this issue, and it may well be at the heart of your conflict. In fact, it may be a significant factor that a court would take into consideration if the matter were to be resolved there. But before having our second conversation based on your business and personal interests, I want to be sure that you both feel you understand the legal reality. Does it seem clear to both of you what your lawyers' arguments would be if you went to court, and what risks you would run?

Rick: Not to me. I don't understand this business of the Constitution and indentured servitude applying to this situation.

Carl: If I may, Rick, with your counsel's permission, the reality is that if you were to have your way, Charlene could publish parenting books only with you under terms that you decided before the books became as popular as they are now. You, on the other hand, could decide tomorrow that you don't want to publish any more books by Charlene, and she would have to live with that. There is no mutuality in that. People's right to work wherever they want and to freely bargain for that is protected by the 13th Amendment.

Rick: But we entered into the second contract freely. Don't people have to live up to their commitments?

Rob: Exactly the point.

Mediator: You are pointing out why you think the constitutional argument shouldn't be persuasive. You don't have to agree with the argument, but do you understand it?

Rick: Frankly, I'm offended by it, but I understand it.

Mediator: How about you, Charlene? Do you understand the arguments?

Charlene: Yes, I think I do. But you cut us off from talking about the marketing investment. And I believe that's the nub of the issue.

Mediator: It may be, and I think it's an important discussion for us to have. I don't want to mix it up with the discussion about the law. If we have as much clarity as we can about the legal reality, I think it will be easier to put it aside when we return to the other conversation that you are eager to have. Is that okay?

Charlene: Okay, but can we do it quickly?

Mediator: We don't have to do it this way.

Charlene: I just find talking about the law intimidating.

Mediator: It can be, and I'm actually asking you to stay with it in an effort to make it less intimidating by cutting it down to size. It looks to me as if there are two competing principles underlying our entire discussion.

■　■　■

The Principles Underlying the Law

The goal of the legal conversation is to make the legal reality comprehensible to the parties. Providing a structured way for the lawyers to talk about the strengths and risks of the case, as we did here, is designed to give the parties a better grasp on how their dispute might proceed if it went to court and to create some greater convergence between the lawyers about what the likely outcome would be.

Another way to make the law understandable to the parties, and thereby reduce the destructive potential of the elephant, is to work with the parties and their lawyers to identify the principles that underlie the statutes and rules. Identifying them in a straightforward manner can be a revelation to the parties and make the connection between the two conversations more graspable.

■ ■ ■

Mediator: The first principle has to do with people's freedom to choose their work, the people they work with, and the terms of their work. The second has to do with respecting obligations that people have entered into, and not releasing people from those obligations just because a better deal comes along. Rob and Carl, do you think that I've accurately described those principles?

Rob: Yes, but they're not on an equal plane. The courts aren't about to let people run away from their commitments because of the principle of freedom. Business would be paralyzed if obligations weren't respected.

Carl: Likewise, people can't be held to their commitments unless the full implications are spelled out with a specificity that everyone understands. You can't force people to work together.

Mediator: You may disagree with each other over which principle the court will consider more important in the context of this case, but do you agree that those are the principles that the court would be weighing?

Rob: I agree.

Carl: So do I, but the facts would make a difference.

Mediator: And one of the crucial facts that Charlene and Rick were about to address is the extent of the financial contribution by BookPro to the marketing of the series, within the circumstances of the arrangement between the two of them.

Carl: That's a central one.

Charlene: So the court would be looking at the same things that we want to talk about.

Mediator: Exactly. But the court would be much more restricted in how it viewed them. While a court is likely to struggle with many of the same concerns that you and Rick are dealing with, the judge is more bound by rules in reaching a decision than the two of you are. And the court would obviously be less familiar with what is crucial to the two of you than you are. Conversely, if the two of you are going to decide this case, you are both intimately familiar with the past and present of your situation. And you'll have more control over shaping the outcome based on what the two of you consider important.

Charlene: That's helpful. I think we've already paid a price— and frankly, Rick, the fact that you are seeking to bind me legally hasn't made me any more trustful. I know that I've been more guarded with you and afraid to talk about some ideas I've had because I've thought you might exploit my suggestions.

Rick: And, as you can imagine, knowing there is the risk that you'd be publishing more books in the series with someone else has made me reluctant to invest more in marketing. I need some peace in all of this. I need to know I can count on several more years of publishing the whole series in order to create a comprehensive strategy for maximizing sales. I can't do that knowing you're threatening to get out.

Charlene: Well, I need to know that I am not locked in for life to you as the publisher if I don't think you're getting sufficiently behind the books.

Mediator: Your individual concerns are very important. As you begin to talk about the personal and business realities that also underlie the legal reality, I just want to be sure you both feel satisfied that you understand the legal realities we've been talking about.

Charlene: I think I do.

Rick: I don't have any more questions for now.

Mediator: I think you should understand one additional aspect of the legal reality before we turn to the other conversation, and that is what it would mean to go to court practically. If we clarify the practical consequences of litigation, it will help us considerably when we explore possible solutions.

■ ■ ■

The Practical Consequences of Going to Court

After discussing the strengths and risks of each side's case, we address the reality of going to court. Lawyers and their clients are often so focused on the rightness of their legal position and how to win in court that they don't consider what's at stake if they lose, which is what the parties have just done. They also may not think about the practical consequences of going to court, not only if they lose but also if they win.

Again, the goal is to make the law comprehensible to the parties in terms of how the legal processes will affect them. Usually, the results are measured in terms of time spent or saved, financial reward or costs, diversion from goals or the ability to achieve them, opportunities secured or lost, reputations enhanced or tarnished, and relationships preserved or breached.

While lawyers and clients may have touched on these elements in their discussions, it is often surprising how little they have actually considered the practical consequences of their battle. We're not trying to convince parties that litigation is always bad, as some mediators maintain. Our goal is for the parties to see and understand the legal realities so they are in the position to make the best choices.

■ ■ ■

Mediator: Carl and Rob, if it's okay with you, what are the practicalities if your clients go to court?

Carl: Well, first, we would seek a declaratory judgment from a court that would release Charlene to enter into a contract with another publisher. Otherwise, no publisher would touch the book.

Mediator: How long would that take?

Carl: I think since the case would go on a "fast track," we could get a decision from the court within six months.

Mediator: And if they lost and appealed?

Carl: Two more years.

Mediator: And if you won, what would you get?

Carl: We would get a judge to allow us to publish the book with another publisher who would be willing to pay her more. It's possible that we would get attorney's fees, especially if the other side appealed and lost.

Mediator: And the cost?

Carl: For the trial, somewhere upwards of $25,000, maybe up to $50,000 on appeal.

Mediator: What other practical consequences would there be? What would be the impact on the book and the series?

Carl: Most important, Charlene would get a big advance from the new publisher and a chance to make a lot more money because she would also get a higher royalty.

Mediator: What about the delay? What effect would that have?

Carl: That might be a problem. Charlene's series reached a high volume of sales last year and there's been a downturn since then, we think largely because of inadequate promotion. We could lose the market if we wait too long. But that would hurt them more than us.

Mediator: How so?

Carl: If Charlene doesn't put out a new book pretty soon, it will affect the whole series' sales.

Mediator: Rob, what would be the impact on Rick of litigation if you won?

Rob: In terms of cost and time, I think that Carl has it about right.

Mediator: That there would be parallel impact on Rick and BookPro.

Rob: Right. But I think that by preventing Charlene from going to another publisher, it would be a wake-up call for her and could give her an incentive to get back to work with Rick. There is no question that we would appeal if we lost, and I do think that it would doom the series. Rick is not about to put any resources into the series until the litigation is resolved, and with a fast-moving market, the series could become history quite quickly.

Mediator: So the delay might doom the series. And that would be bad for both BookPro and Charlene.

Rob: Right. But Charlene's going forward with another publisher would also doom the series with BookPro, and in addition would reflect badly on Rick and the company.

Mediator: In that respect, let me ask both of you, what would be the impact of the publicity from the litigation?

Carl: The publishing industry is pretty vulnerable and Rick would not only be out the time and money of litigation, but the public may well side with Charlene. I know that's not good for Charlene either, since she couldn't force Rick to market the series. But it could be that the publicity would keep the series in the public eye and help sales.

Rob: But once other publishers knew Charlene was in litigation, she'd get the reputation of being trouble, and I think no one would want to touch her. There are some significant upsides if we win—the security of knowing the rest of the series would be published by Rick.

Mediator: And would there be any downsides to your winning?

Rob: There is always some inevitable fallout from going through litigation. It's not a pretty process, and it could damage their relationship. That's why we're here.

Mediator: And from your client's perspective, I imagine that could make this a pyrrhic victory. He would have the right to publish Charlene's books, but Charlene could decide not to write them. Or at least a strained relationship could impair the product and scuttle any positive personal aspects of their interaction.

Rob: Of course.

■ ■ ■

We had reached another interesting point in the process. Both lawyers had conceded that their clients would be at risk if they proceeded in court and, more significantly, even if they were to win in court. This is not an uncommon phenomenon. Often, lawyers and their clients get so caught up in the legal fight that they ignore the bigger picture. In fact, many trial lawyers feel that to even think about a negotiated result makes them less effective as advocates. Many business executives increasingly turn to mediation precisely because they know that, win or lose, legal struggles will be a diversion from business priorities. In this case, the lawyers supported the mediation process, but neither of them had apparently had such a full exploration with their clients of the consequences of litigation.

Litigation was still an option for them if we were not able to find a better solution. Even though there were significant differences in the lawyers' assessment of the litigation risks, there was quite a bit of agreement about the negative consequences for both if they won. That would make our job much easier when we moved to a discussion of the business reality to find solutions that would leave both Rick and Charlene better off than if they proceeded with litigation.

■　■　■

Business and Personal Conversation

Now that it was finally time for the business and personal conversation, the law moved to the background and Charlene and Rick were able to discover and explain what was important to each of them. For Rick, it was the peace of mind that would come from knowing that he could develop a viable publishing and marketing plan for the remainder of the series and that he could count on Charlene to work with him toward that end. For Charlene, it was knowing that Rick would commit the necessary resources to give the series its best chance for long-range success and that she could leave if she felt that Rick wasn't sufficiently forthcoming.

That discussion led to Charlene and Rick negotiating an agreement in which Charlene agreed that Rick would remain her publisher for the next four years, at which time it would be determined whether or not they had reached minimum pre-set sales targets. If those minimums had not been reached, Charlene would have the option to find another publisher. This gave Charlene the out she wanted so that she wouldn't feel that the series was doomed if Rick didn't market it effectively, and it gave Rick the peace of mind he needed to make the next four years as productive as possible. The lawyers played a major role in helping Rick and Charlene determine a workable method to measure success that would be legally binding. While the legal reality never loomed as large again as it had at the beginning of the mediation, it played an important role in bringing Rick and Charlene together, united in their efforts to find something better for both of them than pursuing what was likely to be a lose–lose result.

Commentary: Bringing in the Law

The subject of bringing in the law involves two related but distinct challenges for the mediator, the parties, and their lawyers: *whether* the law will be addressed in the mediation and, if so, *how* it will be addressed.

Since we seek to place the parties in a position to make informed choices about their decision making, we want them to have as full an *understanding* as possible of how the law might inform those decisions. Several crosscurrents complicate that task, but we have found ways to deal with the challenges.

Making the Law People Size

Given the law's authoritative voice in our culture and in most of our psyches, the very inclusion of the law or even the attempt to include it can impede the parties' ability to *make decisions together* that reflect what's important to both of them outside the law. When their respective lawyers give them disparate predictions as to how a court may see their dispute, the parties can find themselves caught in a legally defined *conflict trap,* believing they can prevail in court and that the other side is less than straightforward. They may then decide that they should "leave it to the lawyers." Thus, the law can become all-consuming and overwhelming.

In order to put the law in perspective, the mediator needs to help the parties distinguish the *legal substance* of the dispute from the *legal impact* of the dispute. *Legal substance* is composed of the rules or statutes that govern our legal relations with one another. Since the parties are not usually lawyers, it can be useful for them to be educated on how the law sees their dispute in terms of legal substance.

Legal impact refers to the way the parties experience their dispute because of how they and their lawyers deal with the law. The impact of previous efforts to talk about the law was to make Charlene and Rick reluctant to ever have such a conversation again. Yet their lawyers probably intended to represent them responsibly. The best intentions may have the worst impact.

As these parties became educated about the impact of the law, even when it was initially barred from the discourse, they were open to searching for more constructive ways to deal with the differing views of legal substance.

The distinction here between substance and impact is an important one to keep in mind because lawyers, parties, and mediators (particularly lawyer-mediators) often approach the question of law as exclusively one of legal substance and thus ignore the destructive power of impact. In fact, the complexity and intricacies of the substance of law that may dazzle in the point and counterpoint exchanges between lawyers often conceal the impact of those exchanges on the parties.

Reference Points for Decision

The two conversations—one about the law and one about the parties' business and personal reality—communicate in a very real and sustainable way that there are different bases on which the parties make their decisions. Understanding that law is only one reference point helps to deal with its impact.

Parties to conflict quite naturally approach their dispute from different reference points. To one party, the practical and economic reality may be the most important consideration; to another it is the relationship; to another it is other needs and interests; and to some it may be the law. It all depends on their different perspectives, values, and priorities. The mediator who understands the different bases that could be important to the parties can help free them from the legal reality's restrictive grasp.

Following are some reference points for decisions.

A. Sense of Fairness
B. Interests and Needs of Parties and Others
C. Relationship
D. Law and Underlying Principles
E. Practical and Economic Realities
F. Prior Agreements
G. Other

The Importance of Including the Law

The more clearly the parties, and their counsel, see how law might inform rather than control their choices, the more empowered they are in relation to the law. That knowledge makes "The Law" only the law. There are several ways the mediator can help bring that knowledge into focus.

Comparing Mediation Result with What Will Happen in Court

A central value of mediation is for the parties to decide on a solution that will serve them better than their alternatives. Whether or not they seriously entertain the possibility of going to court, what a court would likely do provides a principal alternative in the minds of most parties and their counsel. In our understanding-based approach, we want the parties to have enough information about the legal alternatives to be able to compare it to what they're considering in mediation.

The problem in most business mediations is that the parties often have received information sufficiently skewed by their lawyers' opposing perspectives that they form widely divergent views of the likely outcome, keeping them stuck in a *conflict trap*. Why should they settle if each side believes it will likely prevail in court and the other side will ultimately recognize that?

Having the legal conversation in the presence of both parties and their counsel allows the gap created by their differing expectations to be lessened. Indeed, the very act of working together to lessen that gap is itself a way out of their *conflict trap*. And once they both realize that it is unlikely that their counsel's opposing views are both correct, they might turn toward one another to look seriously at what they can accomplish together.

Understanding One's Legal Rights

In our culture, parties in conflict often measure what they have or what they deserve in terms of their rights provided under law. For many disputants, understanding their legal rights can prove enormously empowering, since the law often provides some check upon one party to a conflict taking advantage of the other. Even when parties are represented by competent counsel and the mediator can assume they are informed of their rights under the law, it can still make a critical difference to have one legal conversation where everyone hears the same thing at the same time. Having the legal conversation together informs each party of his or her own legal rights, as well as the other's legal rights. Ironically, an open acknowledgment of both parties' "rights" often helps the parties move beyond an exclusively rights-based focus to the resolution of their conflict. It can also lessen the mystique of the law by making the legal information clear and more under the parties' mutual control.

Appreciating the Human Principles Underlying Legal Categories

It often can prove enormously helpful for parties to understand the principles that underlie the legal rules applying to their dispute. These principles frequently parallel aspects of what the conflict is about for the parties at a deeper level, and making them explicit can help give the parties a fuller understanding of what's at stake for both of them in their struggle. In the legal conversation in the Publishing case, Charlene and Rick were better able to understand the law when they saw that that the courts would likely look to two principles: the need to protect individual freedom and the importance of honoring commitments made in business relations. In this way the law can be a useful guide for appreciating how society struggles with legal disputes in terms of fairness, justice, and right relations that the parties can measure against their own personal sense of what they believe to be right.

Reinforcing Agreements Made in Mediation

Finally, there are two ways that having an open legal discussion can protect and reinforce agreements that parties enter into in mediation. The first is the fact that in a significant number of jurisdictions, if a party was uninformed of legal rights when entering into a legal agreement that ended a dispute, that legal agreement may be voidable in court. The second is that when parties choose to enter an agreement that differs from what they believe a court would have done, the fact that they choose differently, knowing the law, may actually reinforce their commitment to their agreement.

Three Steps of the Legal Conversation

The legal conversation is aimed at educating the parties about what would likely happen if they were to seek to resolve their conflict in court. The tricky part is to help them gain that understanding unskewed, to the extent possible, by the usual distortions of the adversarial lens.

As developed in the legal conversation in the Publishing case, we look at clarifying three separate elements:

1. The strengths of each side's legal position
2. The risks of each side's legal position
3. The practical consequences of going to court

Leading with *strengths* is the most comfortable starting point for both lawyers and their clients, since doing so allows each side to support its position. Having that conversation *together*, with the mediator taking time to understand the strengths of each side's legal argument, brings both into focus. We often ask the lawyers to slow down or to state in plain English some of the concepts spoken in legalese. We may try to translate by looping in straightforward language what the lawyers are saying in legal terminology.

Asking the lawyers to loop each other's legal positions also promotes understanding of the differing perspectives. Looping also helps clarify confusions, sometimes for the lawyers, sometimes for their clients, and not infrequently for the mediator. Giving the parties the opportunity to ask questions of their lawyers further promotes their understanding. In these ways, the legal conversation can lessen the mystique of the law by making the legal information clear.

When asking each side to expose its *risks*, we are sensitive to the fact that we are asking a lot. People in general are wary of making themselves vulnerable, particularly in front of those who could take advantage of them. That is even more true of lawyers, given their professional tendency to be risk averse. Making themselves and their clients seem vulnerable by saying what may be a weakness of their case in front of the other side is at best counterintuitive. As more than one lawyer has said to us, "I'm not going to do the other side's work for them." However, as lawyers and parties often acknowledge when facing this question together, to the extent the lawyers do not disclose the risks and the parties maintain unrealistic and divergent views of what would likely happen in court, the chance significantly increases that they will fail to reach a mutually agreeable resolution. As we are fond of saying to the lawyers, there are risks both ways.

The mediator's work is to help the lawyers see that their disclosing the risks of going to court may best serve their clients by increasing the likelihood of an agreement that makes good sense to both sides—the very purpose of their being in mediation. Alternating disclosures, as with the lawyers for Rick and Charlene, through *mutuality of vulnerability* can help build a confidence in the process, as the lawyers start with small risks and see whether they are met before setting out more significant ones.

Exploring the *practical consequences* of going to court is essential, and often disarming. Surprisingly, we find that lawyers have often not spoken in depth with their clients about what would really follow from seeking to resolve the case in court, even the implications of what would follow from a legal victory. The question—where "success" might leave the parties—can prove an eye-opener to both parties as they think through, in one another's presence, some of the real-life implications they may not have previously considered.

By moving systematically in this way through the legal conversation, we work with the lawyers to establish a shared, rather than oppositional, view of the legal reality.

When to Have the Legal Conversation

When lawyers are present in the mediation, as in this case, we prefer to address the law first and so suggest when making initial agreements about *how* we will work together. Our general experience is that a good number of attorneys are more comfortable moving back from center stage and allowing the parties to have the business/personal discussion *after* the lawyers have had their time at the fore. Also, parties generally come into mediation with the legal reality and the personal/business reality intertwined. It's often impossible to have the personal/business conversation with the parties until the legal context is established.

Clarifying the legal reality for the parties is a great incentive to have the business/personal discussion that follows. With the two conversations clearly separated this way, the task of each is clearer. And once the parties have a clearer sense of the legal reality, including the attendant risks and costs of pursuing the legal option, they are primed to see whether they might do better by looking at their conflict through a different lens.

Finally, the legal reality is infused with notions of right and wrong, with winning and losing, persuading or convincing one another. Since the basis of our approach is to seek to resolve conflict through understanding and agreement rather than winning and losing, the notions of right and wrong may prove less central. Indeed, much of what we do in mediation is to educate the parties about the restrictive hold these notions may have over them, challenge that hold, and help them break free. Having the legal conversation can help move toward a shared, rather than oppositional, view of the legal context.

Whose Decision Is It?

What happens if one or both parties simply do not want the law to be a part of the mediation? They want to make their decisions ignorant of the law or at least absent any explicit discussion about the law. On one hand, our goal is that the parties be fully informed. On the other, we want to put the parties front and center in decision making, including how they will work together to resolve their dispute. We respect their autonomy. The parties have the opportunity to be informed about the law, but it's their choice. If they decline, as Rick and Charlene initially did, we urge them again when it becomes clearer that their failure to understand the law may be keeping them caught in their conflict.

But what's a mediator to do if the parties oppose bringing in the law and the mediator continues to think it important? We proceed from the basic principle that reaching agreement on *how* we are going to *work together* includes both the parties *and* the mediator. The conversation cannot take place without the parties' agreement, but it also cannot be abandoned without the mediator's agreement.

The cases in which the mediator and parties disagree about bringing in the law fall along a continuum as we seek to *develop the parties' understanding* and also *support their responsibility*. At one end both parties are represented and fully informed about the law; at the other the parties have neither lawyers nor legal knowledge.

At a minimum, we urge parties to use counsel as consultants to the process. Early in the mediation, the parties will gain the benefit of their lawyers' perspectives on how a judge might view the dispute if it were to go to court. Later, the parties can use counsel to compare any agreement they reach against the reference point of the law, and to help draft a legal contract to formalize the parties' ultimate agreement.

In a case where both parties were represented by competent counsel, and both assured us that they were fully informed about the law, and we believed that to be the case, we would likely agree to work without a conversation about the law if the parties wanted to proceed that way. But we would likely urge them to reconsider having the legal conversation together, as with Rick and Charlene, and would stay vigilant to the possibility that mistaken impressions about the law were undermining their ability to move forward.

In a case at the other end of the continuum where the parties are unrepresented, do not wish to see lawyers, and are without legal knowledge, the mediator can introduce the law in terms of his or her view of what a court is likely to do. Or the mediator can recommend that the parties together consult an independent lawyer with expertise in the field who could be brought into the mediation. We would likely not agree to continue the mediation if we could not reach an agreement with the parties about *how* the law could be introduced.

Remember the Essential Point: Focus on the Parties' Understanding

The essential point of having the legal conversation is to *help the parties understand* how the law might apply to their conflict so that they can give it as much or as little weight as they choose. We are constantly aware of the distorting potential of the legal lens, and we work hard to give the parties a clear understanding of the law and the proper perspective on the law's relevance to their decisions in mediation.

Throughout, we emphasize with the parties and their lawyers that we have the discussion of the law in a manner that supports *the parties understanding* what would likely occur if their dispute were to be resolved in court; informs them of the values and principles embodied in the law; and supports their freedom and ability to give the legal perspective whatever significance it has for them.

Love, Death, and Money: To Caucus or Not to Caucus

9

"I'm sorry now that we didn't go to the other mediator who's an ex-judge," Serena, Stephen's frustrated lawyer, blurted out. "He would be more than happy to caucus with us."

"Let's talk about why you want to caucus."

"What does caucus mean?" asked Jamie, the other party to the dispute, sitting next to her lawyer, Jordan.

> *Mediator:* Caucusing is when the mediator meets separately with each side. My clear preference is for all of us to stay together throughout the mediation. Of course, you're free to meet privately with your lawyers at any time either of you wish. I would hope that either of you or your lawyers would speak up anytime you want to meet alone. I will not meet separately with either side.
>
> *Jamie:* I don't want them to meet separately with you.
>
> *Mediator:* Will you say why?
>
> *Jamie:* I don't trust what they'll tell you. I want to know directly what you're hearing from them.

And there's nothing that I would tell you alone that I wouldn't tell them, too. I have nothing to hide. In fact, I want them to hear it all.

Serena: I feel like I'm being put on the defensive here. I think it could help us a lot to meet separately with you. There are two ways. First, it would enable you to cut through everything that's going on here and give us your opinion about what you think would happen if we were to go to court. That could provide a reality check for both sides. Second, I am afraid that when we get to the point of trying to make a deal, if we don't make an offer that Jamie likes or, if we do anything other than acquiesce to her demands, she'll just walk out and not keep an open mind. There's a lot of bad feeling here.

Mediator: So you think the tension between Jamie and Stephen may make it challenging for them to resolve this together, and if my view of the law favors one side over the other, it might be better to receive the bad news in private. Secondly, you imagine that when we get to the point of dealing with economic offers that might settle the dispute, the two sides might be less reactive to one another if I were to shuttle back and forth to facilitate the negotiation process.

Serena: My experience in mediation is that it can be very helpful. And Jamie would walk out if we offered anything other than what she wanted.

Mediator: Let's talk about both concerns. I would prefer to start with the second one you set forth—that if you and Stephen put out a proposal in response to theirs that Jamie might walk out of the mediation if she considered it too low.

Serena: Right.

Jamie: Look, it was my brother who died and the money—money that came to us when our father died—was never intended to go to Stephen, plain and simple. And I'm not about to turn this into a matter for bargaining like at a bazaar. So if Serena is saying that we might leave if I don't like her "offer," she's right.

Serena: You see?

Mediator: We all agree you are here because of difficult and sensitive issues. Our challenge includes finding a constructive way to talk about an economic settlement of any money in dispute. But we are not there yet. And if when we get there, there is no way to talk about that with one side or the other threatening to walk out, then we might well have a problem.

Serena: Which is why I recommend we caucus and get some parameters on what we're talking about here without having to get to that point. My experience in mediation is that it can be very helpful.

Mediator: I don't have a problem with your raising the issue nor with your reasons for doing so. It's vital to how best to work together. We don't have a basis for moving forward until we have agreement about this. While I do have a strong opinion about the value of our meeting together throughout, I won't decide this unilaterally. And though this might be starting to feel coercive to some of you, we are now in the process. And as I understand it, Serena, you think if I meet with both sides separately, I might be able to help both see a realistic range for settlement that could potentially work for both sides without running the risk of one or the other side dismissing the other as not serious about settling.

Serena: I think that could certainly prove helpful.

■ ■ ■

Within the mediation world, caucusing is controversial. The expectation of many who come to mediation, particularly lawyers, is that the mediator will meet separately with each side, going back and forth between them, in an effort to broker a deal. Indeed, many mediators have the parties together only for an initial meeting and then conduct the entire mediation through caucuses, bringing the parties back together only for a final handshake at the end.

Almost all lawyers have experienced "settlement conferences" with judges before trial, where the lawyers for each side—sometimes with their clients, sometimes without—have separate meetings with the judge in an effort to settle their case. In this traditional adversarial setting, judges commonly seek to help each side evaluate its legal position. But they are also known to put pressure on both sides to settle by pointing out the risks each side faces if the case were to go to trial. If both sides experience sufficient risk in the court alternative, both may be willing to settle based on the judge's prediction. In this way, judges help reduce the court docket, and parties come to accept that half a loaf may be better than the cost of a trial and the risk of ending up with no loaf at all.

While lawyers often prefer this approach for many reasons, a common belief is that when conflict threatens to rear its ugly head, it's best to keep the parties apart and to call in the law. Otherwise, left to their own devices, disputants will too likely end up abusing one another. Most lawyers are generally comfortable with this approach, and many mediators are too.

However, we believe caucusing gives the mediator too much authority. He or she becomes the only one with the full picture. The parties know only what goes on in the meetings in which they participate, plus whatever secondhand report the mediator is permitted and/or chooses to give of what transpired with the other side. Our goal is that *the parties be the ones who resolve their dispute.* In caucusing, the danger is that the mediator will become judge or arbitrator, or use his or her position to manipulate the sides to make a deal as we develop further below. Indeed, some mediators view that as precisely their role. When caucusing, it is natural that the parties look to the mediator as the judge since the mediator has more information about the whole case than either side.

These dangers may not be obvious to the parties or even to the lawyers, so we try to make them explicit.

■ ■ ■

Mediator: Let me explain why I think working together makes sense in spite of the challenge it might pose. I don't want to be the judge in this case. I don't want to try to use authority to move you closer together or to manipulate either side by skewing my analysis of the law for that purpose. As you lawyers well know, what some mediators do in these separate meetings, or what judges do in what are called "settlement conferences," is to put the fear of God into each side—telling one why it may very well lose and then doing the same with the other. That seems coercive and manipulative. My goal is to turn down the heat rather than turn it up to help you make a deal.

Serena: That's frustrating because I think that you could help us come together by giving us the benefit of your independent legal analysis.

Mediator: I intend to be active with regard to the legal alternative, but not how you're suggesting. I don't think that my opinion about the law would be very valuable, because I don't know as much about the case as you two lawyers. I consider the two of you to be the experts about the law. Having said that, I do think that it could be useful for us to have a more in-depth conversation about the law so that your clients understand with more precision where you disagree and where you agree on what a judge might do, as well as what the practical consequences of going to court might be for each of them. While leaving the predictions to the lawyers, I'll certainly seek to clarify the situation with you, and will raise questions or concerns and share any insights I may have. I think I can do that best with everyone together and that we can reach a fairly common view of the court alternative if we are all present for that conversation.

Serena: But if you share your insights with all of us together and your insights favor them, or vice versa, that could drive us farther apart.

Mediator: That's a legitimate concern, and it's one of the reasons that I'll leave the actual predictions to each of you. But it's true, we could discover together that the law favors one side more than the other, and my inquiries or insights might contribute to that realization. But you could also discover that in private meetings, unless the goal is for me to hide the truth and manipulate the process.

Serena: Your insights might be easier to digest in private.

Mediator: You're free to meet with your own clients at any time. They should feel protected and supported by you as well as able to have you help them think through and clarify the situation.

Serena: I can see that I'm losing on this one.

Mediator: It may sound trite, but I'm working toward all of you winning. If you all have full access to the same information, then we're all working from the same basis, and I think that will maximize the chances of achieving the best resolution. If we agree to give it a try and it's not working, tell me.

Serena: Okay, I'm willing to try if Stephen is agreeable.

■　■　■

The events that had brought Stephen and Jamie to this point had been tragic for everyone involved. Stephen, 59, had been in a long-term gay relationship with Jamie's older brother, Eddie, who had, after a seven-year illness, died the previous year at age 64. While brother and sister had been close, Eddie had never told Jamie the full nature of his relationship with Stephen.

In the last three years of his life, Eddie needed increasing medical care. A year before he died, one of his legs was amputated; from then on he required full-time care. Stephen was not equipped emotionally or financially to handle the burden of caring full time for Eddie. His work kept him away for at least nine hours a day, and he came home to an understandably depressed and increasingly anxious Eddie.

Jamie, who had once been a nurse, stayed in regular touch with her brother by phone. As Eddie's health deteriorated, Jamie became increasingly alarmed by her brother's description of his situation. One day she made an unannounced visit and was appalled at the quality of care that Eddie had been receiving. Within a few days, she had moved in with Stephen and Eddie to care for her brother.

Tension between Jamie and Stephen grew and became unbearable. Within a few weeks, Jamie moved Eddie to the house of a friend of hers, where she oversaw her brother's care until he passed away two months later. During this time, Jamie severely limited Stephen's visits in terms of number and duration. By the time of Eddie's death, Jamie and Stephen were so antagonistic that she excluded him from the funeral.

About a year before he died, Eddie had converted several of his bank accounts, totaling about $100,000, into joint accounts with Stephen, who had long been his beneficiary under his will, and did the same with an $80,000 certificate of deposit. After Jamie moved Eddie out of the house he had shared with Stephen, Jamie encouraged Eddie to change his will to exclude Stephen from his estate, and introduced him to a lawyer who would draw up the papers. Eddie executed a new will leaving everything to Jamie and the friend whose house Eddie moved into before his death.

Shortly after Eddie's death, Jamie discovered that the new will was not effective with respect to those assets that had become joint accounts, including the $100,000 in bank accounts and the $80,000 certificate, which together formed the bulk of Stephen's estate. She hit the roof. She brought a lawsuit against Stephen charging him with neglect and abuse of Eddie during his last illness, and because of Eddie's age, a particular action of elder abuse that would entitle her to punitive as well as compensatory damages against Stephen.

When they arrived at the mediation, Stephen and Jamie had not seen each other since Eddie died. They were unable to make eye contact with one another. It clearly was not easy for them to be together, and I was not in the least surprised that Serena had made such a strong case to caucus.

When we were all agreed on proceeding together at least on a trial basis, I explained my rationale for the *two conversations*, the first about the law, to be led by the lawyers, and the second about the personal interests of the parties.

■ ■ ■

> *Mediator:* It is already clear, without having gone into it at any depth yet, that there are very strong personal dimensions that underlie each of your views. Eddie was clearly a very important person to each of you, and the strength of that personal connection to him is, I think, central to how each of you experiences what is going on here. After we finish the conversation about the law, I hope that we can have a conversation that includes what is personally important to each of you. And for this conversation, my hope is that our staying together in the same room will really pay off as we all begin to understand what underlies your separate positions.
>
> *Serena:* That may be true. We'll have to see.
>
> *Mediator:* Let's take it one step at a time.
>
> *Jamie:* It's not just a case of personal connections but of personal actions and personal accountability.
>
> *Mediator:* That, too. Whatever is important to each of you.

Serena and Jordan laid out their clients' legal positions. Jordan made it clear that he believed that Jamie's legal position was quite strong and would be backed by a list of witnesses that included nurses, friends of Eddie, and a neighbor. They would all testify, he said, that Stephen had been unable to properly care for Eddie, feeding him inappropriate food, forgetting to provide him with his necessary medications, and leaving him alone and uncared for while Stephen was at work, all contributing to enormous misery for Eddie and hastening his death. Jordan said that he was confident that a jury would award Jamie up to $1 million in compensatory and punitive damages.

Serena's presentation was equally powerful. She pointed out that Stephen had done the best he could for Eddie; that Eddie had participated in the decisions about his care, that they had had a loving relationship, as their friends would attest, and that all Stephen's efforts had been out of love for Eddie and commitment to him. Indeed, Stephen's willingness to allow Jamie to move in and then to remove Eddie from their home was out of that sense of commitment and sacrifice.

On the other hand, Serena said, Jamie's motives could be seen with some suspicion, particularly in having had Eddie change his will. Stephen was clearly Eddie's chosen beneficiary based on a series of well-documented acts by Eddie, such as his naming Stephen the beneficiary in his will and his adding Stephen's name to his accounts and to his certificate of deposit. If Jamie and Jordan took the position in court that Eddie had been incompetent when he added Stephen's name to the certificate of deposit and his various accounts, it would follow that the subsequent will that Eddie executed would also be invalid, and all of the property that Eddie left to Jamie under the new will would automatically go to Stephen, since Stephen was the beneficiary of the previous will. And, she pointed out, it would hardly sit well with a jury that Jamie had asked her brother to change his will if she believed he was incompetent.

The matter of Jamie having excluded Stephen from what was his domestic partner's funeral was another cruel blow that the court might hold against her. Both Serena and Jordan acknowledged the potential merit of the other's legal points and agreed that the outcome in court would probably turn on the jury's assessment of the relationship between Stephen and Eddie. And that issue would present significant risks for each side. We then talked about the practical consequences of going to court, including legal and expert fees that would be incurred, and the involvement of neighbors and friends who would be called as witnesses.

I actively participated in the legal conversation, asking questions when the lawyers' analyses seemed incomplete or when I didn't think the clients were understanding them.

■ ■ ■

Then we turned to *conversation two*. I asked Stephen and Jamie to each explain their versions of the history of the dispute. We agreed that they would each talk to me rather than to each other, at least initially.

It quickly became apparent that Jamie was unable to contain her vitriol and judgments toward Stephen, who kept his eyes downcast while Jamie was speaking. I knew both lawyers were thinking that this must be one of those cases where we should caucus, while for me the potential of staying together was right there in the room. With enormous power and directness, Jamie described how Stephen had abandoned her brother, referring to phone calls with Eddie and her own observations during the last months of his life. My role was to restate and thereby refocus much of Jamie's accusatory statements about Stephen into statements that admitted this was her own perspective. Slowly, Jamie's own view deepened.

Her pain and sadness about her brother's life over the past several years emerged, as did her feeling of powerlessness in trying to keep him alive. This time had clearly been excruciating for Jamie. Because she felt supported by me and by her lawyer, she was even willing (with her lawyer's permission) to speak about a lawsuit she had brought against a nursing home for failing to take proper care of their father at the end of his life. The suit had resulted in a settlement with the insurance company after her father's death.

Jamie had vowed that she would never again allow a loved one to go through what her father had suffered. This had added immeasurably to the pain of losing her brother, knowing that he too had been ill-cared-for, and that Jamie had not moved fast enough to prevent it. It was particularly maddening for her that the money from the insurance settlement on their father's suffering that Eddie had put into the $80,000 certificate of deposit had legally become Stephen's property upon Eddie's death.

When it was Stephen's turn, he spoke with a resignation and sadness, describing the last years of Eddie's life as overwhelming for both of them. While Jamie had been bursting to explain a myriad of details about the situation, Stephen was reluctant to speak at all and expressed himself in short clipped sentences. As it slowly emerged, he was both relieved and frustrated by Jamie's entrance onto the scene, because her competence was enormously helpful but her anger with Stephen was constantly painful. He had felt increasingly and systematically marginalized by Jamie in Eddie's life and death, capped by Jamie's exclusion of him at Eddie's funeral.

As Stephen spoke, Jamie made frequent efforts to interrupt to rebut Stephen's comments and was clearly having great difficulty living with the agreement we had made to allow Stephen to express himself without interruption. When I pointed that out to her, she was able to contain herself, but only barely, and only until Stephen's next statement. I recognized how difficult it was for her since she saw things so differently, and I told her so, emphasizing several times that the point was to have both their views expressed in the room.

I could feel the enormity of the gulf between them and wondered what if any impact they had made on each other. I was sure that it had been difficult for Stephen to hear Jamie speak, but I hoped that as the focus of the conversation between us moved from a direct attack on Stephen to statements about Jamie's experience, particularly her pain, it might have been easier for him. And for Jamie, I saw that listening to Stephen was very hard, and that she had absorbed little if any of the particulars of what he had said. I only hoped that she could see what was plainly visible to the rest of us: what a toll the whole experience had taken on Stephen.

■　■　■

It certainly would have been possible to have a private conversation with Jamie and then with Stephen and try to transmit their views back and forth between them. I could even have had those separate conversations and then brought the parties together to try to restate their views and listen to one another's. However, doing this with everyone together had had some noticeable impact. Jamie had made a gradual progression from a focus of attack to a more apparent focus on her own experience. Stephen had had excruciating difficulty in expressing himself at all. Both of these efforts had an unmistakable genuineness that could easily have been lost if they remained private or even if they had taken place with everyone together after private "rehearsals."

It was this genuineness that stood out, and I hoped it might provide a basis to build on what had just happened. I asked them if we could take another step to see if they were willing to make the effort to understand each other, even though they saw things so differently. Stephen thought that this could be useful. Jamie had difficulty understanding how it could change anything.

■ ■ ■

> *Mediator:* It might not change anything. If it is going to be valuable to us, it will be because you'll both know that you understand the whole picture. Your perspectives are different. The point of this would not be for you to agree on anything.
>
> *Jamie:* I'll never agree with that man. I cannot understand how he could have treated my brother the way he did.
>
> *Mediator:* Would you like to understand?
>
> *Jamie:* Yeah. Tell me why you took such rotten care of my brother.
>
> *Mediator:* That's not exactly what I had in mind.
>
> *Jamie:* Then tell me how to do this right.
>
> *Mediator:* It may not make sense to do this at all. The only reason to do it is if you would find it valuable to do it.
>
> *Jamie:* Okay. Yeah. Why are you so unappreciative of me for doing what I did?
>
> *Mediator:* Is that a real question?
>
> *Jamie:* Yes, it is.

In my mind I had a somewhat different idea how this part of the process might go—that each of the parties might say what they understood from what the other had expressed and that that might close some of the distance between them. But it was clear Jamie really wanted to know the answer to the question she posed, and I wanted to support that if it made sense to Stephen.

> *Mediator:* Stephen, I can imagine it might be difficult for you to answer Jamie's question.
>
> *Stephen:* I can answer. I was appreciative. You were enormously helpful to us when I didn't know how we could go on.
>
> *Jamie:* Then why didn't you tell me that?
>
> *Stephen:* All you ever did was criticize what I was doing. No matter what I did, you just kept saying how it was wrong. So I learned to just keep my mouth shut.

Mediator: So as a result of hearing only criticism from Jamie, you never thought to voice any appreciation and just kept your mouth shut.

Stephen: Yes.

Mediator: Do you know why?

Stephen: I don't know. Maybe I was afraid of her.

Jamie (exploding)*:* Afraid of me? Why would you be afraid of me? I was there to help.

Mediator: Jamie, I think that might be going on even now.

Jamie: What might be going on?

Mediator: It might be that Stephen is afraid of you now.

Jamie: Is that true?

Stephen: Yes. You can be pretty scary.

Jamie: I've been told that before. How long have you been afraid of me?

Stephen: Since I first met you.

Jamie: You mean when I had you as a guest in my house, you were afraid of me?

Stephen: Yes.

Jamie: When I welcomed you into my life, even though my brother never told me that the two of you were lovers, you were afraid of me?

Stephen: I think Eddie was a little afraid of you, too.

Jamie: What do you mean?

Stephen: I always wanted you to know about our relationship, but Eddie said that he thought you couldn't handle it.

Jamie: I always knew what was going on. I didn't have to have my brother tell me about the two of you. I knew it.

Stephen: Yeah, but he was still afraid to bring it up with you.

Mediator: And you didn't insist.

Stephen: I wouldn't do that. He was scared to say anything.

■ ■ ■

We had reached an interesting point. Jamie was truly shocked to know that she was intimidating not only to Stephen, but to her own brother. This opened the door to some further less-charged exchanges between them and the atmosphere softened little by little. While neither acknowledged it directly, it was clear that they had both cared deeply for Eddie. It was also becoming clear that it was in large measure the strength of their caring for Eddie that had led them to be so hurt and upset by what the other had done or had failed to do.

Throughout this exchange the lawyers had kept quiet except once when Jordan checked in with Jamie to see if she should continue talking about her father's death. But as I viewed it, the lawyers' silent presence and support played a crucial role in allowing the depth we had reached.

We then identified the priorities of both parties in terms of their needs and interests and listed several options for resolving the dispute. Finally, we reached a point where Stephen and Jamie agreed, in consultation with their lawyers, to come in with a written proposal to each other that was intended to take into account the priorities of both sides.

■ ■ ■

When we met again, Jamie proposed that Stephen turn over the $80,000 account to her, that he make a written acknowledgment of having treated Eddie badly, and that certain personal effects that were left in the house where Eddie died be given to Jamie. Stephen's proposal was that he would pay Jamie $40,000, make no apology, and turn over to Jamie Eddie's personal effects.

> *Jamie:* It's very simple from our side. I feel like Stephen has made me into the bad guy because he wasn't invited to the funeral. I think what we did was justified, and the effort that I made to take care of Eddie wasn't really ever appreciated or expressed. I need to have some written acknowledgment that he didn't treat Eddie well enough. As far as the money in the certificate of deposit is concerned, that represents the result of what happened to our father and it doesn't feel right that he should have it.
>
> *Mediator:* So having an acknowledgement from Stephen that he didn't properly take care of Eddie will provide you with the appreciation that you felt that you never received from Stephen?
>
> *Jamie:* It's far too late for him to express his appreciation now. It's not too late for him to admit that he didn't do right by Eddie. That's why Eddie changed his will.

Mediator: So if you were to have this admission, what would it do for you?

Jamie: It would be the truth.

Mediator: And having your truth known is of great importance to you.

Jamie: It's not just my truth. It's what happened.

Mediator: If Stephen were willing to acknowledge this as what happened, what would be the significance to you?

Jamie: It would, with the money that came from my mother, allow me to put all of this to rest, including my Dad's nursing home horror.

Mediator: So for you, the nightmare of all of this was reliving the experience you had when your father died and seeing the same thing happen to your brother.

Jamie (in tears): That's right. That money is blood money from our father. And you're right, I would have done anything to be sure my brother died with dignity.

Mediator: It sounds to me like he did.

Jamie: I think so, in spite of Stephen.

Mediator: Stephen, I imagine it would be hard for you not to react to what Jamie has just said, but I think it would be helpful if we could look to your proposal and help me understand what your thinking is.

Stephen: This is very hard for me. I'm not happy with what happened. It's true that I missed giving Eddie some of his medications. And it was impossible to keep him from eating chocolate. It was the only thing that he enjoyed, and I just couldn't deny him that. And I did leave him for long stretches at a time because my job required it and I didn't have an option to quit.

Mediator: So you felt that you were making as much of an effort as you could to take care of him.

Stephen: I did. You have to understand that I had really been taking care of him for many years, living with the knowledge that he was dying and we couldn't do anything about it. Especially after his leg was amputated, he became very depressed, and I often didn't know what to do.

Mediator: So when Jamie came on the scene, I imagine you felt a mixture of relief and frustration.

Stephen: That's true. Because she was a nurse and cared so much for Eddie, I knew that he was in good hands. But I got pushed aside and basically didn't feel welcome in my own house. And when they moved him and I went to visit, I got the cold shoulder.

Mediator: So this adds an important part of the picture for you.

Stephen: That's right.

Mediator: And the personal effects and money?

Stephen: If Jamie wants the personal effects, it's okay with me. They don't have meaning for me, and they might for her. I know that she made a great sacrifice to leave her family to take care of Eddie, and I know that Eddie cared a great deal for her. That's why it's all right with me that she get some of the money. But you also have to know that Eddie put the $80,000 in both of our names because he wanted me to have it when he died.

Jamie: That's just not true. When he made out his new will, he thought that account was in his name only.

Stephen: I wouldn't be surprised if he told you that, particularly then.

Jamie: What do you mean?

Stephen: There's something that I think Jamie doesn't understand about Eddie.

Mediator: What's that?

Stephen: Eddie was afraid to tell Jamie that we were in a gay relationship, and what that really meant—that we were life partners, that we were like a married couple. He always kept it hidden.

Jamie: I knew that. It's true he never told me, but I knew. I just felt that was his private business. But why didn't *you* tell me?

Stephen: Eddie wouldn't let me. It was really quite painful to me to have to pretend we were just friends.

Jamie: Why wouldn't he let you?

Stephen: That's what I tried to tell you before. He was afraid. He was afraid that you would judge him.

Jamie: How could that be? He knew I would give my life for him. Look at the sacrifices I made for him.

Stephen: But he was still intimidated by you. He just couldn't tell you.

Jamie: My own brother? Why would he be so intimidated?

Stephen: Because you're always right, and you always know what's wrong with everyone else.

Jamie: Then I'll just shut up.

Mediator: I hope not.

Jamie: Why not? I just seem to hurt everyone.

Mediator: Because the two of you are both in a lot of pain about someone you cared a great deal about. You're in each other's lives now because of him, and you're both grieving about him.

Stephen: There is something else I want you to know.

Jamie: What now?

Stephen: It's about your children. Your children were always important to Eddie. He cared a great deal about them. Even though I didn't get to know them very well, I felt as if I did, mostly through Eddie's stories about them. I'm sure he would have wanted you to know that.

Jamie (starting to well up with tears)*:* I didn't know that.

■ ■ ■

We had reached an important point in the mediation. Something had shifted between Stephen and Jamie. Jamie was still angry with him. Stephen was still afraid of her judgments. But there was a perceptible softening toward each other. Stephen felt strong enough to be able to admit that he was afraid of Jamie and to say what he needed to about him and Eddie. Jamie had become a little more sensitive to her impact on Stephen, and possibly on Eddie as well, and had been touched by Stephen's sharing about the importance of Jamie's children to Eddie. It also seemed that it was important to Stephen to have shared that.

With the two of them in the same room throughout, there had been for both a gradual and at times grudging coming to terms with what had happened between them and in their separate relationships to Eddie. A new understanding emerged from their direct interaction. With it, hostility and fear diminished and possibly the parties felt some compassion toward each other. In this case it also seemed significant that they had each acknowledged, implicitly if not explicitly, a connection because they had loved the same person.

From one perspective, it might appear that the mediation had not progressed at all. Jamie and Stephen were still in disagreement about money and any acknowledgment of Stephen's "wrongdoing." But each understood much better how the other saw the situation. There was not about to be a reconciliation between them. But they were less polarized. Although the lawyers had remained largely quiet during this conversation, their presence provided support for the parties. It also provided the lawyers a fuller understanding for later separate meetings with their clients, in which they looked at options to resolve their dispute over the money.

Much of any understanding Stephen and Jamie had gained had been implicit, and would remain so. They had directly acknowledged to one another the full nature of Eddie's and Stephen's relationship. This they could have done only together. If I had met with each side separately, perhaps I might have learned more about their views. They might have said things without each other present that could have shed more light on the situation, including aspects of what was important to them; and the lawyers might have been more open about the risks of going to court. Even if that had happened, it would have been impossible for me to convey to the parties the smallest fraction of understanding that could have affected them in the way they were affected through their direct but painful confrontation.

■ ■ ■

The importance of *gaining understanding directly* is central to our approach to mediation. Parties may not always reach the level of understanding that Jamie and Stephen did, but we want to create the opportunity for them to do so. There can be more to mediation than simply fashioning an agreement that ends the conflict at least on the surface. Assuming that it is best for the parties to avoid dealing with one another does not, from our point of view, serve the parties fully or well.

The *value of understanding* by the parties and between them does more than help them reach agreement. Understanding has value for its own sake, particularly for people who are traumatized, as Stephen and Jamie had been. We believe what they took out of mediation would have lasting implications for them, even if they never saw one another again.

Now it was time to see whether we could take advantage of their fuller understanding to find a solution to the case, which I still hoped they might be able to do. But if they did not, I would still have considered the mediation a success. When mediators judge their success by whether the parties reach an agreement, it may trap them in a position of untenable responsibility for the outcome of the process.

I've always felt that I'm a far more effective mediator without the burden of ensuring that the parties make a deal, although I certainly support them in doing so. Caucusing only furthers the impression that the responsibility of the mediator is to ensure that the parties ultimately agree, but staying together in the same room throughout this mediation, we could all feel the desire for closure.

■   ■   ■

Serena and Stephen asked to meet privately with each other to come up with a proposal. Fifteen minutes later we reconvened.

> *Serena:* We have a proposal that we think could work for all of us. First, Stephen is willing to write a letter acknowledging that he raised his voice with Eddie and that there were times when he forgot to give Eddie his medication and that he regrets that. Second, we've already agreed to return Eddie's personal effects to Jamie. Third, we propose that Stephen put $60,000 into a trust account for the education of Jamie's children.
>
> *Mediator:* Can you tell us what the thinking is behind this idea?
>
> *Stephen:* I know that I made mistakes in taking care of Eddie, but I did the best I could, so I'm willing to acknowledge that. With the money, I feel that it honors Eddie's feelings about Jamie's kids, so it feels good to me that they receive some money. Their education was important to Eddie. I think he would be pleased to know that he helped support it. I would also keep some of the money, because Eddie wanted me to have it and he considered it ours, so that feels right, too.

For a moment, shock registered on Jamie's face. She quickly recovered her composure.

Jamie: That's fine. I never wanted the money for myself in all of this, so if it goes to my kids, that's fine. It is also right that Stephen admits what he did. I need this because there are people who think I persecuted him. So this will help. Stephen, I never meant to do anything but help.

So it seemed we were done. I asked Stephen and Jamie whether they wanted to say anything else. Both said no, and it felt to me that there wasn't anything else for them to say. I expressed my appreciation for their perseverance in attempting to deepen their understanding of the situation and find an agreement that worked for them both. The lawyers also had nothing to add other than questions about crafting the written agreement, which we did on the spot.

I was grateful that Stephen and Jamie had gone as far as they had and that they had done so on their own terms. Could a mediator shuttling back and forth between them, while they sat with their lawyers in separate rooms, have crafted the same or similar financial agreement? It's possible. The numbers, and even the part about the trust for Jamie's children, might well have come out looking similar, although the element of the apology might have torpedoed the entire effort if it hadn't felt authentic for Stephen in saying it and Jamie in hearing it.

But more significantly, could meeting separately have had the same impact on Stephen and Jamie? I'm convinced it could not. There was a sense that they could now each put all the pain and unpleasantness they had experienced behind them. And most important to me, and perhaps for them, was the fact that they had done it together. This agreement rested on a basis that they could both understand. It wasn't just that it worked, but that they understood why it worked.

Commentary: To Caucus or Not to Caucus

In the understanding-based approach to mediation, we place great importance on everyone staying together in the same room throughout the process. It is not that we think that caucusing has no advantages and only downsides. But, if the mediator is motivated and prepared to help the parties *work through their conflict together* and the parties are willing to do so, staying together has many more advantages than risks. Given the values that underlie the understanding-based approach, the differences between proceeding by caucusing and by not caucusing go to the heart of mediation.

The Problems with Caucusing

In the caucus style of mediation, the mediator shuttles back and forth between private meetings with each side, attempting through reason, persuasion, entreaty, or manipulation to bring the two parties together to broker a deal that will resolve their conflict. Given our goal of supporting the parties in *resolving their conflict together*, meeting separately, and very likely holding secrets, is antithetical to how we see the challenges and possibilities posed by conflict. We see two primary dangers in the caucus manner of proceeding.

Making the Mediator a Judge

The first danger is that the parties will look to the mediator as a judge, arbitrator, or informed advisor who decides on the best solution to their problem. If the mediator goes back and forth between the parties, learning more and more from each side, then only the mediator hears everything. The parties express their own views and proposals directly, and they hear the proposals and views of the other side largely secondhand, through the mediator (to the extent that the mediator transmits what has been said).

When the mediator has the fullest view, it follows that he or she is in the best position to formulate the outcome and persuade or pressure each side to accept it. All this without necessarily having to reveal, or even being permitted to reveal, the full basis on which the chosen outcome rests. Many mediators work this way and many parties, and their counsel, naturally and readily expect them to do so.

So what's the problem? Perhaps none, if you don't believe *the parties have the primary responsibility* for resolving their conflict and you don't aspire for them *to do it together*. For many mediators, and some parties, it doesn't matter how heavy-handed the mediator is, as long as a resolution is achieved.

If the parties prefer and knowingly choose that approach, then it may make sense for them. If, on the other hand, they don't know the implications of the approach and the values behind it and if they do not know that there is an alternative, which they usually do not, the matter becomes more complicated.

At a minimum, we believe that the parties should be informed of the option of staying together *and* the potential advantages of doing so. In the vast majority of mediations, however, particularly those when lawyers are present, most mediators take for granted that caucusing is the way to go and don't consider giving the parties a different option.

Manipulation

The second closely related danger of the caucus approach is that the parties will be manipulated, feel manipulated, or both. Manipulation occurs if the neutral takes a strong role in managing the flow of information through confidential caucuses in an effort to determine the outcome, contrary to our aim that the parties have control over the outcome. Many mediators believe that manipulating parties to get them to reach a settlement is not only tolerable, it is their responsibility.

We would ask the parties: if you knew the mediator had such a decisive role, would you feel comfortable having the other side provide him or her with information that you are not privy to and that you may never get the chance to counter? The answer for many lawyers and parties alike might be "yes." If you were to ask those very same people if they felt similarly were the neutral to act as an arbitrator, very few would find that acceptable. Yet how different is this from a nonbinding arbitration?

At a meeting of lawyers who participate regularly in mediation, the moderator asked how many preferred to caucus rather than having the parties stay together. Most did. When asked their reasons, one statement elicited knowing smiles: "I know that I can manipulate the mediator." Often both lawyers have that same idea. The danger of manipulation is very real, either by the mediator, of the mediator, or both.

A familiar opportunity for manipulation arises in caucus when an attorney for one of the parties reveals to the mediator a trial strategy or the existence of some information or evidence that the other side is unaware of, which could increase the likelihood of a favorable outcome in court if the case went to trial. Such a revelation is accompanied by the admonition: "Don't tell this to the other side." Lawyers do this to show the mediator that they have a strong case. Their further intention is that the mediator will use this new knowledge without revealing the underlying information to advise the other side that their case is not worth as much as they thought.

But what is the mediator supposed to do with knowledge that must be kept confidential, particularly if that knowledge could or should influence the outcome of the case? He or she may hint to the other side or simply act as if nothing was said. More likely, the mediator will go to the other side and say something like: "I have some information that I cannot disclose to you but that convinces me your case is significantly weaker than you think. If I were you, I'd seriously reconsider their last offer." That is akin to the settlement conference model, and we believe it puts too much power and responsibility for resolving conflict in the hands of the mediator.

Working together, the parties know what the mediator knows, giving them a much greater ability to evaluate the progress of the mediation and ultimately to have more control over the process. It also ensures that the mediator will not be delivering different messages to each side. This gives the mediator a lot less wiggle room and provides the parties and lawyers with more control and also more responsibility for finding the solution. We think this is a critical difference in our approach to mediation, because we want the parties, with their lawyers' support, to *assume responsibility* for decision making and to determine the ultimate outcome.

The Reasons for Caucusing

Mediators give several reasons for caucusing.

Building Rapport with the Parties

Many mediators say a significant value for them in meeting separately with each party is to build rapport and understanding with the parties. We have the same goal. With Jamie and Stephen, as with other cases in this book, the mediator can serve as a bridge *to understanding.* By looping, the mediator makes sure that he or she understands each of their views and that each party feels understood by the mediator.

We sometimes refer to this aspect of our approach, only half in jest, as caucusing in the presence of the other side. After the parties feel understood by the mediator, they may be willing to deal more directly, effectively, and authentically with each other. When a party sees and feels that the mediator has understood both, they confront the great mediation paradox that "only one of us can be right." And this can break open the *conflict trap.* Though it is definitely a challenge, demonstrating understanding of each side of a conflict with both parties in the room together creates a foundation for all the work and understanding to follow, as it did with Stephen and Jamie.

Preserving Mediator Neutrality

One of Serena's primary reasons for wanting to caucus was out of concern that if the law was set out in a joint session, the mediator might appear to favor one side over the other. We try not to favor one side or the other. We encourage understanding the reality of the law through the legal conversation in our joint sessions. Unless the point is to paint a different picture for each side, we see little benefit in discussing legal matters in separate meetings.

We have often had just this conversation with mediators who say that they must caucus on the issue of the law precisely because they could never give a legal opinion that favored one side in the presence of the other. When asked whether in caucus they give both sides the same opinion about the law, mediators generally insist that they do. Then, we press: "Are you saying that you are telling each side the same thing only not at the same time (because you do not want the side that hears bad news to react in the presence of the other)?" Almost invariably, mediators then say, "Well, not exactly. I tend to emphasize with each side the risks they face in going to court."

We think a more authentic way to assure mediator neutrality is for the parties to see and hear everything that is going on—for the process (and the mediator) to be transparent. If either party, or the mediator, thinks the mediator is favoring one side over the other, it's out there for everyone to see and address. Our idea of mediator neutrality is when the mediator is working to understand both sides and to support both sides. That is not an effort we want to conceal from one side or the other, but one we want to make evident in the presence of both.

Avoiding Conflict

Mediators often believe that disputants will not be able to stay in the same room together or communicate constructively with one another when their controversy is heated and the emotions between them run high. Serena wanted to caucus in part because of her concern that things would blow up between Stephen and Jamie. That is an assumption that underlies how conflict is viewed and experienced by many. We challenge that assumption.

Working through conflict together rather than assuming the parties cannot get through the discord that pulled them apart is possible. We believe doing so even offers a greater potential for them to own their conflict while learning how to resolve it. Many mediators are not prepared to work this way.

A significant reason the caucus model is often relied upon, which is not often discussed, is for *the mediator's* comfort. In fact, the mediators and often the lawyers may be the most uncomfortable with the parties dealing directly with one another. For the mediator, and the participating lawyers, facing one side at a time may be less demanding and more controllable than working with both sides together. And many mediators think they can be more focused and effective by separating the parties, thereby not having to deal with the dynamics that can come up when disputants face each other. Simply put, many mediators, and lawyers, may see their role as managing conflict rather than helping people go through it. For us, supporting the parties in *going through their conflict together* is precisely the challenge

Of course, if the mediator does not believe the parties are capable of moving through the conflict together, there is that much less chance that the parties will see the possibility themselves. In this way, the parties are caught in a *conflict trap*, circumscribed by the limiting worldview of unproven assumptions. We believe people can *work through conflict together*, even when they aren't sure they can and have not worked well together so far. While we don't want to force people to do so, we do want to educate them about the value of doing it this way and give them the opportunity to try.

Coaching Each Side in Its Approach to the Conflict

Typically, most mediators make it a ground rule that they will caucus regularly (or as needed) and will keep all communications confidential unless specifically given permission not to do so. Both mediators and lawyers view the caucus as a place to learn information or perspectives that the party and/or counsel does not want the other side to know. Each side, it is reasoned, will be willing to speak more openly with the mediator alone than they would be in the presence of the other.

Caucusing thereby addresses a concern of many lawyers— that mediation risks revealing weaknesses in their case, prejudicial information, or elements of legal strategy that could later be used against them in court. (However, in our experience, most lawyers pretty much know the likely strategies of the other side as well as the weaknesses in the other side's case.) The privacy and confidentiality of the caucus setting would seem to guard against these dangers and thereby reassure lawyers, pledged to protect their clients, that they can fulfill their responsibility and safeguard their legal options.

We acknowledge that in a confidential setting with participants on one side of the dispute free to talk among themselves, the mediator can help them understand the conflict, their own interests, and the approach they might want to take toward resolving the dispute. Sometimes there are different perspectives or disagreements among the parties on one side of the dispute—problems behind the table rather than across the table, as in the San Francisco Symphony mediation. Parties might well be reluctant to deal with such internal conflicts in front of the other side. But blindly accepting that caucusing is the answer, without assessing with the parties its limitations or dangers, is unfair to everyone.

And there is usually little effort to minimize the use of caucusing to certain limited ends, or to restrict the way that caucuses are conducted to benefit from their advantages while avoiding their all-too-likely problems.

Supporting Parties to Reveal Important Information

Another claim for caucusing is that by revealing information or perspectives to the mediator without the pressure of the other disputant's presence, the mediator can help the party think through whether or how to reveal that information to the other party.

Parties do not always insist that information revealed in caucus be kept secret. In fact, they may even want the other side to know but think the mediator will be better at explaining their view than they would be themselves. Or they may agree, in response to a mediator's urging, that the mediator be free to reveal it if the mediator believes it would be helpful. The hope of many mediators is that once a party has disclosed relevant information in a private meeting, the mediator will be able to convince that party to disclose it to the other party in a joint session. We believe that coaching a party on how best to present his or her perspective in a joint session is one of the best reasons to caucus.

For us, however, there is still a significant potential loss to the communication possibilities between the parties if the information is shared privately and then carried secondhand to the other party or even transmitted by a party after coaching by the mediator. In the case at hand, when Jamie told us that when her father died she had sued the nursing home and recovered a monetary judgment, that revelation was not without some risk. Jordan had to have been concerned that if the case ever went to trial, it could appear that Jamie made a habit of finding fault with caretakers, thereby translating personal tragedy into financial reward. Jordan might have advised Jamie not to bring up this information in front of Stephen and his lawyer, but to reveal it, if at all, in the privacy of a caucus. In a caucus, Jamie might have asked the mediator not to mention it, or to do so only with great care.

When Jordan supported Jamie to make her revelation in front of Stephen and Serena spontaneously, we believe the understanding deepened and everyone benefited. Stephen was likely already aware of the source of the certificate of deposit. More significantly, hearing what Jamie had gone through when her father died provided a vital emotional context that made Jamie's demands of

Stephen and her suffering comprehensible. Even if Stephen continued to see his mate's sister as unreasonable, she had become that much more understandable.

It seems doubtful that the same message could have been conveyed with the same meaning through an intermediary. Even if the caucus had been used to help prepare Jamie to reveal the information in a joint session, it would have meant a less spontaneous delivery and left Stephen wondering what else had been said in caucus.

Not many parties are willing to reveal such charged information without discussing it first in a caucus. Possibly this could be a cost of our approach. Yet it is a risk worth taking, but many mediators, not appreciating the potential in having the parties together for an open exchange, don't create the context for that type of open dialogue, perhaps because they don't feel comfortable with such an open exchange themselves.

We believe that when the parties *develop an understanding* of what is important to both of them, the possibility for finding creative solutions that benefit them both is greatly enhanced. And if a solution honors what is important to both of them, it will enhance the parties' long-term commitment to the resolution they have chosen. If the parties have an ongoing relationship, *going through the conflict together* can preserve, or even enhance, that relationship. For others, like Jamie and Stephen, *resolving their conflict together* still respects the relationship they have had, even if there will be no ongoing direct relationship in the future.

As we view it, *going through conflict together* is an end in itself central to the goals underlying our approach. In a world where conflict is endemic and destructive, finding ways to *work together* can make a meaningful and constructive difference.

The Neighbors: Positive Neutrality

10

Rather than seeking to be equally distant from each party, we strive to be equally close.

■ ■ ■

I don't automatically disqualify myself as mediator if I've had previous contact with any of the parties or have a current relationship with them as friends, colleagues, relatives, or the like. But I am quite wary of mediating with people I know. So alarm bells went off when my assistant informed me that neighbors whose dispute was notorious in our small beach community had asked if I was available. If I were to mediate, I would need to be sure I could be neutral in our particular sense of that term.

Both neighbors had retained lawyers, one of whom I also knew. When that lawyer called my office to set up a meeting, she was clearly sensitive to my previous contacts with the parties, telling my assistant that I was either the best or worst person to mediate their dispute. While cautious, I was intrigued by the challenge. After a phone call with the lawyers describing my approach to mediation and enumerating my previous contacts with their clients and with the lawyer I knew, we all decided that it was worth giving mediation a try, particularly since the lawyers had not been able to make any progress with the case. They were already in court on one matter, and there would be many more possible court proceedings to follow if they were not able to successfully mediate a range of disputes that had accumulated over the four-year period these neighbors had lived side by side.

Nancy, who at 78 was one of the earliest residents of the community, had lived in her well-situated home for 35 years, the last 20 alone. She was an ardent environmentalist and had a well-earned reputation for raising a ruckus over a wide variety of community issues, including significant disapproval over the way my family took care of our dog. Not known for keeping her many opinions to herself, she was viewed as the chief whistle-blower for any actions she thought might threaten the values she held dear.

Henry was a young, successful real estate developer when he moved into his house with his family. Living in a community that largely opposed all real estate development, he was generally viewed with some suspicion. In Nancy's eyes, his work as a developer meant that he started with three strikes against him. From the get-go, she had been continually annoyed with his activities, ranging from his use of a leaf blower to committing what she saw as other "treasonable" acts against nature.

Henry, for his part, came to see Nancy as one who would all too readily act on any suspicion, and he held her personally responsible for compelling him to spend $50,000 to upgrade a septic system that was already functioning properly, in order to comply with county regulations. Nancy, in turn, was sure that Henry was retaliating when about a year ago he made an offer to acquire a vacant parcel between their homes to "protect it for the neighborhood." This action earned him a certain notoriety in the community, which Henry saw as a result of Nancy's perpetual lobbying against him.

It had all boiled over recently. First, Henry removed most of the trees on his property, improving the view from his home while dramatically exposing Nancy's previously very protected home. Nancy considered this both a crime against nature and against her and was outraged that he had not informed her of his plans in advance.

Shortly thereafter, Henry told Nancy that for several unanticipated reasons, he wouldn't be able to protect the parcel he had acquired from development after all. In fact, he was going to build a house there, move into it himself with his family, and sell the home in which they now lived. Nancy, already infuriated by the tree removal, felt deeply betrayed by Henry's turnabout on preserving the land. She made his betrayal known to several people in the community who shared her respect for nature, and she maintained heightened vigilance for any new activity on Henry's part that she felt would further degrade her environment.

She didn't have to wait long. One summer evening she received a phone call from a neighbor who had seen Henry on the south boundary of her property. Nancy jumped into her truck and (depending on various accounts) raced or drove down to where she spotted Henry "on my property!" and brought the truck to an abrupt stop inches away from his knees. How precisely this all came about, as well as what exactly happened, was the subject of dramatically different stories from Henry, Nancy, and a couple of witnesses. Henry called the county sheriff and had Nancy arrested for assault. Nancy threatened to sue Henry for the arrest as well as for his plans to develop the property he had promised to protect.

■ ■ ■

Loosening the Hold of Judgments

As we have seen in the Nature Preserve case, mediating with a commitment to understanding what is truly important to each party means having to deal with one's own all-too-natural tendency to judge the parties. The problem is hardly avoided by simply eliminating from one's practice any parties the mediator has known previously. Most of us are quick to make judgments about people, particularly when they are in conflict with one another. "He's too aggressive." "She's self-righteous." "He's been wronged." Indeed, one way that conflict maintains its restrictive grasp is to make judgments seem so natural and justified.

The question for us as mediators isn't how to avoid judgments. It is what to do as they arise, which they inevitably will, to keep them from blocking or limiting our effort to be fully present for each party. In order as mediators to be able to help the parties escape the hold that judgments have over them and their conflict, we must be able to counter that trap within ourselves.

■ ■ ■

I had already formed many judgments about Henry and Nancy. It was only after I was fairly certain that I could keep the judgments from interfering with my intention to be fully present for both of them that I agreed to see them.

Even though the mediation took place more than a month after the incident that culminated with Nancy's arrest, when Henry and Nancy arrived with their lawyers, the two of them still seemed traumatized—Henry by the incident, Nancy by the arrest. Sensing the fear that was there for both of them beneath their contentious stances helped reassure me that I might be able to identify with both.

Nancy's lawyer began the mediation by demanding that Henry withdraw his complaint to the police so that Nancy wouldn't have the criminal proceeding hanging over her head. Henry's lawyer responded that it was not possible to do that since the case was now in the prosecutor's hands. He also made clear that he was unwilling for the criminal proceeding to be negotiated, or even discussed in mediation, because he believed it was unethical, even illegal, for such a conversation to take place.

Before engaging them about the situation, I wanted first to clarify my role in helping them. I began with more uncertainty than usual about whether I was the right person to mediate with them.

> *Mediator:* Henry, you know that over the years Nancy and I have had many interactions as neighbors in the same community and that I know Nancy's lawyer. Nancy, you know that I've had some interactions with Henry as a neighbor as well. And you both certainly know that as a person in the community I've heard about much of what has been going on between you. If I'm going to mediate with the two of you, all of us need to be satisfied that I can be neutral.
>
> *Henry:* I assume that you can be objective.
>
> *Mediator:* You may feel that way, and I appreciate that. Perhaps more pertinent, I want both of you and your lawyers to

know that my idea of being neutral is not to be objective or to pretend objectivity. I think I need to be neutral through "being there" for both of you in order to help you. My goal is to understand you both as fully as I can. I'll want to stay in the middle by seeking to move closer to both of you and what you care about rather than by keeping equal distance.

Henry: That's not what I had in mind. I was hoping that you would be objective and then tell us what you think is fair.

Mediator: I think of my role differently. As a mediator, I won't decide who is right. My job will be to help you make decisions together. To do that, it would not be helpful for me to remain detached and keep my distance. Even in this moment, I truly want to understand not only what you're saying but what might be behind what you're saying.

Henry: And what do you think that is?

Mediator: Well, because you're wishing for someone objective to decide this matter, I imagine you don't have much confidence that you can reach an agreement with your neighbor yourself.

Henry: That's right.

Mediator: So for me the question is whether you would want to decide with Nancy how your dispute should be settled, if that were possible.

Henry: Well, yes, I'd like to, but as you may know, there's a lot of water over the dam.

Mediator: I suspected as much from the rumor mill, but for me, part of the question is answered by your indicating that you have some motivation to work it out together, even though you don't have much hope. So if Nancy is similarly motivated, then the question is simply, "What kind of help do you need from a neutral to be in the position you'd like?" If I were going to decide what you should do, my detachment might be very helpful. But if the two of you are the decision makers then my role requires getting more directly involved. I'll want to understand what is important to both of you under your dispute, and help you understand yourselves, and possibly each other more fully. If I'm going to do that, you both need to have confidence that I haven't already chosen sides and that I'll never do that as part of this process.

■   ■   ■

Positive Neutrality

Rather than maintaining a stance of objectivity and distance from both parties, the understanding-based mediator tries to achieve a sense of *positive neutrality*. This means trying to be equally subjective with each party and equally close. We work to identify with each party, trying to understand and feel within us what the dispute feels like to each—in a word, to empathize—and to ensure that each party feels understood by the mediator.

Seeking to understand and connect with each party in this way, in the presence of the other party, can make a critical difference in working through the conflict, as would prove the case with Nancy and Henry. To do so means not just working with the parties toward positive neutrality but also working within ourselves as mediators.

■ ■ ■

Henry: What you say makes some sense to me. But how do we test your neutrality?

Mediator: Well, I've already described the nature of my prior contact with all of you and the source of my knowledge of your dispute. While I don't think any of that prior intelligence will interfere with my role, you and Nancy, or your lawyers, should feel free to ask me any questions about my previous relations with any of you. And if at any time any of you feel that I've moved off my neutral position, and become partisan in the sense of being or appearing to be more on one side than the other, I'd want you to bring it up in the mediation. It's quite possible that you'll think I'm not neutral in the classic sense of the term, simply because I'm working hard to understand Nancy, just as she may think that that's going on now between you and me.

Nancy: I was a little concerned about how much attention you're paying to him, but I think I understand what you're saying. I also think that because you are a neighbor, you care about what happens in the community more than any outsider could, and that could be helpful to us.

Mediator: So do I. I do feel some stake in wanting to help you beyond my basic professional stance because we're part of the same community. The danger might be that I'd take on more responsibility because of that connection, and maybe even try to push you to make a deal. My goal is to be noncoercive, and for you to take the major responsibility for reaching an agreement and what kind of agreement you reach. And, of course, you're free to quit this process at any time.

Nancy: Don't worry about me. Nobody's going to push me to sell out. I've been making my own decisions for a long time, and I'm not going to stop now.

Mediator: I have confidence in that.

I then asked Henry and Nancy why they were interested in mediating. Both gave rather lukewarm responses, which concerned me. It was clear that neither was optimistic that mediation would work. I hoped this would change once they had more of a feel for the process and what could be achieved. Henry's and Nancy's lawyers, however, were more optimistic.

■ ■ ■

Lawyers' Support for Mediation

Whereas in the earlier days of mediation, lawyers often cautioned their clients against its dangers, many now espouse its very real benefits. Henry's and Nancy's lawyers were not only well aware of the pitfalls that litigation posed for both clients, but they also felt that the only way to resolve the dispute definitively would be through a result personally tailored to meet their clients' needs. A court-imposed decision would likely lead only to further litigation down the road.

■ ■ ■

After further discussing the mediation process and additional agreements about procedure, we then turned to *conversation one*—laying out the legal context of the dispute. With the court options in mind, our goal was to see whether we could ultimately build a result that was better for both parties than what could happen through litigation. All of us agreed that putting the litigation into perspective would be valuable even though it wouldn't by itself point us in a direction that Henry and Nancy wanted to go. That would depend on the personal context of their dispute, *conversation two*.

After the lawyers laid out the various legal proceedings that would take place if their clients were unable to resolve their differences in mediation, it was clear to all of us that no matter who won or lost, Henry and Nancy were facing the potential for years of litigation. As long as they remained neighbors their hostility and anger would cause major disruptions in both their lives.

I then suggested that in having conversation two, each take as much time as needed to describe their view of the dispute *to me*, and I assured them that I would do my best to understand each side.

■ ■ ■

The Centrality of the Mediator Understanding the Parties

When a mediator makes the effort *to understand each party*, it gives the parties the opportunity to express their views and to reflect on their own experience. Some parties are simply not assertive enough to express their points of view (this was clearly not an issue with Nancy or Henry, as we shall see). And even readily assertive parties can be frustrated when their counterpart is constantly reacting to their every word. Both may be trying to talk but each feels constantly interrupted, and it is not clear that anyone is listening. When it's agreed that the mediator will work with the parties to understand each of them in turn, it means that each will have the time to express his or her views, while the mediator makes the effort to understand.

To maintain our stance of *positive neutrality*, we need to continually work within ourselves to assure that we are fully there for both parties despite how differently they see their situation. Conflict puts pressure on anyone witnessing it to take sides. As mediators, we need to accept the parties' differing views, rather than denying those differences or trying to convince one or the other party to change their views.

As developed earlier in *Bubbles of Understanding*, this effort to understand each party, done well, leads to both parties feeling understood by the mediator. Since in conflict most people feel misunderstood, at least by the other side, receiving authentic understanding from a neutral third party can be enormously valuable. Misunderstanding fans the flames of conflict. *Understanding* can begin to quell them.

When a mediator is simply trying to understand them, rather than lead them or alter their views, many parties deepen their understanding of what is important to them. Once the mediator has understood the parties' respective views, the parties may also attempt to demonstrate some understanding of each other.

■　■　■

I explained to Nancy and Henry how I wanted to work to understand them at this point by having separate conversations with each in the presence of the other, and both said it made sense to them as long as they could "rebut" any misperceptions created by the other. Then Henry's lawyer raised a question.

> *Henry's Lawyer:* We have been mired for some time in the muck of the past. Dredging it up again is only going to inflame their feelings and get us caught in that quagmire. I think we would be better served by avoiding a rehash of the past and focusing instead on the future and what it will take to get beyond where we have been.
>
> *Mediator:* Your inclination would be to see if we can make progress by avoiding a conversation about the past, including the incident with the truck.
>
> *Henry's Lawyer:* I do think it would be a better use of our time.
>
> *Mediator:* We can try that if you all want to, but my experience is that understanding the past is often necessary to release people from the kind of quagmire you're talking about. Also, I'm not sure that some of the problems you've encountered haven't come from how Nancy and Henry have talked about the past. I wasn't there, of course, but my guess is that Nancy and Henry haven't felt that they've had the chance to fully express themselves, or that they've been understood. If we can find a way to talk about the past that doesn't leave us stuck, that understanding can be valuable in pointing us in a direction that makes sense for the future. I think my suggestion might make a difference. Both your clients will have the opportunity to express themselves, hopefully without having to defend against the reaction of the other, and I am going to try to understand what this has been about for each of them.

■　■　■

Looking Back in Order to Look Forward

Henry's lawyer's comments hardly surprised me. Many mediators take a similar view—that speaking about the past serves no purpose other than to reiterate and possibly exacerbate the conflict. Often a breakdown in trying to talk about the past has resulted in the impasse. If speaking about the past serves any purpose, the argument often goes, it is to allow the parties to "vent"—to discharge built-up emotions—and that is best done outside the presence of the other party.

For us, the goal of speaking about the past is to gain a fuller understanding of how the parties believe they have gotten to where they are. Knowing this can open a meaningful dialogue about what is important to the parties in going forward. In fact, avoiding the past can keep people locked in their conflict, fueled by mutually reinforced negative views of each other's past actions and motives. The idea that allowing expression of feeling is somehow to provide space for "venting" suggests that emotions are a contaminant in the process, rather than a valid aspect of the parties' experience. Emotions, authentically experienced and expressed, are often part of the inquiry and may prove key to gaining a fuller understanding.

But the danger of what can happen when people return to the past is very real. The challenge is how to support the parties in having that inquiry constructively.

■　■　■

The dialogue with Henry's lawyer turned out to be short-lived. Both Henry and Nancy were quick to agree that, painful as it might be, if we were going to find a way out of the problem, we needed to review what had happened. I supported them, and the lawyers voiced support, while possibly retaining some skepticism. Listening to each of the parties describe how the problem had developed, I felt myself pulled toward each—first Nancy and then Henry—and my sense of positive neutrality grew.

> *Nancy:* I had successfully blocked the development of this land 30 years ago, when the then owner wanted to build a

monstrosity on it. It was prized land, on the ocean, and I was worried that the fragility of the ecosystem would be upset by the placement of any house there, but particularly the 4,000-square-foot house the owner had in mind. The town agreed with me, or at least refused him the permits he sought. When Henry made his offer on the parcel, he told me that he was committed to keeping the land undeveloped. Fool that I was, I believed him. But he had this in mind the whole time.

Mediator: So, for you, that parcel of land in its undeveloped state has a long history related to your commitment to the environment. And you relied on Henry's word that he would keep it undeveloped, but you now believe that he was not in earnest. Why?

Nancy: Any fool can look back now and see what he was doing.

Mediator: I understand that you thought he was purposely deceiving you. It would be helpful if you could speak more about what *you* went through than telling us what you think was going through Henry's mind.

■ ■ ■

Validating Differing Perspectives

As developed earlier, parties in conflict are usually convinced of the truth and rightness of their view and the falseness and malevolence of the other's. Henry and Nancy were both caught in *conflict's trap* of judging themselves by their intentions and judging each other by the impact of the other's actions on them. The stance of positive neutrality with the mediator's heartfelt acceptance of both views allows the parties to see their confrontation as one of differing perspectives and thereby begin to escape the hold that their conflict has over them.

One of the central guides for helping the parties get out of the blame–counter-blame dynamic is to encourage them to speak from their experience, rather than attributing motives or intention to the other. Even simple efforts in this direction can help break conflict's restricting grasp.

■ ■ ■

Nancy: Okay, I'll stick to my experience, but what's obvious is obvious. I actually told him that I supported him to make his offer. He had lots of money. I had none, so I couldn't help financially, but I was willing to do whatever I could to keep that property undeveloped. If it all became one parcel, so much the better. Henry and I seemed to be getting along fine up until the tree fiasco. He told me he was going to be cutting down three trees. Instead, I came home to find 36 stumps from the clearing his men did in one day. I knew then what a liar he was.

Mediator: You were devastated when those trees were cut.

Nancy: I felt betrayed. I was angry. Not only had we lost those trees forever, but now I was exposed to the beach and had lost my privacy.

Mediator: So you mainly felt betrayed and angry. I also thought when you were talking that I heard grief in your tone.

■ ■ ■

Appreciating Anger

Finding a constructive way to deal with parties' anger in mediation is critical and challenging. Anger is not easy to be around and continually threatens to exacerbate or at least rigidify the conflict. It can be tempting to try to change the focus, perhaps to what the party seeks on a concrete level, or encourage the parties to let go of the anger or at least put it aside and turn to reason instead. Some mediators prefer to caucus precisely to avoid angry confrontations between the parties.

In our approach, we view anger, blame, attack, and counterattack as a way that conflict can become entrenched. So it might seem a good idea to try to stop it or at least confine it. But as we view it, anger is not the issue but rather how it is responded to or not responded to. Anger met with anger, and blame with blame, can indeed perpetuate the conflict, as can denying any opportunity for the parties to voice these feelings. But parties feeling authentically met and empathically understood in their anger— with focused appreciation both for how each party feels and how each views the situation—can dramatically change anger's place in the conflict. It is not a question of simply giving the anger room for expression, what is called venting. It is a question of the mediator authentically seeking *to understand* that the parties are angry and the parties' feeling that that is understood. And it doesn't stop there. Once the fact of each party's anger is understood, the challenge is to *go beneath*.

In exploring Nancy's view of the history of their dispute, I'm trying to understand not just the anger but also the feelings *under* the accusations that she and Henry have been trading back and forth. These feelings are often unexpressed and unappreciated, hidden at times even from the party who holds them. As Nancy spoke more from her own experience and the impact on her, those feelings began to come out, and I helped her find the words to express them. Fear and pain are often at the core of conflict and the source of mutually reinforcing, self-justifying views by which each side defends itself as right and attacks the other as wrong. My realization that those deeper feelings might *underlie* their recriminations against one another would make it easier for me to empathize with each of them. Addressing these feelings with the parties may begin to loosen the hold of the attack/defense mode that keeps their conflict intact.

■ ■ ■

Nancy: You have no idea what those trees meant to me. They were living things and they were murdered.

Mediator: You're saying that for you, losing any tree is a degradation of the environment.

Nancy: Yes, even the tree that overhangs my house that they say could fall on it. I don't believe in destroying nature. Nature protects us and we should protect nature.

Mediator: So the trees provided protection to you, and losing your privacy added insult to injury.

Nancy: Yes. I hate to have the people who use the beach be able to spy on me. I've lived here for 35 years and only now have I lost my privacy.

Mediator: And from the day the trees were cut, your relationship with Henry changed?

Nancy: Of course. Wouldn't you feel that way? And then when I found out that he was going to build a house there, I knew that I was dealing with the devil himself.

Mediator: I understand how angry you are with him. But instead of characterizing Henry, I prefer you talk about your own experience. It will be easier for me to understand you, and less inflammatory.

Nancy: Okay. I'm just telling you the unvarnished truth.

Mediator: I believe you are speaking honestly from your experience of what happened. There is also Henry's view of what happened, which I imagine is different from yours. All I want to do now is try to ensure that there's room here for both your views, and to see whether you can recognize that there may be more than one truth.

Nancy: Okay, this is *my* truth. But the facts speak for themselves. Now he's got a permit, and he's going to build a house there. And he's trying to turn the whole community against me.

Up until now, it had been fairly easy for me to move close to Nancy and empathize with her. She was a legend in our community who was fighting for her home and the environment, values with which I could readily identify. Given what I had already heard about the threatening episode with the truck, however, my judgments about her could cut me off and make it harder for me to be as open to her in this next step. Recognizing that possible block within me, I began.

Mediator: Can you tell me what happened?

Nancy: I had suspicions that he was snooping around my property. There were signs that he had gone through the fence to do some kind of survey. I had warned him not to trespass again. One evening I got a call that he was over on the lower part of the property, so I got into my truck and went down, and I caught him. It's true that when I put on my brakes the truck skidded a little on the loose stones, but I know every inch of my land and drive there all the time. I never intended to hit him. I didn't and I wouldn't. But he knows how to work the system. He yells that he's going to call the sheriff and that if I go anywhere he'll tell him that I've left the scene of a crime. When I got home, I called the sheriff and told him that I was home if he wanted to talk to me. I never touched Henry. It's just his way of trying to get me to back off. And I won't.

Mediator: You were concerned with what might be happening on your property, and went down to check it out. So you drove there at once, and while the truck may have skidded a bit, you had no intention of harming Henry.

Nancy: Wouldn't and didn't.

Mediator: And then the sheriff got involved, which must have been upsetting.

Nancy: You wouldn't like it, would you? But, it isn't going to sit well for him either.

Mediator: You will continue to stand up for what you believe in.

Nancy: He's not going to get me to back off.

Mediator: I'm not trying to get either of you to give up on what is important to you. Right now, I'm just trying to get your respective views on what happened. I believe that with suffi-cient understanding, you'll find a solution that reflects what is important to you both. From what you've told me, it seems that the whole incident must have been hard for you. Do you think I understand what you've said?

Nancy: I don't know for sure. You seem to. And I've been say-ing the same thing for years, so I'm hardly a mystery.

Mediator: Okay. Next I'm going to try to understand what happened from Henry's perspective.

■　■　■

Emotional Reality and Neutrality

In addition to suggesting to both parties that there may be more than one possible view of their conflict, I've begun to try to under-stand Nancy's perspective, including her emotional experience. The more these deeper emotions can be included as part of the effort at understanding, the more likely the parties will feel under-stood and acknowledged for who they are and what they are experiencing. The more they feel understood and acknowledged, the greater the possibility that they can get past their judgments about one another and recognize each other's humanity.

That is also true for the mediator. A key step for getting past my own judgments about Nancy and the stances she sometimes assumed was recognizing how fearful she was and how embattled she kept herself. While I didn't say so explicitly, my own aware-ness of her fear and frailty allowed me to move closer to her experience and to her.

The challenge for me now was to do the same with Henry, which meant being as open to his perspective as I had tried to be with Nancy's, and without letting go of the connection I now felt with Nancy. I also had some personal judgments about "developers" and would have to guard against these impeding my effort to understand him. Putting those judgments aside, I extended a genuine invitation for him to share his perspective.

Henry's version of the events was quite different.

■　■　■

Henry: This has been a difficult situation for me. At first, when I decided to make an offer on the parcel, I was only trying to protect the property from being developed in a way that would have been horrible for me and for the community. Just like Nancy, I didn't want to ever risk what might go up next to my house. I was pretty sure that the parcel was not buildable as the seller presented it to be, so I made an offer that was contingent on its buildability, confident that the price would come down significantly after I proved it to be unbuildable. Two of my other neighbors agreed to share the purchase price so that we could make lot line adjustments that would add to each of our properties and protect the land from development. So I made the offer contingent on the lot being buildable, and it was accepted.

Mediator: You're saying you wanted nothing built on the parcel and were confident that it would be shown that no one could actually build on it. So when you told Nancy about your plan, you believed that the property would remain undisturbed. This was before the trees were cut?

Henry: Yes. We actually cut down three trees altogether. The rest were . . .

Nancy: That is absolutely not . . .

Mediator: Nancy, I know there may be many things you see differently. But please try to wait until after Henry has finished his description of what happened. Then you'll have a chance to add anything you want to.

Nancy: Facts are facts, but I'll bite my tongue for now.

Henry: What I was saying is that aside from the three trees, the rest were bushes and brush that needed to be cleared away so that we could test the leach fields, which would prove the lot unbuildable. At least that was what the expert I had hired believed. Then several things happened that changed the picture dramatically. First, the seller informed me that she wouldn't change the price if the property were to be proved unbuildable. Second, the neighbors who were going to contribute to the purchase backed out. Finally, a backup offer came in for twice the price I had agreed to pay, so I had no choice then but to try to find out whether the property was buildable. As it turned out, the tests proved to our surprise and dismay that it was. Now I was in an economic bind. I couldn't possibly pay all that money on my own just to protect the land. And if I withdrew, the lot would be sold to the person who had made the backup offer and none of us would have any control over what would go up there.

Mediator: The economic factors changed dramatically when the seller refused to lower the price, the other neighbors did not want to contribute to the purchase, a higher offer came in, and the leach test actually established that a house could be built there.

Henry: Right.

Mediator: Where did that leave you with Nancy?

Henry: I knew she was already upset about the trees, but that was a miscommunication. I told her that we would be cutting down three trees, which is what we did, and when we cut the trees and brush, I actually thought she would be pleased because we opened up her view of the ocean. But apparently that wasn't what she wanted. And when she heard that there was no way to protect the land, she was more upset.

Mediator: So relations felt pretty strained. This all preceded the truck incident?

Henry: Yes. I knew she was pretty upset, but I was now under a time constraint to go ahead with a building permit. Meanwhile, she built a fence that was supposed to be on our common property line, but actually went over the line onto my property. I was down there investigating that one evening, and at the moment actually trying to figure out how to save a tree when I looked up to see Nancy barreling down the lane toward me in her truck at high speed. I had no place to retreat because I was standing in front of a concrete barrier. If she had gone a matter of inches further than where she stopped, both of my legs would have been crushed.

Mediator: So for you the truck coming so close felt really threatening.

Henry: I was terrified. I knew she was angry enough to want to hurt me. But I was also enraged. I called the sheriff because this time she had gone too far.

Mediator: You were really upset, and then called the police.

Henry: I've developed a lot of properties and dealt with lots of problems before, but it's really different when it's your home. This has been really hard for me personally and for my family.

Mediator: I understand that the whole experience has been difficult for you.

After confirming with Henry that I had understood what he had said, we reached the point of finding out whether Nancy and Henry were willing to say what they understood each other to have said.

■ ■ ■

Inviting the Parties to Try to Understand Each Other

We had reached a critical and subtle point in the mediation. Both parties had had the opportunity to express their views; and each now felt understood by the mediator. This may have already helped detoxify an atmosphere poisoned by misunderstanding.

Henry and Nancy have both agreed that the mediator has understood them, or at least begun to do so. But paradoxically for the parties, the mediator has also seemed to understand the other, whose view seems totally contrary. In fact, the mediator seems to be holding both perspectives side by side without one canceling out the other. That is the promise of *positive neutrality*. We call it the mediative perspective. The mediator being there fully with and for both parties in empathically understanding them; and doing so with both present makes this next step possible. That possibility is for a *deeper understanding* within and between the parties. Having witnessed the mediator do it, perhaps the parties will take a step in that direction as well.

If a fuller mutual understanding seems a possibility, we invite the parties to give it a try in a more structured way. While it often proves fundamental in *working together*, we don't require it. We are careful to proceed with the task of moving toward mutual understanding only if it makes sense to the parties. If done under pressure, it could easily prove to be a step backward. Sometimes the dialogue about whether to do this task changes the tenor of a mediation.

■ ■ ■

Mediator: Right now, I believe I understand each of your perspectives, which I've found very valuable. And I hope and expect that the two of you have a somewhat fuller understanding of each other's perspectives. There is an opportunity now for the two of you to test that—to see whether you understand and are understood by each other, if you are willing to try.

Nancy: I don't think Henry understands me at all. If he did, he wouldn't think that I tried to run him over with my truck.

Mediator: And you want him to understand that?

Nancy: He should.

Mediator: Do you think that you understand what he has said?

Nancy: To some degree, yes.

Mediator: Would you both be willing to demonstrate what understanding you have of each other? And fill in any gaps where you think it necessary? What about you, Henry? Do you think you understand Nancy's perspective?

Henry: I hope so.

Nancy: Why would we want to do this "demonstration"?

Mediator: You don't have to do it at all. But since the two of you are the decision makers, the better you each understand the whole picture, the better chance you have to make decisions that take both of you into account. Right now, I'm the one who seems to understand both views but you're the ones who will be charting the future.

Nancy: It is important to me that Henry understand some fundamental things about the situation.

Mediator: I think it could also be important that you understand Henry's perspective.

Nancy: If that's the price you're asking me to pay, then all right.

Mediator: You'd be willing to do that?

Nancy: Yes. You don't have to worry about me. I can take care of myself.

Mediator: That's true. I know that.

Nancy: Look, I agree that we are pretty tangled up here, and if this might help disentangle us, it's worth a try. At least, I know that if Henry can do that, it'll help.

Mediator: How about you, Henry?

Henry: I'm not sure that this will take us any place, but I'm willing to give it a try.

Mediator: Why?

Henry: It would make a difference to know that Nancy has some sense of what she put me through. If we're ever going to trust each other in the future, I need to know that she gets what happened.

■ ■ ■

The Parties' Motivation to Understand Each Other

If the effort to understand each other is supported by motivation rather than simply acquiescence, it is more likely to succeed. Not surprisingly, this task seems to make sense to most parties in conflict if it means that the other will understand them. That is where many parties start. The thought that there may also be value to them in understanding the other is not so readily apparent. But it may follow.

Even if the parties decline to make the effort or do not succeed in doing it well, this inquiry into whether they will try to understand and be understood by each other is a step toward considering that differing views need not cancel each other out. With that realization, the parties have loosened some of the hold that conflict has had over them.

■ ■ ■

We agreed Nancy would begin, and I asked her to tell me one thing that she remembered Henry describing that was a significant part of his view.

Nancy: I think he always had it in mind to develop the property.

Mediator: Is that what you heard him say here?

Nancy: No, but I am not about to be suckered again.

Mediator: And I'm not trying to set you up to be. I'm simply trying to see if you heard what he said, so that you and he both know that you did, if you did. And vice versa. If you're still willing, what did you hear him say here?

Nancy: That he didn't always plan to develop the property. But I don't believe him.

Mediator: I'm not asking you to believe him. This is tricky. I'm not suggesting that you change your mind about what you think is true. It's only important to demonstrate that you understand what Henry is saying. The truth is that you don't know for sure what was going on in his mind, nor he in yours. Just see if you can tell me what Henry reported about his view.

Nancy: But I think he's lying here.

Mediator: But if you hold that as the only possibility, you can see where that leaves us in this process. Later we'll talk about what was happening inside you when you were driving your truck. I imagine it will be difficult for Henry to accept that you didn't intend to put him at risk. You are each ultimately going to have to decide what you accept as true.

Nancy: I can see what you're saying about the truck. As long as no one thinks that I'm agreeing with Henry's report, I'm willing to go forward.

Mediator: Understanding doesn't mean that you agree. That is fundamental here.

Nancy: I'll try, but you have to understand you're dealing with a nerve being touched.

Mediator: I can see that. It might well be true for both of you.

Nancy: All right. I heard Henry tell us that his plans changed.

Mediator: I heard that, too. How and why did they change?

Nancy: He said at first that he wanted to protect the property from development.

Mediator: And what did he say changed that?

Nancy: He was counting on lowering the price once the property was proved unbuildable. But the owner wouldn't do that.

Mediator: Henry, does she have it right?

Henry: Yes, she does.

■ ■ ■

Teaching the Parties to Loop Each Other

Now the mediator, as needed, can correct one party's misunderstanding of the other or ask the other party to do so, serving as a bridge between them. In effect, the mediator is a looping coach. Here, the loop is complete when Henry confirms it.

■ ■ ■

Nancy: Then the other neighbors changed their minds about participating in buying the property. I know that's true because they told me that it was going to benefit Henry a lot more than it would benefit them.

Mediator: Good. Was there anything else?

Nancy: The backup offer. I didn't know anything about that. I'm not sure that's true.

Mediator: If it is true, could you imagine that it contributed to changing the picture for Henry?

Nancy: Sure. I understand that Henry doesn't have infinite resources. I know if he builds on this lot, he'll have to sell his old house to recoup some of his money.

Mediator: So you can see that the owner's firmness on the price, supported by the backup offer, made the problem more difficult for Henry?

Nancy: If that's true, yes. But he never told me about the backup offer.

Mediator: Good. Has she accurately described your dilemma, Henry?

Henry: Yes. Once the numbers changed so dramatically, I knew I couldn't afford to keep it undeveloped, especially when it turned out to be buildable.

■ ■ ■

Something else significant may be happening here. Both parties may begin to take seriously the possibility that the other could understand their perspective and may even want to do so. They may also realize that they can be helpful to one another in making that happen. When these types of realizations begin to occur, the parties may further shift how they experience their conflict, and the possibilities for dealing with it expand.

■ ■ ■

Mediator: Henry, tell me one thing that you remember that was important to Nancy in her version of what happened.

Henry: I never knew that she felt that the trees protected her privacy. I thought I was doing her a favor when I cut the trees and brush because it gave her a better view of the ocean.

Mediator: It wasn't your intention to do anything that hurt her but it turned out differently. That's your perspective. And hers?

Henry: I always knew that she was against all tree cutting, but I can understand now that exposing her property was not what she wanted.

Mediator: Has he got that right, Nancy?

Nancy: Yes. And he was in such a big hurry. I left my house in the morning having no idea that the trees were going to be cut and when I got back that evening, he had devastated the area.

Henry: It's true that I moved quickly, but I was afraid that if I didn't, Nancy would make it harder. Also I needed to know as soon as possible whether we could put in leach lines, which we couldn't know until the trees were cut.

Mediator: You're explaining why you acted as you did. Right now I'm asking if you can understand Nancy's perspective. Can you imagine how cutting the trees as you did might have added insult to injury?

Henry: I know how precious the trees were to her, but I have to reiterate, only three of the cuts were actually trees. The rest was brush.

Nancy: They were not. They were mostly pittosporum and had been there for 20 years.

Mediator: So you have different perspectives on many things here, including the definition of a tree. Can you understand Nancy's view about that, Henry?

Henry: I know that she thinks of every living thing as sacred. I know that killing even one living thing is truly a serious matter to her. She does not make the distinctions that I do.

Mediator: Is that right, Nancy?

Nancy: Of course.

Mediator: So for her. . . ?

Henry: So for her, particularly when it happened all at once, it was a shock. Antagonizing a neighbor was not what I was trying to do. Nor what I am trying to do.

Nancy: A hell of a shock.

Mediator: Good. Let's try another round.

■ ■ ■

Mutuality of Vulnerability

It was important not to ask Nancy to express her full understanding of all that Henry had said before asking Henry to do the same. We go back and forth because the party making the effort to understand is in a vulnerable position. We don't want that party to feel overexposed if the other proves unable or unwilling to make the same effort. We therefore seek also here to have *mutuality of vulnerability*. If a step taken by one party is met with one by the other, it can reinforce the willingness of both to go one step further.

■ ■ ■

Mediator: Nancy, what else do you remember that is an important part of Henry's view?

Nancy: He said that the situation was hard for him. If it was, I didn't realize it. It seemed to me that he was just a businessman and wasn't taking this personally. I get now that he would have liked there to be peace between us. At least he says so. He has a misguided idea of how to get there, but I can recognize that it would be better for him if we could work things out. Even with our differences, nobody likes to be hated by their neighbors.

Mediator: I imagine you can appreciate that at least partly because it's true for you as well.

Nancy: I've been under a doctor's care for nerves for the past six months. But don't go thinking I'm going to give up.

Henry: I don't think that, but it's good to know you have some feeling for what it's like for me, too. And I can see that it's difficult for you.

Mediator: Your turn, Henry.

Henry: I can understand Nancy's suspicions of me. It's not true that I don't care about the beach. This is where I am raising my children, where I want to live the rest of my life. But I can see how it could look like I just wanted to build a house all along, particularly when she didn't know that the backup offer had come in and eliminated my negotiating ability with the seller. I see how she might feel betrayed by the change from the plan to ensure open space to learning that I had received a building permit.

Mediator: Especially when she believes so strongly in preservation. I think that's a core belief for Nancy.

Henry: I know that. It's important to me too, but for me, it has to be balanced with practicality. For Nancy, it goes deeper. And you must know, Nancy, that if I build a house on this property, I'm going to be much more sensitive to your concerns than a stranger would be.

Nancy: You're going to have to prove that to me.

Mediator: Does that mean that he understood you correctly?

Nancy: Sure, it goes much deeper. But that doesn't mean I believe that he is going to be sensitive to my concerns.

Henry: I understand that.

We wrapped up this stage in our mutual understanding effort by my reiterating that understanding the other's position did not mean agreeing with it, and expressing my admiration for their work so far. Then I asked them to take another step.

Mediator: Would you each be willing to say how you understand the other's perspective about the incident with the truck?

Nancy's Lawyer: Don't you think we've gone far enough? You know there's a pending criminal proceeding.

Nancy: No, I'd like to do it.

With the understanding that there would be no negotiation about the criminal proceeding, everyone consented, and Nancy went first.

Nancy: Okay. Henry had no way of knowing that I wasn't going to try to run him over. Maybe he didn't realize that I had complete control over the truck.

Mediator: So when you put yourself in his position, what do you imagine that was like?

Nancy: I would have been scared seeing a 78-year-old woman barreling down on me. He did have room to get out of the way. I think that was pretty obvious. But he says he didn't know that, so that would have made it doubly frightening.

Mediator: Is that right, Henry?

Henry: Yes. In addition there was loose gravel near where she brought the truck to a stop, and there really was no place for me to retreat. A few more inches and she would have broken both my legs. I was terrified.

Mediator: Can you put yourself in her position?

Henry: Yes. I know that she was surprised that I was working down at the corner of the property and that she was really angry. But in this particular moment, believe it or not, I was just trying to figure out how to save a tree that we thought we might have to cut, but she had no way of knowing that. And I'm sure that being arrested was no piece of cake for her.

Mediator: Is that accurate, Nancy?

Nancy: It's true that I was really angry. It's also true that the arrest was a horrible experience. Seventy-eight years and nothing like that had happened to me before. But I have to also say that I felt great when I knew that I had caught him red-handed. I'd had my suspicions that he was poking around, but when I actually saw him standing on my property, I felt that I wasn't just paranoid. I was actually relieved to know I wasn't crazy.

Henry: That's why you felt justified in running me over.

Mediator: Henry, I heard what Nancy was saying differently. Nancy, can you clarify what was going on in your mind then?

Nancy: I never wanted to hurt him. But I certainly wanted him to know that I would be vigilant about his trespassing.

Henry: I hear that you didn't intend to hit me. And I want you to know that I will not tolerate ever being put in that position again.

Nancy: I know.

The room was quiet as Nancy and Henry both found themselves uncharacteristically at a loss for words. It was a poignant moment. Several seconds passed, and then I asked them whether they found this helpful.

Henry: It feels like a step in the right direction. I'm hearing things come out of my mouth and Nancy's that I never would have dreamed possible this morning.

Nancy: This doesn't solve the problem, but I think it is helping.

■ ■ ■

Something had definitely changed in the room, although it wasn't easy to put a finger on it. Nancy and Henry seemed to understand themselves and each other better than before. And they somehow had met in a way different than before.

And just as the atmosphere and emotional tenor had changed and deepened, so too had the understanding of the content of the dispute that had been uncovered. When we charted their interests beneath the surface of their heated conflict, it looked like this:

Nancy	Henry
Protect and preserve nature	Protect his investment
Protect her privacy	Provide home for his family
Preserve her independence	Make own decisions
Enhance value of her property	Enhance his view
Preserve community values	Ensure his safety
Have good neighborly relations	Have good neighborly relations

The inquiry that had become possible for each, and the dialogue between them, had also touched at times, with care, on the deeper level of meaning or life direction. For Nancy, it was when she talked of her connection with nature and her desire to have good will between neighbors. Henry perhaps came closest when he described his dream for the house he wanted to build for his family and the peace of mind he was seeking in his relationship to Nancy and the community.

After each had the opportunity to fill in anything additional that they felt they needed to, there seemed a sufficient basis of mutual understanding to start to look forward. Both expressed what was important to them for the future and both made the effort to understand each other's priorities. They were now in a position to resolve their problem based on an appreciation of what they both cared about, and in a way that would allow them to live amicably side by side.

Although the lawyers had not been very active in the dialogue up to this point, their presence had been indispensable in providing their clients with both legal and emotional support. This allowed them to take more risks in openly expressing their differing views, and understanding each other's, than they might otherwise have been inclined to do. If we were able to continue in this positive direction, the law-yers would likely prove very helpful (both outside and inside the room) as we sought to fashion solutions individually suited to their clients.

As a neighbor, I felt especially good about helping to de-escalate what had been a problem for the entire community. As a mediator, the challenge had been to work within myself, as well as with the parties, to be fully present for each. But as usual when a mediation works, it is because the participants themselves have the courage to go beyond the limits of comfortable discourse to venture into difficult emotional territory.

■ ■ ■

The solution Nancy and Henry arrived at with the help of their law-yers had two elements. The first called for a joint exploration of the possibility of a nature conservancy buying the disputed parcel, which would preserve the land as open space for generations to come. Henry was for it but thought it was a long shot. If it proved not to be pos-sible, then a process was agreed on to move forward with a design of Henry's house that would minimally intrude upon the land and restore Nancy's privacy. It was clear to all that while the first solution was preferable, both were far better than any kind of solution a court or administrative agency might impose.

Still remaining was the question of what would happen with the criminal prosecution of Nancy over the truck incident. Henry's lawyer had consistently maintained that it would be unethical and probably illegal to have any negotiation about the criminal proceedings. But after the mediation, Henry wrote a letter to the prosecutor to indicate that his only interest had been to be assured that there would be no repetition of such an incident. This was somewhat less than the full request for dropping the charges that Nancy and her lawyer had hoped for, but with Henry no longer actively seeking prosecution, it appeared that the prosecutor might be less inclined to pursue the case.

■ ■ ■

I next saw Henry and Nancy a couple of months later. By now, it was clear that there was almost no possibility that the nature conservancy would buy the land, but it was also clear that the effort had had Henry's full cooperation. The parties had moved to plan B: a design of Henry's new house that would meet Nancy's concerns as much as possible. Nancy also thought it was important to get community consensus on the design. Together they composed and sent out a letter to their neighbors describing their process of coming together and their hope that others in the community would provide input without having to go through any formal administrative process. While the lawyers were no longer directly participating in our meetings, both Nancy and Henry were consulting productively with them in between our sessions.

■ ■ ■

Another two months passed before Nancy and Henry asked to meet with me again. The criminal charges relative to the truck incident had been dismissed, and Henry was to present his final plan for Nancy's approval. Nancy arrived late with her adult son who had been kept apprised of our progress. She appeared to be less vigorous than usual, but she still retained her sense of humor. She pointed out specific glitches in the design that none of us had seen, and Henry noted them. At one point, when we were discussing how Henry's architect had changed the plans in a way that disappointed Henry, Nancy said, "You know, Henry, I'd like you to be happy with this, too."

The moment passed without comment from any of us, but it was clear that Henry was both surprised and touched. There was a palpable sense of appreciation in the room for how far we had come. With a few clarifications, we concluded the mediation.

Those last moments became all the more poignant when I received a letter from Nancy's son, who had supported her involvement in the mediation and was present at our last meeting. He wrote:

> After we left the mediation, I stayed overnight at the house with my mother. She seemed quite tired, but also peaceful about the situation, which, knowing my mother and what she had been through, was a blessing for her. We talked for a while after dinner, and then she retired to bed. That night, she died in her sleep. I am so grateful that she had been able to put this behind her in the way she had. And, were it not for the fact of our meeting that day, she would have died alone. The house will now pass to me, and I plan to live in it with my family. And because of the work completed between my mother and Henry, I expect that we will have good neighborly relations.

From Understanding to Resolution

Part

4

Radix and Argyle: From Interests to Options and Creating Value at the Options Stage

11

When we first met with the executives and lawyers in Radix and Argyle, as detailed in Chapter 2, the two companies had been locked for years in court struggles, the current being a $300-million, winner-take-all legal dispute. Years of further litigation loomed, with continued strain on both companies. The entrenched hostility between them projected well into the future and seemed as inevitable as it was draining. Once the key executives began to see how the traditional protective stance of their lawyers had kept them trapped in their conflict, they began to consider other possibilities; and the two corporations agreed to work together to try to resolve their differences.

The mediation unfolded over a period of several months, with the CEOs from the two corporations present and active throughout. During the contracting phase, we made a number of agreements to support the process, including that after clarifying the issues, we would proceed with *two conversations*: the first about the law and the second about the business reality and what was at stake for each company.

At its core, the nature of the dispute was fairly simple. While the two sides experienced and presented it from very different vantage points as buyer and seller, they agreed on the essential facts. Executives from each side had been involved in establishing a series of long-term contracts between the two companies for the sale and purchase of a commodity. The climate in which the agreements were reached was a period of relative scarcity of the commodity, so the buyer Radix (which also was a seller to others), wanting to ensure a continued supply, locked into a relatively high price.

Several years into the contract, the market price shifted dramatically due to an unpredictable increase in the availability of the commodity. Radix now wanted Argyle to change the contract to reflect the current market reality and, after carefully examining the terms of the contract, concluded that there were sufficient legal grounds for them to cancel the contract outright if they could not work out a new price. Argyle wanted to hold Radix to its original commitment because of the risk it had originally run to guarantee an uninterrupted supply to Radix, which could have resulted in minimal profit to Argyle, or possibly a loss, if the market hadn't shifted so dramatically. If Argyle were able to hold Radix to the contract, it would mean a profit to them of $300 million. If Radix were able to escape the contract, they would be able to save $300 million through purchases from an alternate source.

In the beginning, executives from both sides were concerned that focusing on the law could lead to further polarization between the parties. However, both agreed to look carefully at the legal probabilities to guide them in their negotiations. So both sides invited the lawyers who would litigate the case to make a presentation about the legal reality to the executives, with instructions to both lawyers to present not only the strengths of their case to the assembled group but also the risks their side faced. The lawyers wanted to spend a day presenting. The executives decided that each lawyer would have 30 minutes to present.

■ ■ ■

When the lawyers entered the room, the tension was quite palpable. First, the lawyer for Argyle spoke, confidently assuring the group that if the case were to go to trial, a jury would very probably find in favor of his client. When it came to presenting the risks his client faced, he admitted that there was some small possibility they could lose, but that it would be highly unlikely.

Then the lawyer for Radix spoke, looking directly into the eyes of his target audience, the Argyle executives. "I want you to know up front that if this case goes to trial, I think there is a significant risk that we could lose. In fact, I would go so far as to say that it might be equally likely that we could lose this case as win it."

The tension in the faces of the Argyle executives visibly eased as the Radix lawyer allowed a moment before he proceeded. "Before you become too comfortable, you ought to know a couple of things. First, while I might have the short end of the stick here, if we win this case, you're going to lose a lot of money, about $300 million. So my law firm has supported my taking this case on a contingency basis. We are more than willing to roll the dice, because the reward more than warrants the risk."

The tension crept back into the Argyle executives' faces. The Radix lawyer had been so forthright that it was impossible not to feel the ring of truth in what he had said. While affirming his client's risk, he had gained credibility with everyone in the room. By the time he had finished his presentation, the motivation of the Argyle team to settle the case had clearly been tapped even more strongly than before.

In fact, both lawyers agreed that the result of a trial would not be an in-between verdict. Given the law, the verdict would be either $300 million or nothing. The case would turn on a factual determination of how an ambiguous escape clause in the contract would be interpreted. The clause allowed for Radix to cancel the contract if Argyle couldn't fulfill all of its orders. Bolstering each side's case were many written communications as well as competing accounts from executives for the two companies recalling past conversations about whether Argyle had complied with the requirement.

The litigating lawyers then left the room and the executives reconvened in the center of a circle, with the in-house lawyers and support management sitting on the outside. This set the stage for the second conversation with the executives in which they set out their views about the history leading up to the dispute.

■ ■ ■

The Nature of the Dispute

From the outside it was easy to understand the economics of why Argyle wanted to hold Radix to the original agreement and why Radix wanted to be free of the contractual obligation. The legal conversation had focused solely on whether the conditions of the ambiguous escape clause had been met. But as the executives related the history of the contract negotiation and execution, it became clear that considerations other than profit and loss were at stake for each side.

In addition to the contracts for the purchase of the commodity, where they were in a competitive situation, Radix and Argyle had other ventures in common where they were partners for the extraction and sale to others. This created somewhat complicated relations between them that had resulted in a continual succession of lawsuits. Thus they had been in court with one another for most of the previous two decades.

At our initial meeting, this continued legal embroilment with each other had led them to consider mediation. Now the executives from both sides recounted the history of the litigations that had cost both companies not only enormous legal fees but the diversion of energy from operating effectively in the broader marketplace. As a result of changing market conditions, a number of industrywide changes were causing both companies to re-examine very basic questions about the future direction of their companies.

Also present was an underlying personal dynamic of distrust between several executives on each side of the dispute. While the contracts had been negotiated by the executives and ultimately by their lawyers, each executive's retelling of the history revealed strong feelings that litigation had damaged the personal relationship they had established with each other.

Executives on each side were such significant players in the industry that it was clear they could not avoid future business interactions with each other, and that there would be opportunities to damage each other in terms of reputation and economics.

■ ■ ■

Developing the Parties' Understanding

We asked the executives to loop each other—to demonstrate their understanding (not agreement) of the other side's perspective. With approximately 30 people in the room (an inner circle composed of executives who participated in the creation of the contract and the ensuing dispute and an outer circle of middle management representatives and lawyers), the executives on each side recited their views about the history of the dispute, and the main executives then looped each other's views. By previous agreement, when each executive spoke, the others made sure to listen carefully, even taking notes, as they knew they would soon be put to the test of demonstrating their understanding. While there were clear differences between their accounts, the fact that both sides seemed to make an honest attempt to understand each other's views seemed to ease tensions considerably.

We were presented with the next challenge: to understand what was important to each company underlying the dispute.

> *Radix CEO:* So we understand now what is at stake—$300 million. And we heard the lawyers' different assessments. So clearly now what we need to do is to find some number between zero and $300 million that would be acceptable to both companies. It's time to compromise. I think we both know how to do that.
>
> *Mediator:* Yes, we certainly could do that, but I think we might be able to do better than that.
>
> *Radix CEO:* What do you have in mind?
>
> *Mediator:* Both companies have a lot at stake in this dispute. If we can identify what is important to both companies underlying this dispute—your interests—then we might be able to use that as a springboard when it comes time to look at solutions. That could lead to a different result than if we simply figured out now how to cut up the $300 million.
>
> *Argyle CEO:* What do you mean?

Mediator: You've each hinted at this when you described your history. Obviously, maximizing profitability is important for both companies. But your companies each have other interests that, once identified, could lead us toward solutions that might actually expand the pie, beyond the $300 million.

Argyle CEO: You mean our business plan. We are not about to disclose that to our biggest competitor.

Mediator: Of course you needn't disclose anything that doesn't make sense to you. Clearly you need to keep certain things confidential, but would there be some areas that you might be willing to talk about, particularly if you knew the other side was doing the same?

Argyle CEO: That could be interesting. But it does feel risky.

Mediator: You don't have to do this if you don't want to, but when you think about risk, it would be interesting to weigh the risk of disclosing against not disclosing.

Radix CEO: I clearly see the dangers inherent in disclosing.

Mediator: The risks of disclosing are important to assess, and you are all aware of them. You don't want the other company to take advantage of that information. The risk of not disclosing may be less apparent but no less real. To put it simply, if you reveal your real interests to each other, we might find a solution that would be better for both of you. That's what you need to think about.

Radix CEO: Well, if Argyle were willing to do this too, we would consider talking somewhat more openly about what is important to our company.

Argyle CEO: We both probably know more about each other than we realize. This could be worthwhile.

At our next meeting, both CEOs came in willing to explore interests behind their positions. Besides profitability, each company was thinking long and hard about its future direction in the fast-changing marketplace. Both were rather cautious about disclosing particular options under consideration, but a significant door had been opened *to deepen their understanding* of what this dispute was about, and how they might solve it.

After we had developed a list of interests and posted them on flip charts, we put them aside to brainstorm options for solving the dispute without worrying at the moment how well those options might meet both sides' interests. The goal at this stage is to support the parties' creativity. Specific ground rules for encouraging that creativity are discussed at the end of this chapter.

> *Radix CEO:* We've thought a lot about possible outcomes in this dispute. But as we mentioned before, it still comes down to finding a mutually acceptable number to compromise, obviously, some place between zero and $300 million.

> *Argyle CEO:* We are in complete agreement with that. We ought to restructure our contract to take whatever number we settle on into account.

The options included litigation, arbitration of the figure, splitting the difference, readjustment of the contract price based on various external indices, termination of the contract, and a variety of partnering arrangements with others that mitigated market risks. All were based on a fairly static way of looking at the problem and the possibilities for its resolution, with some form or another of the division of the $300 million at their core. We reached an interesting point when the mediator suggested a different way to think about the solutions.

■   ■   ■

Working Together to Create Value

> *Mediator:* Certainly we are going to have to find some mutually acceptable number to resolve this dispute. Before we finally accept this as a negotiation to try to find some number both sides can live with, I wonder if there aren't ways to think differently about the possibilities for the future that could potentially leave both of you better off than if we simply try to divide up the $300 million.

> *Argyle CEO:* Like what?

> *Mediator:* Well, you both take on many different functions with respect to the purchase and sale of this commodity. I wonder if there might not be ways to cooperate with each other that could increase the profits for both companies.

> *Radix CEO:* Settling our lawsuit would save our companies an enormous amount of money and energy presently being spent on the lawsuit.

Mediator: Good. That's a start. But I wonder if there are other ways in which you could cooperate with each other that could be mutually beneficial.

■ ■ ■

To have suggested such possibilities at the beginning of the mediation would have bordered on heresy. With their previous warlike stances toward each other, such an idea would have been inconceivable at an earlier stage and well beyond the scope of what any judge would impose on the parties. But they had worked so hard to get to this point that it seemed useful to try to build on the working relationship that had begun in this mediation. And one of the distinct advantages of having *the parties work together* in the same room throughout the mediation is to use that *working relationship* and *understanding of the whole problem* to create new ideas.

■ ■ ■

Argyle CEO: I do think that's possible, but our technical people would know best.

Mediator: Do your technical people ever talk to each other?

Radix CEO (laughs)*:* Yes. They are at each other's throats all of the time.

Mediator: That's for the purpose of fighting about the mechanics of executing the contract.

Radix CEO: Yes. There's a lot of animosity there.

Mediator: I wonder what would happen if you put technical people together in the same room to see whether there are any creative ways that they can imagine the companies cooperating with each other.

Argyle CEO: That would be complete chaos.

Mediator: Because?

Argyle CEO: Because they are so used to fighting with each other. Any new idea would simply be something new to fight about. That is the culture of both companies.

Mediator: But what if we gave them a different task?

Argyle CEO: You mean instructions not to fight with each other?

Mediator: Something like that. What do they fight about?

Radix CEO: Our side always feels as if the other guys are trying to reduce our profits on the contract.

Argyle CEO: Our guys feel much the same.

Mediator: Suppose you gave them specific instructions that their job would be simply to create new ideas of how the companies could cooperate. In fact, for this purpose they could imagine that they were all working for the same company, as if the two companies had merged.

Radix CEO: That might work. We would have to make clear that they have no responsibility for deciding how to implement the ideas.

Mediator: Right. Ultimately the two of you with your management teams will have to make those decisions, particularly when it comes to dividing the profits for any new ideas. They just come up with possible recipes for enlarging the pie.

Argyle CEO: I think that could work. We would also have to make clear that we will figure out how to divide up the pie. Their job is to create new ideas to make it bigger.

Radix CEO: But they will still be worried about that.

Mediator: Naturally, but if you can make it clear that their only task is to create new ideas, perhaps something new can emerge.

Radix CEO: Interesting.

Argyle CEO: I agree.

■ ■ ■

Radix and Argyle chose teams of approximately 10 people from each side. We then spent several hours with representatives from both sides to negotiate ground rules for *working together* to brainstorm new ideas. They were surprisingly receptive and actually felt relieved that they would not be negotiating with each other. They spent three days together, then wrote a joint report describing their ideas and estimating the potential financial value of these ideas. At our next mediation session, a representative from each side who participated in the brainstorming session presented the joint report.

The task force (as we had called them) identified 25 different ideas for cooperation between the companies on new projects. Despite moments of tension, the leaders of the meeting had managed to keep the group on task and avoid regulatory restrictions that could derail them.

As the leaders presented the report, a definite shift in the atmosphere in the room was noticeable. Once the dust cleared and we had digested the reports and winnowed the options down to realistic projects that could all begin in the near term, it was clear that the group had added value to the $300 million already at stake somewhere in the area of an additional $200 million. Carrying out these projects could result in an additional $200 million of profit to share.

As this information was revealed, a new tension developed in the room. Up until now it had been unclear whether Radix and Argyle would be able to successfully negotiate a division of the $300-million pie. The additional $200 million increased the pie to $500 million. It was obvious to all that Radix and Argyle choosing to litigate would negate the additional $200 million as well as any other future projects not yet considered. These new projects would require a great deal of cooperation between the companies that would be impractical if not impossible in the face of ongoing litigation.

Both sides now recognized that it would be irrational for either side not to negotiate a settlement. Our job now was to face the tension the CEOs had agreed to take on, to negotiate a division of a $500-million pie, knowing that the alternative of litigation was even more unappealing than before.

This required the mediator to allow the momentum the parties had created to carry the mediation forward rather than "turn up the heat" to try forcing a solution. The challenge was to continue to use the *power of understanding* rather than coercion to deal with the tension of dividing the pie. It was also important to continually link the numbers being discussed with the interests that the parties had previously identified, so that the numbers wouldn't take on a life of their own apart from the priorities of each company.

This required a new proposal that would be better for each side than the alternative. That part would be easy. We also had to find a solution that both executives could present to their boards of directors and that both sides would feel was fair. What was new was that neither side could credibly threaten litigation. They knew now that they needed to settle the case to each party's satisfaction, or there would be no deal.

The final negotiation, drafting of the documents, and implementation of the agreement took another two months of meetings, but the spirit of the mediation had changed. Instead of seeing the dispute only as a problem, they now had joined forces in the marketplace to effectively deal with their competitors. They had to carefully work through various minefields that awaited them, dealing with regulations governing the industry, perceptions from their competitors about their new-found cooperation, and obtaining consent to the agreement from their boards of directors and stockholders.

Commentary: Developing and Evaluating Options

As described in our definition of mediation, the goal is to help the parties reach a result that is better for both than their alternative. Mediation provides the opportunity for the parties to create their own result responsive to the uniqueness of their situation. The necessary atmosphere to unleash the creativity of the parties is critical to opening this possibility. It is the fourth stage of the mediation—*developing and evaluating options.*

All that we have done prior to this stage of mediation has been directed to this effort. At the start, the parties agreed to try the *understanding-based approach* to mediation—to *assume responsibility* for resolving their conflict, to *work together* with everyone in the same room, to reach agreements about how we will work that make sense to all of the participants (including the lawyers), and to *go beneath the problem* to identify what is most important to both sides underlying the problem. These aspects of the understanding-based approach often make more sense to the participants when they can see the possibility for reaching a mutually satisfying result.

When we reach this fourth stage of the mediation, it is time to use *the ground of understanding* achieved between the parties as the basis for *developing options* to resolve the conflict and then for *evaluating* them.

We separate the creation of options from the evaluation of them for a basic reason. In a negotiation, there is always the potential to create value and always a tension between cooperative and competitive moves. Competitive moves advance individual interests, and cooperative moves look at what is jointly possible and desirable.

Developing Options

The mediator should seek to have the parties brainstorm ideas that create value either in terms of quality or quantity. This should be structured so that the parties do *not* analyze or evaluate the ideas as they seek to create them.

When parties are value claimers, they believe the object of negotiation is to win. Their strategy is to start high and concede slowly, and to play their cards close to their vests. They believe the pie is limited and they want to maximize what they get of it. As value creators, the parties look for ideas that make the pie bigger or better, expanding it in terms of quality or quantity. In this mode, parties are inventive, cooperative. Here the strategy is to communicate and share information to create joint value, and the negotiation becomes a joint problem-solving task as we seek to brainstorm together to invent creative solutions. As we work with parties at the options phase, we seek to separate value creation from value claiming so that the creative process can have its full expression.

We find several ground rules helpful in encouraging creativity at this stage of developing options:

1. No Evaluation
2. No Attribution
3. All Options Are Encouraged (seeking to create value opportunities)
4. Mediator's Options Are Included (preferably several, once parties have contributed ideas)

First, we separate the creation of ideas from their evaluation. Separating the creation of ideas from their evaluation serves several purposes. Creativity and evaluation use different parts of our brains, so premature evaluation can shut off creativity. We also want to be sure that the parties don't negotiate prematurely, so postponing evaluation keeps open many possibilities before the parties fasten on one as the ultimate solution.

This was why in Radix it was so helpful for the CEOs to instruct the managers not to worry about negotiating amongst options when they were inventing them. The CEOs would do that later. Also, the best ideas often come after everyone has exhausted all of their thoughts of possibilities and no one can think of anything more. Sometimes one person's suggestion, even an idea that seems to make little sense, can trigger a valuable idea from someone else.

A second ground rule is that we agree not to attribute any option to the party who suggested it. Thus, no party will be expected to agree to a particular option. (We use a flip chart to list all of the options without identifying their source.) Any option that goes up on a board can later come down just as quickly, allowing parties the freedom to make all kinds of suggestions.

We are particularly interested here in encouraging parties to suggest options that expand the pie, either through increasing income, reducing expenses, or making qualitative changes that have the potential to leave both sides better off through a sharing of the increase in value. We separate the creation of value from deciding about how the increased value is distributed, to minimize strategic behavior and keep the parties focused on the creative function of brainstorming options. Because the Radix and Argyle companies had been locked in a decades-long struggle, they had been focusing only on trying to maximize their share of the existing value of the dispute. This was a natural result of their feeling imprisoned by their conflict.

By challenging them to think beyond the way they had viewed the conflict and its possible resolution and to imagine both sides being part of one company, they were free to think differently about the problem and possible solutions. After recognizing the power of the possibility, the executives in Radix and Argyle embraced it enthusiastically.

Finally, it can be valuable for the mediator to participate in this brainstorming process, but without any special role and with a certain amount of self-discipline that will avoid the danger of the parties giving any special weight to the mediator's ideas. This danger is lessened when the mediator makes multiple suggestions rather than one and waits until the parties have suggested as many possibilities as they can.

Evaluating Options

With Radix and Argyle, after the parties worked together to create the new options that expanded the pie, it was time to test all the options against both companies' interests. The value-creating options were clearly exciting to both sides. One executive said, "We should have been thinking about them anyway, but we were so locked into seeing each other as adversaries that they didn't even occur to us. I only mean it half-facetiously when I say we're lucky to have this lawsuit."

Of course we were still going to have to figure out how to distribute the value created, but both sides were so clearly intrigued by the creating value opportunities that it changed the entire context of the $300 million problem. Now that the parties are ready to negotiate, the tension which often eases during the creation phase comes back into the room. As mediators, we worry if this does not occur since however big we made the "pie" during the creation phase, now that we are dividing it up, both parties must now make concrete decisions about dividing it up. With Radix and Argyle, this phase took place over two months, as each company worked internally to determine what would be workable and acceptable.

Ultimately, the $500 million was not split in half, but rather 60 percent went to Argyle and 40 percent to Radix, because the projects would require more effort on the part of Argyle. They had discovered how to work together with a competitor on a mutually profitable basis. They also agreed to restructure the existing contract to mitigate future market risks in a clear and mutually acceptable form.

It's All About the Money: Evaluating Options and Testing Them Against the Parties' Interests **12**

A day before the first meeting in a scheduled mediation, I was surprised to find a memorandum in the mail from a lawyer whose name I didn't recognize. It made reference to a construction mediation I was about to start and was marked "private and confidential." Two days earlier, I had had a pre-mediation conference call with the two lawyers scheduled to come with their clients to see whether they could resolve a dispute in which a contractor was being sued by a homeowner for defects in his remodeling of a family home. Neither of them had referred to any other lawyer who would be participating in the mediation. This would not be the only surprise awaiting me.

The receipt of the confidential memo created a dilemma for me. Normally, I ask lawyers to prepare memoranda about the case to be submitted to me *and* exchanged with each other prior to our meeting so that I have some familiarity with the case and their various views. The reason that I want them to exchange their memos with each other is that, as I explain to them, I want to work with everyone together, and in no event do I hold any information received from one side secret from the other.

So I called the lawyer who had sent the memo. He turned out to be representing the insurance company for the contractor. We had the following exchange.

> *Mediator:* I didn't know that you were part of the case, and I'm sorry that you weren't included in the phone call planning our session.
>
> *John:* I've been in lots of mediations before, so I didn't think I needed to be part of any phone call.
>
> *Mediator:* Well, you might find my approach to mediation somewhat different from your other mediation experiences. One thing that is different is that I don't want to be in possession of any information that I can't share with the other participants.
>
> *John:* Too bad. I sent you a confidential memo, and I expect you to keep it confidential.
>
> *Mediator:* Lucky for both of us, I stopped reading it as soon as I saw that it was marked "confidential." So, I think that leaves us with at least a couple of alternatives. I can send it back to you unread, and you can either send me a replacement that isn't confidential or, if you want me to read what you have sent, you can decide that it isn't confidential and send the others a copy of it.
>
> *John:* You know, it's kind of inflammatory, so I think it would be better if you sent it back to me. (He hesitated for a moment.) Nah. What the hell. It's all about money, and they might as well know how upset we are and that we are onto their game. I'll send them a copy.

■ ■ ■

Lawyers' Memoranda

The reason I want memoranda sent to me before a mediation in cases where lawyers are going to participate actively is to give me a sense of the situation, including their legal perspectives. Usually this necessitates a 5- to 10-page memo from each side, which allows me to get enough of a feel of the situation that I can hit the ground running when we begin. It also makes the lawyers more comfortable to be able to provide the mediator with information about the case in their role as advocates for their clients. I learn a lot from these memos not only about the facts of the case and the law, but also about the attitudes of the lawyers toward seeking resolution.

Most lawyers don't show these memos to their clients before the mediation, although it would be a better practice, and I encourage but do not require them to do so. The primary reasons I don't insist on this are that I want to respect the lawyer-client relationship and I don't have the power to implement the suggestion. Nor do many lawyers show their clients the letter I usually send the lawyers in advance describing my approach to mediation and a suggested way of going about *working together*. I wish they did, but I don't assume they have.

Whether or not the parties are educated in advance about the process we are about to undertake, I find it important to have an in-person discussion at the start about how we will *work together*. With lawyers present, it is important for the parties and their lawyers to understand and reach agreements about their and their lawyers' participation that make sense to them. The lawyers' knowledge that I have already read their memos makes this easier. In this case, it was my turn to be surprised once again on the day the mediation began.

■ ■ ■

The mediation was set for 9 AM, but at about 8:30, participants began to arrive. I knew that Linda, the lawyer for the homeowner, Larry, was planning to be there with her client and that Connie, the lawyer for the contractor, Colby, also planned to be present with her client. And I assumed John, the lawyer for the insurance company, would show up. The people who arrived first, however, were experts who had been hired by each side to determine whether Colby had made errors in his work and if so, what it would cost to complete the job. All told, by the time the lawyers arrived with their clients, 20 people were jammed into my waiting room, with the overflow spilling out into the street.

I asked the lawyers and their clients to come into my office, which could comfortably accommodate about eight people, so we could plan how to work together. When I asked them what they had in mind, John spoke.

John: I assume that you ought to meet first with our side, including our experts, and then with the other side.

Mediator: I have a different idea, which I talked about with Connie and Linda when we spoke by phone a few days ago. My goal would be to put all of your clients in a position to decide together what would be an acceptable settlement. To do that, I would prefer that we all meet together in the same room, so that they have the benefit of all of the expertise to get a full picture of their situation.

John: That seems crazy to me. How do you expect us to be able to openly negotiate with each other in the same room? Look, this case is only about money, and we have already been through one unsuccessful mediation process. I think that you're setting up a guaranteed failure.

Mediator: I'd like to think I'm not. It sounds to me as if you are concerned that at least when it comes to the negotiation part that neither side will feel that it can be open in each other's presence. That makes sense to me. I do think it will be challenging for the negotiation to be open enough to be successful. That would ultimately depend on whether you and your clients think it could be valuable to do it that way. It sounds like at the very least, this would be something that would be new to you. Could you imagine that it could be valuable for you and/or your clients to do this together?

John: You're the boss. If you think that we ought to do it this way, I'm willing to give it a try. I just am quite pessimistic that it could work.

Connie: I hate to interrupt this, but I think that this is not such a good use of our very expensive time. We have about 11 people here who are all being paid for their time. Linda and I just assumed they should be here, like in an arbitration. We should have told you, but they are here. And every hour is costing our clients thousands of dollars.

Mediator: I can appreciate that. What do you have in mind?

Connie: I think we need to put these experts to work to see whether they can make progress in narrowing their differences.

Mediator: So while we're in here working, we could have both sets of experts working together in another room.

Linda: That could work, but I think they might need your help.

Mediator: If this makes sense to all of you. I've never worked in quite this way before, but I would be willing to check in with them as we continue to meet here until the experts have reached a point where they can make a joint report to the rest of you and meanwhile come in here to help you make progress. If we go forward in this way, what could prove critical is for them to know from you that you jointly support their working together to narrow their differences.

Linda: That sounds right.

The lawyers and their clients agreed that was a good plan. So we crammed everyone into the room in which we had been meeting. I explained the plan, and the lawyers and clients gave it their support. The experts agreed to try to work together. I then met separately with them in the other room to set up some ground rules for their discussion. They said they would let me know if they needed me.

■ ■ ■

Using Experts

Generally speaking, if I start to work with parties prior to their hiring experts, I strongly recommend that they hire neutrals who will work with them to bring their expertise to bear as problem solvers where the only agenda is to provide as accurate an opinion as they are able based on the facts and their expertise, acknowledging the subjectivity of their opinions as well.

Working with experts who are hired as adversaries is very similar to working with adversary lawyers. Even though they are hired as "neutrals," the experts tend to align themselves with the side they "represent" either because of the nature of the adversary system or the nature of conflict. Each side's experts readily see the evidence and apply their professional focus from a one-sided perspective, and they easily become caught in an *expertise conflict trap.*

The challenge, as with adversary lawyers, is to help them get beyond defending the singular "rightness" of their opinions and look at the problem from a larger perspective that includes the strengths of their view and also takes into account their doubts.

Of course, this requires the support of their clients and their clients' lawyers. But it also represents a challenge for experts who have convinced themselves that the only way to see the problem is their way. Having them talk with each other outside the presence of the lawyers and their clients can reduce their polarization. They often know and respect each other and recognize that if they had been hired by the other side, their perspective on the problem might well have been that of their counterpart. I hoped that might happen in this case.

■ ■ ■

I returned to the room with the lawyers and clients.

> *Mediator:* I want to clarify something. I am not the boss here, but I do have some strong preferences. One of those preferences is to engage you as much as possible in designing this process with me. While I don't want to rule out entirely any possibility of meeting separately with each side, I find the possibility of a mutually beneficial solution greatly enhanced by our staying together, so I'd like to see how much progress we can make with all of us here. If we reach a point where you all agree that I should meet separately with both sides, I'm open to considering that as a possibility, but I would not anticipate that those separate meetings will be necessary and, in any event, would not want them to be confidential from the other side if we all agree to have them.
>
> *John:* Let's just move ahead.

For the next few hours, we did move ahead in both rooms. The experts reached a point where they had dramatically narrowed their differences about the cost of replacing a retaining wall that had failed from their starting figures of $15,000 to $75,000 to $30,000 to $45,000, and their difference about the cost of completion of the remodeling of the house from $5,000 to $75,000 to a range of $25,000 to $40,000.

In effect, the differences between the experts had gone from $60,000 to $15,000 regarding the wall and from $70,000 to $15,000 regarding the remodeling of the house. That meant the gap between the estimates for completing the work that had been as much as

$130,000 was now narrowed to $30,000. Everyone recognized the significance of that movement. The divergence in the experts' opinions would likely not prove an insurmountable obstacle to resolution.

Clarifying Differences

In meeting together with the parties and their lawyers in the other room, we proceeded with *conversation one* about the law. The lawyers had a significant disagreement about how to interpret a clause in the original contract that called for the completion of the house by a particular date and whether the initial contract had in fact been amended by a writing signed by both parties a few weeks before the initial contract was to expire. Although none of the lawyers gave up on their legal positions, neither did they claim that their positions were without risk. As a result, the differences between them were slightly narrowed when we emerged from the conversation about the law, and both clients recognized that there was not a single view that would clearly prevail if the case were to go to trial.

We then proceeded to *conversation two* and heard from each of the parties about how their dispute had developed. Larry described a relationship with Colby that began with great optimism and a shared vision of a significant remodeling of his house while he and his pregnant wife and their three-year-old child were living there with a definite schedule and agreed-upon price. As the remodeling progressed, the workers fell behind schedule and changes were made that resulted in increased costs. Close to the due date on the contract, Larry prepared a new agreement that called for both the termination of Colby working further on the project and what he understood to be a financial penalty to be suffered by Colby in the event that the house was not completed within the new time frame.

Larry's version of the events that followed accused Colby of inadequate workmanship, construction of a faulty retaining wall, and a failure to meet the new deadline. He was clearly frustrated by the situation, blaming Colby for the fact that now, one year later, work on the house was still incomplete because of the litigation. He had relied on Colby's expertise in constructing the retaining wall, and it had failed, resulting in potentially serious undermining of the house's foundation.

Colby's version differed in his feeling that Larry and his wife continually changed the plan, resulting in the delays and increased costs. He described signing the new agreement as a supplement to, not a replacement of, the original, and he never understood that there would be any financial penalty for failing to meet the deadline. In any event, he was shocked when he did not receive the agreed-upon amounts for various stages of completion of the work, and he was forced to file a lien on the house to secure the unpaid portions of his work. Colby felt that he had been taken advantage of and that he was underappreciated. The decisions regarding the retaining wall had been made by Larry in a cost-cutting mode. He felt that the "failure" of the wall had been greatly exaggerated and that it was never meant to protect the foundation, which he believed was never at risk.

■ ■ ■

Helping the Parties Broaden Their Views

Colby and Larry had both taken self-protective stances, each blaming the other for the creation of the problem, a natural reaction of each side to accusation from the other, until they had become solidly ensnared in their *conflict trap*. From my vantage point as mediator, I could see that they had each made assumptions about the other's intentions in terms of how it affected them while judging their own actions in what they viewed as their own justifiable and honorable intentions. In this manner, they each cast the other in a negative light, while justifying their own actions as necessary protection. I knew that if I could help them see this pattern, it might reduce some of the acrimony and harshness that had characterized their relationship and help them each see beyond their own views of the problem.

■ ■ ■

As I worked further with Colby and Larry to help them to clarify their own views and seek to understand each other's, Colby acknowledged how frustrating it must have been for Larry to deal with the delays and cost overruns and how from Larry's perspective, Colby had not communicated clearly enough for Larry not to be surprised. Larry could understand how Colby had worked hard and done the best that he could under the circumstances and how Colby felt entitled to be compensated for the value of his work.

We then focused on charting the interests of both sides:

Colby	Larry
Fair compensation for efforts	Finishing work at a reasonable cost
Fair allocation of responsibility for consequences of changes	Safety for family
Reputation for reliability	Protection of investment

I had the sense that there were more interests on both sides, but that they might come up later as we worked toward possible solutions.

Evaluating Options

We then explored a variety of options for completing the house and managing the risks associated with that, without evaluating the options.

- Colby finishing work on the house
- Hiring someone else to finish work on the house
- Selling the house in its present state
- Leaving the house in its present state
- Colby remitting cash payment to Larry
- Colby receiving compensation
- Basing the compensation on the actual cost of finishing the house after the fact

When we evaluated these options against the interests, it became clear that the preferred option for all was to agree on a monetary resolution of the cost of completing the remodeling, dealing with the retaining wall and compensating Colby for work done. At this point John again raised the question of caucusing.

John: I do feel that up to this point it's been helpful for us all to be together, but if we're going to make progress now, we ought to be meeting with you separately. I'm here to represent the insurance company, which, as I have explained, doesn't seem to have much responsibility here. So our interests are different than Colby's. We are not going to talk about that openly here.

Mediator: John, you seem to feel that meeting separately makes sense now, at least partly because the interests of the insurance company are different than those of your insured, Colby. Perhaps it would be helpful if each side met on its own, without me, to consider possible proposals or whatever else you might wish.

They agreed. Colby, Connie and John then met together for about 20 minutes. At the same time, the other side was meeting together to think about how they would be proceeding.

■ ■ ■

Putting Out Proposals

Proposals can be put together in a variety of ways. Normally, I prefer to have each side prepare proposals in writing, ideally more than one, for each side to keep the process fluid.

■ ■ ■

When we came back together in the room, John began.

John: We have a proposal. We are concerned about a couple of things if we put it out. First, if the other side doesn't like it, they might just walk out and end the mediation, and second, they might jack up their numbers just to respond to our offer.

Mediator: It sounds to me like you have developed a proposal that you think makes sense for your side, but you are concerned that it might be considered inflammatory to the other or that they might see it as an opening offer and respond strategically. Is that right?

John: Yes. We have thought this through and given where we are now, we think this is a good place to start.

Mediator: A testing-the-waters kind of solution. But you would like the commitment of the other side to continue the conversation, no matter what they think of the offer.

John: Right.

Mediator: Linda and Larry, what do you think about this?

Linda: We'll agree to stay in the room, but I have to tell you, if this is a lowball offer, which it sounds like, we are not about to respond with reasonableness.

Mediator: So you are also concerned about not placing yourselves at a disadvantage through some kind of strategic bargaining. What's good about this is that you both sound like
you want to move forward in a serious manner, and there is
naturally some tension about how to get the ball rolling in a
way that neither of you feel disadvantaged in the negotiation.

■　■　■

Dealing with Numbers

Once we reach the point of putting numbers on the table in a
joint session, sophisticated negotiators are naturally reluctant
to start the bargaining close to the point where they believe that
the case should settle. The tendency of each party is to put out
a number that gives them a lot of room to move, because they
anticipate that the other side will be doing the same. So the different sides are often feeling out one another, as each announces
their opening offer to see the reaction of the other. Thus ensues
a time-honored classic way of bargaining where each side moves
slowly toward the other from their extreme starting positions. It
is a challenge to find a way to cut through this usual dance when
all of the parties are in the same room.

A mediator can help in a variety of ways. The first is to simply
identify this typical way of bargaining and see if the parties are willing to deviate from it. Of course, this doesn't make the problem go
away, especially if you have sophisticated negotiators in the room,
but it helps to have some discussion and even agreement about
the *how* of this part of the process before we get into the *what*.

The mediator can help the parties act in a less strategic way by
working to ensure some *mutuality of vulnerability*. In the dance of
strategic extremes, one way to reduce the tendency of the parties
to react strategically to each other's offers is for the different sides
to write down their offers and pass them to the mediator simultaneously so that he or she can review them before providing them
to the other side. If the mediator feels that only one of the parties is
operating strategically, there is the option of not passing them on.

Most critical is using the relationship between the interests of
the parties and their numbers. Here the idea is to recognize the
relationship between the parties' solutions and their interests and

to use the interests to ground the solution. The point is that any mutually acceptable solution has to meet the interests of both sides. The goal then would be for the parties to be able to explain how any number meets both their own interests *and* the other side's as well. That would prove my main effort in this case.

■ ■ ■

Mediator: My goal is that both of you feel there is a mutuality here in our moving forward. For that to happen, it would be helpful if you each come up with proposals that have reasoning behind them that you think should be appealing to the other. The reasoning will then give us a better understanding of where you might differ and agree. And to minimize the part of this where you could be reacting to each other or feeling that the focus is just on one side, you might want to prepare the proposals in writing and pass them to each other through me.

John: No. Let's just put this offer on the table and go from there.

Linda: That's all right with me.

Mediator: Okay, if we get stuck we can always take up my idea later, if it makes more sense to you to proceed in this way.

John: Well, we've looked at this carefully from the insurance company's point of view as well as Colby's. And for this purpose, the company would be willing to pay $30,000, which we think would be close to the company's exposure in this case for the water damage to the retaining wall, and that Colby should be paid the remaining $25,000 he is owed for unpaid work. These numbers are scaled down from what Colby is really owed, and the wall damage represents something that is close to the high end of what the company would have to pay if we lose in court.

Linda: I'm sorry now that I promised that we wouldn't walk out of here when we heard their offer. I can't believe what I'm hearing. This represents a net offer of $5,000. You've got to be kidding. This is probably worse than if we went to court and lost everything.

Mediator: So you're disappointed. I'd like to see if we can go through the reasoning behind it to see where the divergence might be. Rather than bargain over numbers, let us see what the numbers rest on for both sides. Is this okay?

John: Sure.

Linda: I'd like to respond. First of all, even if we use their numbers for the cost of the retaining wall and the completion of the house, that is $55,000 right there. So offering $30,000 is even lower than where their expert's numbers would put them. There is no dispute that the retaining wall failed, and there is no dispute that the remodel is incomplete. And as for paying Colby, we have an agreement signed by him that if he failed to complete the house in time, he would not be paid anything further.

Mediator: So this is your reasoning for why the offer is inadequate. Would you like to hear from John what his thinking is about the offer?

Linda: Not really.

John: Why don't you make an offer then?

Mediator: That could be the next step, but I would find it helpful at least for me to understand what's behind your offer. Is that okay with you, Linda?

Linda: Go ahead if you want, but frankly I'd rather make our offer first.

Mediator: All right, but I do want to come back to the reasoning on both. That's the best prospect for having a basis for moving forward.

Linda: We'd settle for $125,000 from the insurance company, and no further payment to Colby.

John: This is exactly what I expected from you. This is completely off the wall, beyond your wildest dreams of what could happen in court.

■   ■   ■

Once again, what seemed most likely to help with this kind of positional bargaining that they had assumed would be to turn the attention from the *what* to the *how* and see whether we could find a more constructive way to proceed that would get us out of the strategic trap.

■ ■ ■

Mediator: So far, you've each managed to unsettle the other with your offers.

John: We need your help here. This is where I would expect you to meet separately with us to move us closer.

Linda: I don't want to do that. I'm still here and I'd like to see if we can do this all together.

John (to me)*:* Then how do you think we can proceed?

Mediator: Well, it's clear to me that we need to have more discussion about what would happen in court since you seem to have such different perceptions about that. We also need to go back to what the priorities are for each side and look at these offers in those terms. And I think we need to create some understanding about how to present another round of offers that will feel less polarizing to both sides.

John: All right. But I have to tell you, I'm worried that if we put out another offer that is close to the best we can do, we could find ourselves in a position we don't want to be in.

Mediator: Which would be?

John: We've put out a good-faith offer, and they just sit there.

Mediator: So you would like this next round to feel as if there is more mutuality.

John: Yes.

Mediator: And you, Linda?

Linda: Yes, but they are going to have to get realistic.

Mediator: If this next round is going to move us forward, it would be helpful for each of you to put it together in a form that you think should be appealing to the other side and be prepared to explain why. Otherwise, it just continues the number trading and taking potshots at each other. In order for that to work, it would be helpful to establish that you understand each other's priorities as well as your own. So it makes sense for us to review those priorities.

■ ■ ■

Testing Numbers Against Interests

Because we had identified the parties' interests at an earlier stage, we could use that as a basis for the particular options that we had been discussing, particularly with respect to focusing the parties on how they believed their solutions met the interests of both sides. As the mediation progresses, a dynamic relationship between the level of options and interests can be used to clarify interests or even identify new ones as well as create new solutions that are responsive to those interests.

■ ■ ■

Linda: Larry has made it clear that his primary objective is to finish the house at an affordable cost.

Mediator: That's true. He also said that he wanted to be sure that the house was safe for the kids and would not require a lot of maintenance in the future. Was there anything else, Larry?

Larry: I said this before, and I meant it. I am not out to rip off anybody. If Colby had completed the house on time and properly, we wouldn't be here. I never meant to punish Colby.

Mediator: So one of your goals in addition for you and your family to have the house you wanted is for Colby to be fairly compensated. Is that right?

Larry: I have never said otherwise.

Mediator: That's helpful. Let me add that to the list. And how about Colby and the insurance company?

Colby: All I want to say is that I have retired as a contractor now, and I feel that I put myself out to do everything I could to give Larry and his family the best I could do, but they kept changing their ideas.

Mediator: One of your priorities is to have a result that fairly allocates responsibility for those changes.

Colby: That's right. And they need to take responsibility for making choices based on their budgetary concerns that have created the retaining wall problem. I told them I would build whatever they wanted, and Larry said he wanted to cut costs.

Mediator: So you want recognition of responsibility for decisions that were made as well as constraints on the budget that were not of your choosing?

Colby: That keeps getting left out of the mix.

Mediator: Is anything else important to you that we haven't identified here?

Colby: Yes. One of my greatest disappointments in all of this is that I felt I bent over backwards trying to make this work for Larry and his family. A number of things were beyond our control, but whatever we could do, we did. We worked overtime without charging for it. I took people off other jobs to try to keep to our schedule.

Mediator: What you would like is some recognition of the effort you made to do this job well and efficiently.

Colby: That's right. Very few contractors would have been willing to work under the same conditions.

Mediator: Then why were you willing to do that?

Colby: I felt like we were helping a family in a difficult situation.

Mediator: So this had a personal dimension for you in terms of your relationship to Larry and his family. Now with this in mind, I think if each side could prepare offers that you think respond to what has been identified clearly by each of you as your priorities here, this could give us the impetus for the next round. What we haven't identified is whether anything from the insurance company's perspective needs to be thrown into the mix.

John: We wouldn't be here if we didn't want to help solve this problem, but Linda, you're going to have to be realistic if we are going to get anywhere.

Mediator: Settling this case on a basis that you can justify to your carrier is why you're here.

John: And that means that you need to recognize that our coverage would be limited only to any problem with the retaining wall. Our exposure is really quite limited.

Mediator: So you're emphasizing that your coverage relates solely to the retaining wall. And the other economic factor, I assume, would be the cost of defense.

John: That's right. Paying the experts plus our legal fees is also of concern to the company. But we don't settle cases on that basis. Otherwise we'd be in a position to compromise cases that have no merit.

With new interests identified through testing of the options against the interests, we add those interests to the chart so that we can all see the relationship between the options and the interests.

■ ■ ■

Testing Against the Legal Reality

No matter how fully we focus on the parties' interests in helping them negotiate a resolution, at some point it is almost always necessary to refer again to the legal reality. Doing so helps to test any particular solution, since the ultimate goal is to help the parties reach a result that is better for both of them than their alternative. While we have already had *conversation one* about the legal reality at an earlier stage in the mediation, it is often necessary to have another version of it at this final stage, particularly because both sides are comparing the likely result in court with the resolution being considered in the mediation. Part of that legal reality includes the transaction costs, which can be a significant element of that determination, whether made explicit or not.

■ ■ ■

> *Linda:* I suggest we exchange offers through you and then be prepared to talk about them.
>
> *John:* I'm willing to try it, but again I don't think we will be able to have the frank discussion that might be necessary to settle this case without meeting alone with you. But we'll do it. We will meet again with Colby and come up with a joint proposal for the defense.
>
> *Mediator:* You've registered skepticism, and what I can tell you is that if you can share control of this process with each other and want to settle the case, you will.

Each side met separately and within 15 minutes came back together and submitted numbers to me which I then passed on to the other sides. Linda's offer was $95,000 reduced by a payment to Colby of $20,000. John's was a $55,000 payment to Larry, of which $30,000 would be paid from Larry to Colby. The net cost of Linda's offer was $75,000 and the net offer from John $25,000. They were $50,000 apart.

> *Mediator:* Now I think it would be helpful to understand what the reasoning is behind these numbers and particularly how you think your numbers take into account the interests that we identified on both sides.

■ ■ ■

Looking at the Problem Together

This is where *working together* provides a real opportunity. If the parties have both clarified and expressed their own interests and made efforts to understand each other's as well, when we undertake this task with everyone in the room together, we are all looking at the whole picture. Each person's problem is everyone's problem. Since no agreement will occur if we don't find an option that meets the interests of each party, we can engage the parties in a conversation to examine the options in light of the interests of both sides. This makes for a very different dynamic than each party looking only at their own interests. In this way, the parties are also encouraged to look at the problem from the perspective of the mediator.

■ ■ ■

John: The $55,000 number is a very generous offer. I think it is close to the maximum of the company's exposure if we lose the case. It gives Larry the ability to finish the house.

Linda: It doesn't come close to that. Your own expert recognized that it was going to cost a lot more than that to deal with future water damage on the wall, and this doesn't begin to take into account all of the unfinished parts of the house that make it uninhabitable. On page four of the expert's report, he admits this.

John (to Mediator)*:* This is exactly what I was afraid of. We've made a legitimate offer, and she's just trying to poke holes in it. I'm withdrawing this offer.

Mediator: So John, you see your offer as going a significant distance in meeting Larry's interest in finishing the house while also being realistic in terms of the legal alternative, while Linda, you feel the gap between the offer and that reality is too great. And you both seem frustrated with each other's response. Of course, you're free to withdraw any offers you make at any time. But before you react to each other's offers, I'd like to understand why you each came to the conclusions that you did and, more particularly, how you think your offer meets the other's side's interests as well as your own.

Linda: We're really far apart. I don't think we're going to be able to settle this.

Mediator: I don't know whether we will or not. But if we are, I think it could come from each of your better understanding how the other's offer is responsive to your priorities.

Linda: I'm listening.

■ ■ ■

Connecting the Numbers with the Interests

Although the parties remained focused on the numbers, it was important to keep the connection alive between the numbers and the interests rather than get caught in an argument about the numbers alone. Asking the parties to explain to each other how they think their offer meets the other's interests helps maintain that connection.

■ ■ ■

John: We think that the $55,000 will go a long way toward Larry completing the house. Because Larry changed the design of the house so much, it shouldn't be our responsibility to provide a completion that wasn't contracted for. We also think that there are cheaper ways of fixing the wall that will be safe for the kids and the structure. This is better than the wall that Larry originally had in mind. Colby's compensation is dramatically reduced here, and we think this takes into account more than his share of responsibility for where things stand.

Mediator: Linda, do you and Larry understand what the reasoning is behind their offer and why they think it meets Larry's interests?

Linda: I think so. I just disagree with it.

Mediator: Then let's hear from you about how you believe your offer meets Colby and John's priorities.

Linda: Well, first we are willing to pay Colby $20,000, basically out of the goodness of our hearts, because we are not legally obligated to pay him anything. The contract was clear that if he didn't meet the deadline, no further payments would be made. This is an important gesture here, and a significant movement on our part. We have also reduced our demand to $95,000, recognizing that there is at least some ambiguity about whether changes were made by Larry. Our view is that those changes were necessitated by the structural problems that were Colby's responsibility, but we recognize that as the project developed, Larry and his wife made some decisions that had some impact on the scope of the job.

Colby: I am not, and never represented myself to be, a structural engineer, nor was there any need for an engineered wall.

Linda: Our experts say otherwise, and even your expert recognizes a potential danger from leakage.

Mediator: Colby, you still disagree about the degree of responsibility you should assume for the wall, but I also hope you recognize the effort that Larry and Linda have made here to offer compensation and assume some responsibility for changes made to the project.

Colby: I do, but I just wanted to point out this problem that keeps coming up.

John: What do we do now, Mr. Mediator?

Mediator: First, I think we need to recognize that there has been considerable movement on the part of both sides, so that there is now only a $10,000 difference in compensating Colby, and there is a $40,000 difference on payment from the insurance company to Larry. My suggestion would be that each side come back with another offer in an effort to close, or at least narrow, the gap.

John: I do think it would be helpful if you met separately now with each side or if you gave your opinion as to where the case should settle.

■ ■ ■

Mediator Opinion

It is often quite tempting for the mediator to fasten on a number that could or should settle the case, and, of course, even in our model, this would not be the end of the world. The dangers, however, remain. Relying on the mediator to determine the outcome gives the mediation the potential to become much like an arbitration. Having worked so hard to reach this point, now the parties might readily cede their power to the neutral as a way to relinquish responsibility for finding their own meeting ground. The other danger is that one or both of the parties will be alienated by the mediator's number, jeopardizing the relationship of neutrality.

The value of the mediator's suggestion of a number is that it is an outside opinion by someone who has no agenda other than to settle the case, and that having a number come from the mediator rather than themselves can help the parties feel less vulnerable. While on occasion, we are willing to point out a number where experience suggests a case might settle, we are quite reluctant to do so. On a fundamental level, we feel strongly that this is the prerogative of the parties, which for us is the whole point of mediation.

■ ■ ■

Mediator: You have expressed wanting me to meet separately with each side and to suggest a number where I think you ought to settle. I think you are making a lot of progress without my having to do that. Obviously, we could take an approach to try to split the difference, but I think it might be useful to have some more discussion about the cost of the wall and the degree of protection needed to guard against future problems. It also might be helpful to talk some more about the two different prongs of the agreement, to better understand how we might go about closing the gaps.

Connie: I've been quiet up to now, but it needs to be said that the only thing that matters to Colby is getting paid for his work. The company doesn't really care a lot about that.

John: And I have to say that we are getting pretty close to the limit of what the company can pay Larry. Personally, I'd like to see Colby get paid, but the company doesn't benefit from that at all.

Linda: Larry needs to be able to finish his house, so any money that he pays Colby cuts into his ability to do that.

Mediator: I find this conversation to be quite helpful. We still have some tension in trying to come to the right figure for everyone, but I find this to be a good tension that recognizes the different realities. Are we ready to do another round of offers or is there anything else that any of you would like to say before we do that?

■ ■ ■

Accepting Tension

One of the greatest challenges for the mediators and the parties at the end of the mediation is to be able to live with the tension that accompanies the final stage of the mediation. We can all sense the possibility of an agreement, but the differences remain, and we don't want either party or ourselves as mediators to fall into the trap of making an agreement just to relieve the tension of the parties' differences. As the mediator, I have learned to recognize that this tension is good for the mediation. If I am feeling it, it means I am exactly in the place the parties have hired me to be in. It is also important for the parties to be able to live with the tension than either to pretend that it doesn't exist or, more dangerously, to give in to make the tension go away.

■   ■   ■

Linda: I'd like to ask Connie and John a question. Would your expert actually fix the wall for the amount that he is saying the repair would cost?

This turned out to be crucial toward narrowing the gap. Connie and John left the room to ask the expert whether he would fix the wall for the amount he estimated. A few minutes later they returned.

■   ■   ■

Testing the Options Against Reality

Once we start to focus on a particular solution, we not only need to test the options against the interests, but to test the options against reality, often requires outside information. Whatever the interests have been, it is critical that the parties not make a commitment to an agreement that won't work. If the parties are reluctant to do this because they are afraid that there might be a problem, it is up to the mediator to press the point to ensure that the progress is not an illusion.

■   ■   ■

Connie: Our expert is willing to make his estimate a bid and be bound by it.

Linda and Larry then left the room to confer and came back a few minutes later.

> *Linda:* We're willing to reduce our $95,000 demand to $70,000, and we'll stay with our last offer to Colby of $20,000.
>
> *Mediator:* Why?
>
> *Linda:* Since our costs will be reduced, we think we can make this work for Larry to finish the house.

Connie and John then conferred with Colby, and a few minutes later they returned.

> *Connie:* We'll pay the $70,000, but we need Colby to receive no less than the $30,000 we talked about before.

Linda and Larry conferred again, and within a couple of minutes, they returned and accepted the last offer. We were done and a sense of relief permeated the room. The deal felt good to me. Larry would be able to complete his house, and Colby would have enough to begin his new life. Larry and Colby shook hands with each other and wished each other luck. The moment felt genuine.

■ ■ ■

I would like to think this process worked better for these parties than the usual settlement process in which the neutral would have met separately with the parties and put pressure on them to settle. What had worked was that the result wasn't simply an agreement about money. The money was a basis everyone understood. One side had been able to take advantage of the other side's expertise to accomplish the result of completion of the house. The insurance representative had a sense of what was meaningful to Larry and his family, and that may have been a motivating factor in settling. So it wasn't just the net result that mattered. It was the particular configuration of the two amounts and what that could accomplish for the parties that had ultimately directed us to the particular solution we reached.

As we left the room, John pulled me aside.

> *John:* You haven't made me a believer, but I must admit I'm a little less skeptical about this idea of staying together. There aren't many cases it could work for, because most of the cases I handle are just about the money.

Mediator: I thought you felt that way about this case in the beginning.

John: I guess I did. I'll have to think about that some more. But I've got to run to another case, and let me assure you—that one's really all about the money.

■ ■ ■

I was glad that we hadn't caucused because I think that kept the reality of the people's lives in the forefront. While it clearly had been uncomfortable for everyone, including me, to stay in the same room together, I think it was more efficient than if I had shuttled back and forth, leaving half of the participants in one room wondering about what was happening. We had been able to take advantage of everyone's expertise, we all had an understanding of what was important to the parties, and there was a sense of *working together*—all of which I'm convinced made a difference in the end.

Commentary: Evaluating Options and Reaching Closure

Once the parties brainstorm options, they have three central steps for evaluating them: prioritize, assess against interests, and needs, and negotiate outcome.

1. Prioritize—Each party designates the most and the least workable options.
2. Assess Against Needs and Interests—Each party assesses all promising options in terms of how they meet *all* parties' needs and interests.
3. Negotiate Outcome—Parties refine, test, and choose options.

Prioritize

Once we have a list of all of the possibilities, the next task is to determine which ones can work best for all parties. With all the options listed on flip charts (or another display equally accessible to everyone participating), we begin the evaluation process by having each party separately rate each of the options. The point is to see which options the parties have an interest in exploring further and which they do not. While there is no one set way to do this, we often have the parties record their ratings for each option—A, B, or C—with A signaling interest in exploring further, C indicating no interest, and B somewhere in between.

Then each party gives the results to the mediator who records the ratings on the flip chart that has been used to identify the options. The parties can then see how interested they both are in each of the options. This not only saves a lot of time going through a discussion of every option, whether of interest to the parties or not, but provides the parties with a lot of information about each other's preferences and, by giving the priorities first to the mediator, it reduces strategic maneuvering.

Assess Against Needs and Interests

Once the options have been rated, then it is time to test them against the interests both parties have identified. (We usually start with the double As, if there are any, or A-Bs.) To this end, we refer to the chart on which we earlier recorded the parties' interests and options. Then the mediator works with the parties to test the options the parties have chosen to explore further.

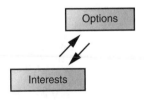

FIGURE 12.1

Going back and forth testing how the options are grounded in the parties interests is often an iterative process. By looking again at the interests from the perspective of the options, parties may realize that they have interests that they had not previously articulated. And, similarly, new options might also emerge.

By this point in the mediation, we would hope to ask each side to talk about how the particular option might or might not meet the interests listed for *both parties*, particularly if there has been real understanding between the parties. When the parties are able to do this, not only the mediator but they too are looking at the whole problem. We call this perspective "mediator consciousness." As with Larry and Colby, the parties' *working together* in this way can prove crucial to their ability to reach closure in a manner that truly resolves their differences.

Bringing the interests to the foreground can seem like a step backward. Not at all. The whole point is that the options be solidly grounded in the interests. Testing the options against the interests naturally makes for a fuller view of the whole problem and its resolution. When the options stand solidly on the foundation of the interests, the endgame can be more a mutual searching for common ground rather than simply bargaining and trade-offs.

With Larry and Colby, testing the options against the interests meant translating the numbers into the completion of the house, and Colby also affirmed that he too wished Larry to have the house he wanted for his family. For Colby, it meant the economics of his contracting business were important for them both to see as they moved toward closure. Larry recognized that and also affirmed that he wanted Colby to be fairly compensated.

By testing the options against the interests, we have narrowed the possibilities and refined the ideas sufficiently to require further exploration to test them against reality, and set the stage for negotiation.

Negotiate Outcome

Now that the parties are ready to negotiate, the tension that often eases during the creation phase comes back into the room. As mediators, we worry if this does *not* occur. However big we made the "pie" during the creation phase, both parties realize that they must now make concrete decisions about dividing it up.

To work most effectively with the endgame, the mediator does well to maintain bifocal vision—on both the *what* and the *how*.

Working With the *How*

The last part of the mediation, where the parties negotiate the final result, is often fraught with tension, particularly when the parties recognize that however creative they have been in developing options, they must still make decisions to divide what is before them. If the tension between the parties has been eased during the creation and evaluation of options, it can be surprising, even jolting, to the parties and the mediator to feel the tension creep back in the room.

As mediators, we experience the discomfort of this tension, and taking action to make it disappear could easily undo all of the good work that has gotten us to this place. Here we return to one of our guiding concepts—*allow tension*. The mediator can work to allow the discomfort of this tension within and between the parties and the mediator.

As mediators we face several dangers at this phase:

1. Trying to impose our own solution;

2. Allowing one party to coerce or manipulate the other;

3. Trying to speed up the process by pushing the parties to make decisions before they are ready;

4. "Laying back" too much and allowing the negotiation to turn into an exchange of numbers that disconnects the parties from what is important to them;

5. Losing our neutrality and favoring one party at the expense of the other.

Here we need to face a central internal challenge as mediators—not to measure the success of the mediation or our success as a mediator by whether the parties reach an agreement. This is particularly difficult when much of the outside world wants to use such an external test of competence. There are several problems with using such a test that can jeopardize the success of the mediation.

Our view is that whether the parties reach an agreement is not necessarily a statement about the quality of the mediation. For us, success is not achieved when agreements are not solid or were not the product of joint decision making. Many cases mediators can feel good about are those where the parties did not reach an agreement, but where some authentic exchange occurred that represented an important movement between the parties. And for the parties, reaching an agreement is not the only important factor. It is *how* they reached it, if they did, that sticks with them, and what went on between them, if they did not.

So what does this all mean about *how* to work with the parties in this phase? Remember the principle: *let the parties own their conflict.* It truly is up to the parties to find their own solution and accept the *primary responsibility* for that. Once liberated from the self-imposed pressure that as professionals we carry the burden of whether the parties reach an agreement, we can actually feel freer to help them.

Second, we are monitoring the process to observe and, if necessary, comment on the communication between the parties. Are they both making the effort to speak up for themselves and take each other into account? Do they both understand their situation—where they are and what they are trying to achieve?

With lawyers in the room, who is doing the negotiating? Are the lawyers encouraging the parties to speak for themselves or are they taking over? Are the parties feeling supported by their lawyers?

We also try to ensure that as much as possible the process feels fair to the parties. To that end, we can help the parties move forward by creating mutuality of vulnerability between the parties—where one party is not left feeling overexposed in relation to the other.

Working with the *What*

A variety of techniques can be used to keep the playing field level and create forward movement during the endgame, particularly when the mediation seems as if it may be stuck. We will suggest a few of them here, not to try to catalog them but to illustrate how mediators working with both parties in the room at the same time can productively use the tension present and help deal with the age-old negotiation problem of who goes first, and without coercing the parties.

Maintaining the Connection between Solutions and Interests

In order to keep the mediation from turning into simply a numbers game, it is important to continually look for the essential relationship between solutions and interests, as this case illustrates. Even when the parties are close to a solution, tracking their movements in relationship to their own and each other's interests helps keep that connection alive and can open doors that might otherwise seem closed, as it did for Colby and Larry.

Simultaneous Offers

Sometimes the parties have reached a point where there is a significant disparity between their last offers. Perhaps, as in this case, the lawyers are used to caucusing and don't want their clients to make a move unless they are sure it will be reciprocated. One way to deal with that is to ask for simultaneous offers. After explaining the goal of trying to avoid the strategic trap, we may suggest, as in this case, that (1) each party write down a number that they will be prepared to explain works for the other side as well as for them and (2) then give those numbers to the mediator to see if they pass a threshold test of whether they have each taken the task seriously before (3) the mediator passes on the offers to each side as the basis for (4) a dialogue in which each party explains why they believe the offer works for both sides.

Exploring the Advantages and Disadvantages of the Last Offers

Here, without either party having to signal any movement, we ask each side to consider what it might mean for them to accept the other side's last offer and what it might mean if the other side accepted their last offer. This often provides more understanding in the room that can be the basis for some real movement.

Exploring the Law Again

As the mediation moves toward the point where parties recognize they may actually end up in court, having another conversation about the law (*conversation one*), examining the risks and probabilities of a court judgment, particularly in relation to the last offers of both sides, can help parties reassess where they are. This also might entail looking more closely at the practical consequences of going to court, including the impact on the relationship between the parties and the time and money that would be spent.

Accepting Closure

For some participants, coming to the end of the mediation makes real the fact that a chapter in their lives has come to a close. A mix of sadness, relief, joy, and pain may accompany that recognition. In these moments, particularly when it is not clear an agreement will be reached, the parties need to decide whether they are willing to *work together* toward a decision that allows them to let go of the conflict.

For Colby and Larry, this meant coming to terms with cutting their losses and allowing each other to move on. Whatever was bound up in the difficulties of the past, it was now time to decide whether they were willing to try to understand each other's perspectives. Both were. Sometimes, as here, it can prove essential to face the underlying emotional reality of the situation, including returning to their reasons for mediating in order to bring closure to the conflict. In this case, it included the money, *and* so much more that the money represented for each.

The Stigma of Mental Illness: Seeing "The Impossible" as Possible 13

Deep beneath our conflicts is a humanity that connects us all. At times, that deeper reality is clearly present in helping guide parties in mediation toward resolution.

■ ■ ■

We were in trouble right from the beginning. Lawyers for the three parties appeared with their clients with one glaring exception. Al, the lawyer defending St. Mary's School, had unilaterally decided that the presence of someone from the school who had directly participated in the situation was unnecessary since the school was covered by insurance and the insurance adjuster was present. That was a surprise. In a conversation I had with all the lawyers two months previously, they had agreed upon who the participants would be, and specifically that someone from the school would have to be present at the mediation. After consulting with their clients, the lawyers had suggested several names of people who would be acceptable.

While it was certainly important to have the lawyers present, it was also important to include people from the school with firsthand knowledge of the situation. We would be unlikely to have any authentic sense of the situation from the school's perspective without someone who had been directly involved. While this case, like many others, was seemingly about money, it went much deeper. Reaching the humanity of those in the room, the parties and also the lawyers, was to make a critical difference. Limiting participation to agents alone would likely have kept us within the traditional confines of the conflict's trap.

Martha, the mother of Donna, had sued the school, believing that the school had conspired to make her daughter a pariah after she had suffered a psychotic episode there. Donna had walked into one of her classes, stood on her desk, talked incoherently about seeing "devils," then jumped from the desk and left the classroom as quickly as she had entered. She was found a few minutes later on the school grounds face down in the mud.

It was now a year later and Donna sat quietly next to her mother, looking younger than her 18 years. She appeared anxious and uncomfortable in this room full of adults, but in all other aspects, her appearance bore little sign of the trauma she had experienced. After several months of intensive therapy following the incident and with the help of medication, Donna had begun to reenter the world, but the school year had ended and she had been abandoned by her friends, leaving her isolated. Her road back to a normal life appeared to be quite complicated and would be prolonged, and her psychiatrist felt that she might need medication indefinitely to control her impulses. Martha took a strong protective stance toward her daughter, sitting very close to her in the room. She had made it clear through their lawyer that she wanted Donna there.

> *Mediator* (to Sally, lawyer for Martha and Donna)*:* With your permission I'd like to talk to your clients to see how they might want to proceed.
>
> *Sally:* Go ahead.
>
> *Mediator* (to Martha and Donna)*:* It's up to you to decide whether you want to proceed today or postpone the mediation until someone acceptable to you from the school can participate.
>
> *Martha:* This is very disappointing to me. In fact, this is the problem that brought us here. The school has just dismissed

us once again. The main reason I wanted a mediation was to let them know just how harmful their actions were to me and Donna. But no one is here.

Mediator: You and Donna had expected, and frankly so had I, based on my conversation with the lawyers, that someone with firsthand knowledge of what happened would be here.

Al (lawyer for the school)*:* I am sorry for this misunderstanding, and if you want to postpone this until someone from the school can be here, I am willing.

Martha: I want you to know that being here is traumatic for me and certainly difficult for Donna too. I can feel my heart pounding, and I am very anxious. This is all about what happened at the school, and they promised someone would be here, but once again they've let us down. After finally getting here today, I don't think it would be good to put it off. So I would rather proceed, but I am quite upset. It's a bad choice to be forced to make.

Mediator: So you are ready to proceed today, but in the course of the day, if you change your mind, I'd like you to tell us. Al, is there any possibility someone could come later even on short notice?

Al: I think the school counselor might be available. If we don't finish today and Martha agrees, I can assure you that I will make available someone acceptable to you.

Mediator: Martha, Donna, would you like the school counselor to come?

Martha: That woman never really understood what was going on, but neither did any of the rest of them. That's the problem. They never got it. I'd really rather have the principal come, but it would be better to have the counselor here than nobody. At least, maybe she'll be able to tell them what is going on.

Mediator: Then let's see if that might be possible.

We took a short break, allowing time for Al to contact the school and for Pat, the school counselor, to join us.

■ ■ ■

Opening Possibilities

In working with conflict, we often find ourselves looking beyond the limits of what the parties (and their attorneys) view as "possible" and "impossible" given how they experience the conflict and the possibilities for its resolution in mediation. Indeed, one way conflict keeps the participants ensnared is by making the possibilities seem more limited than they have to be. We always stand ready to challenge that sense of limitation on what might be possible in dealing with conflict. Opening possibilities was to prove vital to turning this conflict around.

■   ■   ■

When we resumed, I took time to explain the understanding-based approach to mediation, where we would all be meeting together and having the two conversations. I was initially met with skepticism.

> *Tom* (insurance adjuster): This is not what I call a typical mediation.
>
> *Mediator:* My concern about doing this in a traditional way, where I meet separately with each side, is that it puts me in a position of being like a judge deciding for you or possibly manipulating you and your clients to reach a deal.
>
> *Tom:* That's what mediation is. It's manipulation. That's your job.
>
> *Mediator:* That's not how I see my job. I think we can make a lot of progress if you're interested in working together to solve this problem without my having the power to decide or try to do things with either side that the other side can't see. This process is really all about the parties here being in a position to make decisions together based on their understanding and working through their conflict together.

I then started to describe the two conversations—the first about the law with the lawyers describing both the strengths and risks of going to court. I was quickly interrupted.

> *Sally:* This is really over the top. You want us to reveal the risks that our clients run by going to court. Why would we want to do that in front of each other?
>
> *Mediator:* For a couple of reasons. First, it is more honest and gives a bigger picture to your clients, if they are willing to have you do it. Secondly, I think it actually changes the atmosphere in the room. If all of you lawyers are willing to do this, it will set the stage for a better and fuller conversation by your clients when it's their turn to speak about how they experienced what happened

and to understand what is important to each side that might need to be taken into account to reach an acceptable result.

Sally: But when we talk about our risks, we'll be strengthening the other side.

Mediator: That's why it doesn't make sense to do it unless both sides agree. The real question is whether doing this would give your clients a clearer picture of the legal reality and whether this is something they would find valuable.

Sally: I'm going to have to talk to my clients about that.

Mediator: I think that's a good idea. The whole point of this process is to be able to put your clients in a position to make intelligent decisions.

After the lawyers took time to consult with their clients, we then proceeded with the legal conversation. Sally described how her client would succeed on the claims of invasion of privacy, slander, and a violation of the Unruh Act (a law that prohibits public institutions from discriminating against any particular classification of people), and she expressed optimism that they would recover the million dollars they claimed. Al responded in kind by pointing out the deficiencies in Sally's case, exuding complete confidence that Sally would be lucky to get to a jury. While it was clear to him that Donna had suffered, he was confident that the evidence was insufficient to hold the school responsible. We then agreed to turn to a discussion of their risks.

Mediator: Why don't we start with one of you telling us one reason you would give to explain a decision that went against you.

Al: Well, St. Mary's is a Catholic institution, and someone on the jury who had it in for the church could decide to take it out on this school.

Mediator: So if people's prejudices were tapped, the school could lose even if the evidence pointed in the other direction.

Al: That could happen.

Mediator: How about one from you, Sally?

Sally: Well, that same prejudice could go the other way. Someone who felt the church could do no wrong, or even had some feeling about the same diocese, might support the church even when it is clear that they didn't handle this properly.

Mediator: Good. Another one, Al.

> *Al:* We just finished taking Martha's and Donna's depositions. I have to admit that they will both be very appealing witnesses. They are both honest and quite sympathetic, and it will be hard for a jury to turn away from them.

Martha looked quite surprised. Tom looked somewhat irritated and shot Al a look of mild disapproval. The conversation continued with Sally and Al continuing to describe some more technical risks, but something had shifted in the room. It seemed that for a moment, Al had revealed to Martha a hint that he might be more personally involved and affected than he had previously appeared. A chink in his legal armor had appeared. While this conversation had been confined to the law, the personal dimension had begun to open in a way that would prove crucial, and it had opened with everyone together.

After finishing the conversation about the law, Martha finally had the opportunity to speak. I was somewhat taken aback when she pulled out of her purse a single-spaced, seven-page, typewritten statement. While it was clear that her deep concern over the case had led her to want to make a formal presentation, I wanted to be sure she had the opportunity to personally connect with the others in the room, which might be harder to do reading from a prepared statement.

> *Mediator:* Martha, you know this isn't a formal process, and I'd like you to have a chance to tell us all what you went through.
>
> *Martha:* I know; that's why I wrote this up, so I wouldn't forget anything. I feel so emotional about all of this that I was afraid that if I didn't put it in writing, I'd be incoherent.
>
> *Mediator:* So you'd like to refer to your statement. Is it okay if I stop you from time to time to make sure I understand what you're saying?
>
> *Martha:* Sure.

I thought that it would be particularly important to loop Martha, including the emotional impact on her and Donna, since part of what upset her so much, and possibly Donna, was the absence of anyone from the school, a further indication to them that no one had been listening.

Martha then began to read her statement, periodically interrupted by me to make sure I understood and that she felt understood. Doing so slowed her down and ensured that she had time for the full expression that was so important to her. When she reached the point of describing how she was called to the school to bring her daughter home, I interrupted her again.

> *Mediator:* I imagine that you were shocked when you arrived at the school.
>
> *Martha:* To say the least.
>
> *Mediator:* Can you say a little bit more about what that was like for you?
>
> *Martha:* I had never experienced anything like this before. I sent my daughter off to school a healthy, happy girl; and I arrived three hours later to see her look like she had been hit by a bomb.
>
> *Mediator:* The change in her was devastating to you.
>
> *Martha:* Yes. I couldn't imagine what could have happened for her to look like that.

After describing that time poignantly, she resumed reading her statement. She explained how after the incident the school administrators had continually shut her and Donna off from teachers, other students, and the rest of the school, and that they felt painfully isolated. I interrupted her from time to time particularly to allow her the opportunity to bring out the emotional dimension that was so telling but often missing in her reading of her report. Then we had the following interaction.

> *Mediator:* Your experience seems to have ranged from puzzlement to disappointment to devastation.
>
> *Martha:* Yes, but I would like you to stop interrupting. It's making it hard for me to stay with my statement.
>
> *Mediator:* I'm sorry if you feel as if I am interfering. I am trying to understand what it was like for you to go through this experience. Your factually based statement is thorough and helpful. For me, it is often missing this dimension of the emotional impact on you and Donna, so I am trying to bring it into the room.
>
> *Martha:* My lawyer told me to stick with the statement.
>
> *Sally:* It's okay, Martha. Al and Pat need to know what this was like for you, and I think the mediator is helping to bring that out.

■ ■ ■

Including Underlying Emotions

One way conflict keeps its hold is to limit the deeper emotions that those in its grasp can express with one another. Anger, distrust, blame, frustration, disappointment—the emotions that often separate us—can be expressed or implied. Pain, hurt, frailty, sorrow, fear—the emotions that promise to connect us—are more likely to be kept out of view. Lawyers' understandable desire to protect their clients both legally and emotionally can contribute to the understandable caution that their clients not be too vulnerable before "the other side." Sally recognized the different possibility that was emerging in the room. Regardless of the legal frame, it was now palpable on a human level how devastated this family had been.

■　■　■

Martha: It's so hard for me to have to talk about my feelings during this. You have no idea how much my life was turned upside down by this experience.

Mediator: I know that. That's why I'm trying to give you more room to tell us about that.

Martha: The school will never be able to understand this. Pat, you just stonewalled us and wanted to protect the other students. Al, you aren't even part of the school, so you have no way of being able to bring this to them.

Al: I don't know if you can see me taking notes. I plan to bring all this to their attention. I promise. And Pat is here too.

Mediator: So, Martha, as you have viewed it, the school never did get the impact of what happened and never will be able to, and you felt stonewalled by Pat. And Al, as a lawyer, has no way of getting through to the school. While, Al, you are saying that you intend to bring all this to the school's attention.

Pat: Can I say something?

Mediator (to Martha while also looking at Sally)*:* Is this okay?

Martha: Sure, but where were you when we needed you?

Pat: My first obligation was to protect the other students, and I made a judgment call. Of course I cared about Donna, but I felt I could be more helpful to her if we got her off the campus. Then every time I tried to contact you to talk to you and Donna, you refused.

Martha: You didn't get it and you still don't get it. These were her closest friends. You told them not to talk to her. The last thing Donna wanted to do was to be labeled by you, but you did that to her.

Mediator: Pat, it seems like you were in a bind. You were concerned for the other students, and you were concerned for Donna. But you felt that to help everyone, it was better to separate Donna from the other students. And Martha and Donna, you took that as a condemnation of you.

Martha: And so did the other students. The parents wouldn't even let her best friends talk to her. I assume that Pat had instructed them.

Pat: I did not. The parents were scared for their own children. The truth is that none of us really understood what was going on.

Mediator (to Pat)*:* So it was difficult for the other students and parents too, and also for you.

Pat: Yes, it was difficult for me. I was afraid for everyone. The students were getting very upset, and Donna seemed unreachable. And Martha insisted that we keep her at the school. But finally when the principal ordered me to have her removed from the school, we had to do that. I'm so sorry it came down to that, but we didn't know what else to do. Donna seemed so disoriented and out of control, and we couldn't make contact with her. She started babbling incoherently, and we were frankly scared for her and for the others around her as well. This went on for some time until we realized we had to get her out of there for both her sake and everyone else's.

Martha: You really have no idea of the impact of what you did. It took us months before anyone from the school would even talk to us.

Pat: I know. I didn't like that either.

Martha: Then why did it happen?

Pat: I'm not entirely sure. You wouldn't return my phone calls. I know the principal felt strongly about just getting the other students through the remainder of the year, and the parents were adamant about keeping their kids away from your family.

Martha: That's got to be because you told them to.

Pat: I never told any parent or kid to stay away from you or Donna.

This exchange had been rather electric. I noticed that Al too seemed to be touched by what was going on.

Mediator: Al, I know you weren't part of this, but you seem affected by this conversation.

Al: I want you to know something. I have two teenage daughters. This is not as far removed from me as you might think.

Mediator: Can you say some more about that?

Al: This is every parent's nightmare. I don't want to talk about my own life, but believe me, I get how hard this must have been for you, Martha, and you, Donna.

Al's eyes glazed for a moment, and the room was completely silent for the first time in this mediation. It was the last thing any of us might have expected, a lawyer bringing his own humanity and empathy into the room. One more development that would have been considered impossible had become palpable and very real.

■ ■ ■

Behind the Professional Mask

The moments when professionals are touched by the humanity of the situation in legal disputes are not commonplace, but when they do occur, they are important for everyone in the room. Normally, the professional masks that we wear keep that from happening, or if it does happen, from being visible to others. As mediators, while we can not make this happen, we try to create an atmosphere that encourages that level of authenticity through our own willingness to allow the humanity of the situation to touch us and be visible to others.

■ ■ ■

The feelings in the room had softened. As Martha continued, she referred increasingly less to her written statement, and the feeling of her experience permeated the room. Something important had happened between Martha and Al. Martha had a sense for the first time that someone representing the school, even if he had had no participation in the school or the events in question, had a real sense of what her experience had been, perhaps more even than Pat, who had been part of it.

Donna had been quiet throughout the mediation. When Martha finished, I asked her if she had anything she wanted to say.

> *Donna* (on the verge of tears)*:* I'm just so sorry that I caused all this trouble for everyone—Mom, my friends. I didn't know what was happening to me. And no one else seemed to either. What I hated most was that my friends' parents wouldn't let them talk to me.
>
> *Pat:* I know this has been so hard for you.
>
> *Donna:* But you didn't help me either, and that's supposed to be your job.
>
> *Pat:* I did the best I could, but it wasn't enough and I'm sorry.

The human dimension was breaking through in stark terms that would lay an essential foundation for our work together. It was a challenging moment for everyone in the room to face the pain of the situation.

Tom was looking increasingly uncomfortable. Glancing alternately at his watch and papers, he looked like he wanted to leave the room. It was clear to me that the openness of the exchange was something he was not familiar with. We had to find a way to integrate what had happened into our understanding of how we would move forward. I hoped that there might be a way that he could address his discomfort with the others from the school side, without losing the importance of what had just happened.

> *Mediator:* I just want to remind you that any time either client or lawyer wants to meet with each other, we can take a break.

Tom was out of his seat in a flash, and we came back in about 15 minutes. We then spent some time helping Martha and Pat understand each other. Some softening came out of this. Martha got more of a sense of Pat's bind in wanting to be helpful to Donna but experiencing tension with the school administrators who were her bosses and the parents who were alarmed by the situation. Pat understood better that Martha and Donna felt isolated and unable to reach out for help. But Tom's impatience was palpable.

> *Tom:* Let's get to the bottom line.

Mediator: I, too, think it's time to start to move toward resolution if that is okay with all of you. As part of that, I'd like to see if we can identify the priorities of Martha, Donna, the school, and the insurance company that would need to be met in a solution, before we negotiate the actual result. Is this okay?

Tom: It's just a matter of dollars.

Mediator: We will have to decide about dollars, but I'm not so sure that it is simply a matter of dollars for everyone. And even if it is, the inquiry I am suggesting could give us an underlying ground that could even help us figure out the dollars.

Al: (looking at Tom) I think this could be helpful.

Sally: I think Gary's right. There's more here than the money.

■ ■ ■

Eliciting the Parties' Interests

We moved into a conversation about the underlying interests, which we developed on a flip chart.

Mediator: From the perspective of the school and the insurance company, can you help us identify what would be important to you in any solution?

Tom: This is really just a question of money for us, so the sooner we can get to it, the better.

Mediator: From the insurance company's perspective, your goal is to find a financial result you can justify to the company, taking into account the legal reality. Is there anything else?

Tom: No, that's it.

Mediator: Al and Pat, how about from the school's perspective?

Al: Some things here are important to the school. Its reputation is very important. The impact of this situation on the teachers, administrators, and the other students is important.

Mediator: Let's see if we can clarify what you're saying. First, the school. One interest the school has is to have a reputation for being responsive to the needs of its community.

Al: Protecting them.

Mediator: Yes, it's not just reputation but protection. Protection of all the students.

Pat: Right. It's also important that the students know that the school cares about them when they are in trouble.

Mediator: Good. What else?

Pat: That the school stands behind the teachers and administrators.

Mediator: That includes you.

Al: And others as well.

Pat: And that we have a school to run.

Mediator: I'm also hearing that maintaining the educational atmosphere is important to the school.

Pat: That's fundamental. And educating the students. That is what the school is about.

Mediator: Does that include what happened with Donna?

Pat: Absolutely.

Then it was time to help Martha and Donna identify their interests. It took considerable time to articulate what was important to them in a way that did justice to the depth of their suffering while building hope for moving forward. The sequence with them began as follows:

Mediator: Martha and Donna, can you identify what's important to you underlying any solution?

Martha: I think the school should be punished.

Mediator: What would that do for you?

Martha: We'd be vindicated. People might start talking to us.

Mediator: Identifying the school's behavior as wrong would help you in some way to reconnect with people. Is that right?

Martha: Yes. Donna has no relationship with some of her dear friends because of the way the school handled the whole situation.

Mediator: So for Donna to be cut off from people she was close to must have made the whole experience that much more traumatic.

Martha: We feel as if we have been put through the wringer.

Mediator: Can you say what you mean by that?

Martha: The whole experience was just so traumatic for me, Donna, and our whole family. Donna has been marked for life as a crazy.

Mediator: So it wasn't just the experience of what Donna went through that was so hard for you. It was the way that everyone responded that added so much pain for all of you.

Martha: That's right. They cast her out, they cast me out. It was as if we were shunned. They still don't even understand that Donna has gotten better. She can function now.

Mediator: So one of your interests is to lift the stigma so the community can see that Donna is better.

Donna: I'd like to be able to move on in my life. I don't even have a diploma.

Al: You haven't completed your coursework.

Mediator: So completing your high school education is important.

Donna: Yes it is.

It was a touching moment when Donna spoke up. And that Al was the first to support her was not lost on anyone.

Martha: And she can do it. One of the things about all this that has been so difficult is to be marked in the way that Donna and our family have been, to be whispered about, talked about behind closed doors, to be looked at by other students, parents, school people as if we were all crazy. Donna is the third of our children to have gone to that school. We have been connected to it for over 12 years.

Mediator: You felt that you were all a part of that community.

Martha: It was really out of this that we brought the lawsuit. Our frustration ran so deep, we didn't know what else to do.

Mediator: So it would mean a lot to you to feel as if Donna and the family were part of the school community again. Is there more?

Martha: Well, of course, there's money.

Mediator: What is the significance of that?

Martha: We have had significant medical bills, psychiatrists, doctors, you name it, the professionals. More than we would have had if the school hadn't handled it so badly. We even had to have the psychiatrist talk to the school administrators.

Mediator: So fair compensation for the added costs and difficulties created by the school is another of your interests.

During the course of this dialogue, through much difficulty and pain, Martha and Donna developed several interests, including the importance to Donna of resuming her life through completing her high school education, acceptance by the community, and compensation for the difficulties created by the school. The exchange about how Donna and her family had been stigmatized led Martha to turn to the larger context—educating the community about mental illness. The last of these interests developed from an exchange that included the following.

> *Mediator:* What else is important to you?
>
> *Martha:* What we have been through has been so hard. I don't want anyone to ever have to go through what we suffered in relation to the school.
>
> *Mediator:* So you're interested in having something occur that would help others in similar situations.
>
> *Martha:* There was so much ignorance and helplessness. We didn't know where to turn, nor did anyone at the school seem to know either. Like so many other problems that kids have, they just seem to be buried when it comes to the school.
>
> *Mediator:* So one of your and Donna's interests might be to raise the level of awareness about how to deal with these situations.
>
> *Martha:* It would really help us to know that we were not so victimized by this situation, that we were able to use it to help ourselves and others.
>
> *Mediator:* To know you were helping others as well as yourselves would make a big difference to you.

Martha and Donna affirmed that they could see the value in that.

After further dialogue, the following chart was developed of the interests of both sides.

Donna and Martha	School and Insurance Company
Completing high school education	Protecting students
Restoring Donna's relationships with her peers	Educating students
Receiving fair compensation	Preserving the school's reputation
Lifting the stigma of mental illness	Maintaining educational atmosphere
Educating the community about mental illness	

Having reached this point where we now had a basis of understanding about what was important to both sides, my hope was that we could use this as a springboard for thinking about possible solutions.

Developing Creative Options

Mediator: It's time to start thinking about solutions. What I'd like to do is to see whether we can do that in a free-flowing way where we all participate in identifying any idea that might be a piece of a solution and to do that through a process called brainstorming. In order to do that, I would suggest that we agree that anyone can suggest any idea without having to decide whether it would be acceptable even to them and that we all postpone evaluating any option until after we've created them. Okay?

Tom: Frankly, as I've said, we're here to settle this case for money. Let's get real here.

Mediator: So including anything beyond a monetary number doesn't make a lot of sense to you right now. Of course, financial terms may well have to be one of the components of the settlement, but there may be other parts that also could be important for Donna and Martha or the school. We have already identified what underlies those possibilities. Would you be willing to bear with us to see what other ideas we can consider?

Tom: Okay, but I'd like to see a proposal from them.

Mediator: Before we reach that point, I think what we are about to do might be useful to see if we can identify all of the elements of a solution before we try to quantify it with specific proposals.

■ ■ ■

It can be important that the parties not move too quickly into a mode of making specific proposals until they have had a chance to exercise their creativity, building on the solid base of priorities strongly felt and expressed by those in the room. To start narrowing down options prematurely would risk losing the value of joining together to think about possibilities no one has yet considered.

■ ■ ■

Martha: Donna still hasn't received a diploma from the school.

Al: The school doesn't give diplomas without completion of the educational requirements.

Mediator: Let's put off evaluating what is possible or impossible, appropriate or inappropriate, until later and just put this as an element, to see what would be necessary for Donna to receive a diploma.

■ ■ ■

In the brainstorming process, the priority is to create an idea without worrying about refining it or deciding whether it is viable or what would need to happen to make it work. It can be important to generate ideas before examining specifics, which would need to happen in the evaluation stage.

■ ■ ■

Martha: Al has been helpful here, but no administrator from the school has yet been willing to sit down with me and try to understand what the school did to Donna.

Mediator: So, another element might be some opportunity for a further meeting that would include others from the school who participated in the situation.

Martha: I don't know if they are even willing to do that.

Mediator: Neither do I, but I can see this is important to you. Later, we can look to what is possible.

Donna: This might seem silly to you, but I never even received a yearbook of my graduation class.

Mediator: It's not silly. You want some feeling of what you took part in.

Donna (starts to cry)*:* Most of my friends won't even talk to me.

Mediator: Losing contact with your friends has been hard, and reconnecting with them might be important for you. If so, we could give some thought to how that might happen.

Donna: No. I don't want that. I do want the yearbook.

Martha: I don't think we need to discuss that further here.

It was clear that losing her relationships with her classmates had been extremely painful for Donna. I was hopeful that the ground had been laid for Martha to pursue this question with Donna outside the mediation, and that she might even turn to Pat for help.

■ ■ ■

The Interplay Between Interests and Options

At this stage, ideas for options often trigger an understanding of additional interests or clarify those that have already been articulated. This dynamic interplay between interests and options is an integral part of this stage of the mediation and can often prove very helpful.

■ ■ ■

Mediator: What other ideas does anyone have?

Pat: Maybe a letter from the school to Donna's fellow students that explains what has happened.

Martha: I think a specific letter from the school to the parents, particularly of Donna's friends, might open those doors again to Donna.

Mediator: Good. What else might be helpful to Donna or the school?

Martha: I'd like to see an educational program that gives the students more information about mental illness. I wouldn't want anyone else to have to go through what we did.

Mediator: That builds on what you were saying earlier about educating the community. It looks to me as if we have some promising ideas that go beyond money, and there may be more. If you're all ready, we can turn to the financial aspect now, knowing that we can always come back to these other categories if anyone has any new ideas. Before we talk about specific numbers, any ideas about how to structure the payment of money?

■ ■ ■

Addressing Financial Options

Even when we talk about money, the conversation is not just about the amount. Timing, tax impacts, and other concerns are valuable to examine before we get into a particular discussion of the amount of money, because these considerations affect the actual number. Of course, it's also possible to try to find a number and then deal with these kinds of adjustments later, but in the interest of transparency, and particularly where there may be some difference in the degree of financial sophistication, we find it valuable to address these matters first. Most of these considerations, like the nonmonetary kinds of solutions, are beyond what a court could order, so it is another advantage of a consensual process to adapt to the individual needs and priorities of the parties in the case. If money is the only frame, everything is only in shades of green.

■ ■ ■

Sally: Are you talking about payments over time?

Mediator: That's one possibility. I guess there are also tax considerations in terms of how the money is characterized, so that the money would not be taxable to Martha or Donna.

Pat: So far we're talking about what the school can do for Donna and Martha. But I think there are also things Donna or Martha can do for the other parents and students, if they're willing.

Mediator: We can come back to the question of payments. What do you have in mind, Pat?

Pat: Most of the students have just gone on with their lives. But some got caught in the crossfire between Martha and Donna and the school. How about having a meeting between Martha and some of the parents?

Martha: I don't think so.

Mediator: This is another option. Obviously, it would come about only if Martha is willing. Let's just identify it as a possibility for now.

■ ■ ■

Expanding Options and Deepening Interests

We identified several other possibilities, and charted them all on the flip chart without any attribution as to who had suggested them before we started to evaluate the options. The brainstorming of options continues until we all feel we have exhausted the possibilities, knowing that new options and interests can always emerge in the evaluation stage. It is particularly important to keep the distinction clear between the levels of options and interests so that our thinking is expanded through creating options and deepened through examining interests.

■ ■ ■

> *Mediator:* We have all assumed that we are also going to have to talk about money as part of the solution. Before we identify specific amounts, let's see how these ideas we've developed take into account the interests we've identified.
>
> *Al:* Costs are associated with some of these ideas, so you need to know that less money will be available to Martha and Donna if we undertake them.
>
> *Martha:* That's okay with me. It really does make a difference to me and to Donna to know that you'll take measures that would keep this from being handled in the same way again.
>
> *Mediator:* There may be some other ideas about how to do that that we didn't think of during the brainstorming. Does anyone have any thoughts?

■ ■ ■

Brainstorming more options can come back into the picture when new interests are identified, so that we use the new interest as the springboard to think about new possibilities.

■ ■ ■

> *Al:* How about a training program to educate the teachers and administrators about these psychological difficulties?
>
> *Martha:* And how about a program to educate parents about this as well?

■ ■ ■

Testing Options Against Interests

As each option was articulated, it also went up on the flip chart. We then reached a point where we were ready to test the options against the interests. The ultimate goal is to find the option or options that best meet the interests of both sides. Testing the options against the interests—with everyone looking at the interests of *both* sides—helps us all to focus on what is important to both sides.

■ ■ ■

> *Pat:* I want to say something. It feels to me as if you are asking the school to take all of the weight for what happened to Donna. In fact, the school didn't create Donna's illness. Sure, we could have done some things better. We didn't control the flow of information as well as we could have. We could have attended better to the parents and the students. And we paid too much attention to our lawyers. Martha, I know that you were in over your head on this, but I'd like to think that with the benefit of hindsight, you might have done better, too.
>
> *Martha:* I do appreciate your acknowledgment of how the school didn't support us, and I don't blame the school for Donna's illness. No one is responsible for that. It just happened, and no one saw it coming. But there is a stigma that not just Donna but our family carries around. And while Donna is not clear of her problems, she's come a long way, and we can see a light at the end of the tunnel. I have sometimes blamed myself for what happened, and it has been frustrating recognizing how little the professionals seem to understand about all of this. If only the principal could have called me and set up a meeting, we could have talked about this and not become so polarized.

The honesty and vulnerability in this exchange was palpable. Pat and Donna had met, and the authenticity of that meeting was likely clear to all of us, although I was unsure how it might have affected Tom.

> *Mediator:* I hope you both find this exchange as helpful as I do. What feels particularly important is your mutual recognition of what could have happened that would have reduced your polarization. Could anything from this help us in thinking about solutions here?
>
> *Pat:* Definitely. I'd like your active support, Martha, and Donna, too. I know your priority is and ought to be your recovery, but maybe your participation could actually help you as well as others.
>
> *Mediator:* What do you have in mind?

> *Pat:* I'm not sure, maybe something like a joint statement from all of us, including others at the school that explains the situation without anyone trying to paint anyone black.
>
> *Mediator:* In terms of the interests that you identified before, that's pretty interesting because it looks to me like it meets several interests of both sides.

The process had taken an interesting turn. Because it clarified the interests of all of the parties, everyone was looking at a bigger picture than they had seen before and translating that understanding into some concrete solutions that might work for everyone.

We still had to deal with money. But because we had a bigger picture of the whole situation and had laid the foundation for a variety of nonmonetary solutions, money was less likely to become the exclusive and potentially polarizing focus that it might have if we had talked about it earlier. I was confident that these other solutions could help us bridge differences regarding money, so this seemed like a good time to begin that conversation.

> *Mediator:* As we examine the money part of the settlement, I want to point out a danger. My concern is that each side will come back with proposals playing out the negotiating game, asking for more than you would take and offering less than you are willing to settle for. My hope is that you would each come back with offers that you think would be attractive to the other side and, to make that feel less locked in, not necessarily numbers that you know for certain you would finally agree to, but that capture your serious intent. If we can recapture some of the spirit of how we developed the other options, we might avoid some of the strategic parts that could make this feel harder.
>
> *Sally:* How do we know that if we do this, they will too? And who is going to go first?
>
> *Mediator:* My suggestion is that you put the proposals in writing with the reasoning underlying them and give them both to me before you exchange them with each other. If it seems to me that both are legitimate offers then I will pass them on to both of you. If one or both are not, I will simply report that to you, and we'll have to figure out what to do about that. I hope we won't have to deal with that.

■ ■ ■

Proceeding with Proposals

Proposals can be put together in a variety of ways. In this case, since the nonmonetary parts would need to be integrated into the overall proposals, each side putting together a full package would serve two purposes. First, it would give Al and Tom a chance to examine the economic impact of the nonmonetary parts and integrate those into their overall proposal. Second, by asking both sides to put together proposals simultaneously, it would reduce their reactivity to each other. If one side makes a proposal and the other responds, it invites the second party to react to the proposal by pointing out what is wrong with it. If both sides simultaneously put together proposals, then it creates more mutuality since neither proposal is a reaction to the other.

In many situations where the parties seem to be polarized around a particular issue, we'll ask each side to put together more than one package. That should include one proposal where, if the other side agrees to move in their direction on the most divisive issue, the remainder of the package compensates for that, and a second package tilted more favorably toward the proposer where the divisive issue goes in the other side's direction.

The hope is that with at least one proposal from each side on the table, we can move toward a mutually acceptable solution. Or a new idea might emerge. We are always trying to use the interests as the touchstone to see how these concrete solutions can be workable for both sides, with each side challenged to explain how their proposal(s) work *for both*. Specifically, we revisit the interests and ask each side how each proposal meets both their interests *and* the other side's interests.

■ ■ ■

Al: This isn't specific enough. The only time we talked about money, it turned out we were $200,000 apart. A lot has happened here today, and I hope we can settle the case now. But we need to do something more specific in terms of the financial aspect to help us with the proposals.

Mediator: So it would be helpful to you to get a more specific sense of whether your inclusion of the nonmonetary issues in a proposal will change Martha and Donna's stance on the money.

Al: Yes, we simply can't pay your previous demand under any circumstances, and certainly considerably less if we include these other items we have been discussing.

Sally: I understand that. I want you to know, Al, that we are not expecting to settle this case for $210,000 and are open to thinking about this in a new way as a result of these other components.

Mediator: Al, is that enough to help you put together your proposal?

Al: I'd like to think so. It's helpful but I want you to know that there is no way that we will be able to settle this case for even six figures.

Sally: I understand that.

Mediator: Is this enough, or do you want to say anything more?

Sally: This is enough for us.

Al: Yes. Tom, you and I need to speak, but I also need to speak with people at the school.

Mediator: Let's take a break to do that.

Thirty minutes later we reconvened.

Al: I've had a chance to talk to everyone, and I'd like to make a proposal. I don't need to have you make one, Sally, and I'd like to explain why. When we came here this morning, I had a figure in mind and as a result of our conversations here, I am satisfied that that figure isn't enough to settle the case. So we have put together a comprehensive proposal for more money than Tom has authority to settle the case for. But if you say yes to this, I can promise you that both Tom and I will go to bat for you with the insurance company. And while I can't guarantee that they will say yes, I think it's highly likely they will based on both of our relationships with the company.

Mediator: While beyond Tom's authority to settle, you'd like to propose a number that you believe that you and Tom can persuade the insurance company to accept.

Al: Yes.

Mediator: I think that puts Sally, Martha and Donna in a rather awkward position. If they say yes to this, the rug could be pulled out from under them by the company.

■ ■ ■

One of the tensions in any case where the people negotiating in the room don't have sufficient authority to support an offer is that progress can be illusory, and it is also a danger that the parties will use the people with authority outside the room in a strategic manner that could undermine real progress. In pointing out the danger, Al was taking me at my word that he could make a suggestion that his side was not absolutely committed to, and he was being transparent about it.

I wanted to be sure that Sally and her clients would not be disappointed if there was an agreement and then the school and insurance company pulled back from that and that they would take that possibility into account in their response. It was important here to preserve *mutuality of vulnerability*. So Al's suggestion made sense to me that Sally not be asked to be vulnerable with an independent proposal when he wasn't sure that the company would support the offer he and Tom were making. Or perhaps this was all a strategic move on Al's part. I had no way of knowing for sure other than my gut sense that something important had happened in the room that created more trust between the lawyers, and perhaps with Martha, than they had previously experienced.

■ ■ ■

Al: That's true, but highly unlikely.

Sally: I understand this risk, but we've come a long way today, and I'm willing to talk to Martha and Donna about proceeding in this way.

Martha: I'm willing to go with your judgment on this Sally. I don't think we need to talk.

Al: I appreciate this, because I don't think we would have another chance to settle this case for another several months, if we don't do it now. And by then there will be at least another $100,000 spent in legal fees and costs, which will make it much harder to settle the case.

Mediator: If you are all satisfied with proceeding this way, it's fine as long as you all understand the risks of doing so.

Sally: We do.

Al: All right. First, with respect to Donna's diploma, we have identified two papers that need to be written and that if they are completed, I can assure you they will be looked upon favorably. Second, Donna will receive a yearbook. Third, the school has agreed to have a meeting with Martha and Donna and any four individual teachers or administrators that Martha and Donna would like to be present specifically for the purpose of their understanding what they can learn from this experience. You name the time and place. Fourth, we are willing to put together a program for education of the faculty, the students, and the parents about mental health where Martha and Donna can participate in any way they would want, but I think that would naturally evolve out of the meeting with the school. Finally, with respect to money, we are willing to recommend that the company pay $55,000.

Mediator: I expect the thinking behind your first four points is clearly related to the interests we identified and the discussions we have had. Can you tell us what the thinking is behind the monetary offer?

It was important to have the monetary piece explained so that there was an underlying reasoning that held the whole package together.

Al: Yes, we believe that this is a significant amount of money. It is, of course, very hard to determine either what would happen in court or what would actually amount to fair compensation. But we think that this accurately reflects the legal risk and exposure given the actual costs expended, especially when the school could at most be exposed to responsibility only for the additional problems experienced by Donna and Martha that the action or inaction of the school contributed to, rather than Donna's basic condition, which necessitated the greatest medical and psychiatric expenses.

Mediator: Al, can you also explain how you think this meets everyone's interests?

Al: First, this feels like a sufficient amount of money to provide for Donna's additional medical costs. Of course, it's very difficult to know exactly what that incremental cost attributable to the school's actions would be, but this feels like a significant contribution. Secondly, this is intended to be able to open the door for the school community to reconnect to Donna and to Martha, and to have everyone learn from the experience. It also allows the school to facilitate education about mental health concerns, which feels right.

We took a break for Sally to confer privately with Martha and Donna. Fifteen minutes later we reconvened. Martha looked somewhat upset.

Sally: We talked this through. The nonmonetary parts are good, and this is the first time that there has been a reasonable monetary offer, but it's not quite enough.

Mediator: So you are pleased by the response to the need for educating the community and bringing you back into a relationship with the school, but the money is not enough.

Sally: That's right.

Everyone looked at me.

Facing Impasse with Creative Good Will

Tom: Now what are you going to do? We put out our best offer and now we're sitting here with egg on our faces.

Mediator: You feel you have really extended yourselves and have given a lot of thought to how to restore relationships and have the school play a central role of educating its community. Let's find out more about what Sally, Martha, and Donna are thinking.

Tom: That's okay, but we can't go any further.

Sally: We really want to settle this case, but part of the problem is that we have already invested a fair amount of money in the litigation to get to this point, and there would be very little money left over for Donna to cover her further treatment.

Mediator: Given the costs you have had, how much more would you need to make it work?

Sally: Ideally, we would like $80,000, but we appreciate the nonmonetary parts of this agreement, and if we can get $70,000, that will settle the case.

Al: Let me talk to Tom.

We took a break for them to call the insurance company and in 10 minutes they returned.

Tom: The company isn't willing to go beyond the $55,000. Now what?

Now we were faced with an apparent difference between what the people in the room felt was right and the people in charge from the insurance company were willing to do. This was an important tension, and we needed to figure out how to address it.

Mediator: There are several ways of going forward. You have come a long way to get to this point. All of the nonmonetary issues have been agreed upon, and you have narrowed the difference between you to $15,000, which is significantly less than the incremental legal fees would be to litigate. Right?

Tom: Our company doesn't think like that.

Mediator: But it's true, isn't it?

Tom: Yes, but it's irrelevant. I don't think we're going to get another dime out of the company.

Mediator: So I wonder if there are other possibilities here?

■ ■ ■

Opening Possibilities Yet Again

We had come too far to get stuck at this point. But it certainly looked like both sides might draw lines in the sand, and we seemed perilously close to exhausting the possibilities for bridging the remaining gap. I did not want to act in a coercive way although I felt tempted to try to push through. In these moments, it is again important for the mediator to hold the attitude of looking for possibilities that go beyond the feeling of impossibility that we were all experiencing. As I was searching for something more than we could see in the room, I had an idea for an option, which came from stepping back from the situation and asking what might be possible that we hadn't been thinking about.

Sally: What other possibilities might there be?

Mediator: I know that the school's insurance is going to be paying to settle this case, but I wonder if there would be a way in which the school itself might be willing to participate financially, either by contributing to the settlement with Donna and Martha, or indirectly through creating something that responded to Martha and Donna's interests?

Sally: I don't know. We would like to settle this case, but Martha's costs have been significant, so we would need some more money directly.

Al: Let's take a break. Pat and I need to talk to the principal.

Later when we reconvened, Al spoke.

Al: We've talked to the school, and they are willing to consider contributing $5,000 to Martha, and they are also willing to put up an additional $10,000 to put together a conference to educate the other schools in the diocese about the problems of mental illness in students. But we need to be sure that this would be acceptable before we go further.

Sally: Let me talk with Martha and Donna.

A few minutes later, they returned and reached an agreement. Tom looked a little disgruntled. We all experienced a tentative relief, eased a lot by Pat's turning to Martha and Donna, telling them that she would need their help on the conference, and Martha responded, "I will do everything I can to help."

Al smiled a little. By the next morning I received a fax. "Case settled as discussed. We are now fans of the 'new mediation,' although I'm not sure about Tom."

Commentary: The Possibilities Inherent in Conflict

Conflict has always been with us and always will be. It is often one of the most difficult and challenging aspects of our experience. But it can provide the opportunity to honor the best and highest in the human spirit. In the understanding-based approach, we seek to allow and move toward that possibility.

Conflict is all about the human dimensions of life. The depth of human experience often lies buried deep beneath our differences. Sometimes we sense it is there, unacknowledged. Sometimes we touch it slightly. In this mediation it became palpable, central, and helped guide us toward a solution,

Conflict is about human differences, becoming mired in them and trying to deal with them or failing to deal with them. Inherent in conflict resolution is the possibility for understanding our differences, respecting them, and working through them together. It also allows for the possibility, in facing those differences, of honoring our underlying connection, and of coming together anew. The work with the parties in the Stigma of Mental Illness case seemed to touch that possibility as they moved through their conflict.

Conflict often touches upon human frailty and tragedy. Here it was mental illness. That reality, and the stigma attached to it, had them caught in a conflict that impacted them and touched everyone connected with the school. In their *work together* in this mediation, these parties transcended the confines of their conflict. Through assuming responsibility, allowing vulnerability, communicating directly, honoring commitments to themselves and others, and exploring together creatively, they were able to resolve their differences in ways that benefitted the individuals, the school, and the larger community. Together they learned about the reality and myths of mental illness and about dealing with conflict. The challenge they succeeded in meeting proved not only how to overcome their conflict, but also how to make it of service.

The premise of our approach is not to accept the limitations that conflict imposes, which can keep people ensnared within it. Crucial to the movement in this case, as in many, was to reach beyond what is normally thought of as "impossible" to find what might, in aspiration and actuality, be possible.

Afterword

Alfred North Whitehead wrote: "If civilization is to survive, the expansion of understanding is a prime necessity." If only it were possible.

In our early days of working together on the development of this approach to conflict resolution, we had the wholehearted support and collaboration of our friend and colleague, Harry Sloan, who worked with people about the possibilities open to them in their development and their relationships. Going beyond the limits of what was thought of as possible was central to his vision and strongly influenced us in how we and others experienced the world of conflict.

Our friend died much too young, but in his final years and months we continued our active collaboration and continued to learn from it. He approached each day with the attitude—"Well, let's see what's possible today"—and lived that possibility fully. We seek to bring that aspiration to our work with people in conflict and the professionals who serve them.